A TOUCHSTONE BOOK
Published by Simon & Schuster
New York   London   Toronto   Sydney

FOXES
IN THE
HENHOUSE

How the Republicans Stole the South and the Heartland

and What the Democrats Must Do to Run 'em Out

STEVE JARDING and DAVE "MUDCAT" SAUNDERS

TOUCHSTONE
Rockefeller Center
1230 Avenue of the Americas
New York, NY 10020

Copyright © 2006 by Steve Jarding and Dave "Mudcat" Saunders

TOUCHSTONE and colophon are registered trademarks of
Simon & Schuster, Inc.

Lyrics for "Warner" campaign song on pages 90–91 reprinted by permission of
Lansdowne-Winston Music Publishers.

Excerpt on pages 127–28 from Max Cleland, *Strong at the Broken Places*
(Athens, Georgia: Longstreet Press, 1983).

For information about special discounts for bulk purchases,
please contact Simon & Schuster Special Sales at
1-800-456-6798 or business@simonandschuster.com.

Designed by William Ruoto

Manufactured in the United States of America

10   9   8   7   6   5   4   3   2   1

Library of Congress Cataloging-in-Publication Data

Jarding, Steve, and Saunders, Dave "Mudcat."
    Foxes in the henhouse : how the Republicans stole the South
and the Heartland and what the Democrats must do to run 'em out /
Steve Jarding and Dave "Mudcat" Saunders.
        p.   cm.
      1. Republican Party (U.S.: 1854–.   2. Democratic Party (U.S.)
    3. Politics, Practical—United States.   4. United States—Rural conditions.
    5. United States—Politics and government—2001–.
    JK2356.J37   2006
    324.70973—dc22   2006042215

ISBN-13: 978-0-7432-8651-0
ISBN-10:   0-7432-8651-0

Acknowledgments

This book is the culmination of nearly three decades of observing, studying, and working in electoral politics. That's a long time, and as such it would be impossible to thank all of the individuals who helped educate, inspire, and shape us along the way. So we won't try to do that—but with a couple of exceptions.

With regards to this book, we would like to offer thanks to the handful of people who were most instrumental in making this project happen. To start with, we would like to thank a group of Harvard University students we enlisted to help gather the volumes of research needed for this book. Their work and attention to detail was nothing short of superior. These "Dukes of Harvard" as we came to call them were recruited by and organized by Harvard student Joey Hanzich, whose passion for goodness and justice is overwhelming. The "Dukes" also included Brittani Head, Alex Burns, Brigit Helgen and her sister Erika Helgen, Angie Guerrero, Max Newman, Chris Crisman-Cox, Harlan Piper, David Kaden, and Andy Frank. These students provided countless hours of research—all on their own time and while taking full course loads. They have given us great faith that America is still a place that breeds selfless, compassionate, thoughtful, and dedicated leaders. America and the world will see and hear these names again as they take their places as leaders of the next generation.

And speaking of terrific and worthy organizations, we wish to thank the extremely talented people who put together The Progress Report (www.americanprogressaction.org), who deliver an honest, hard-hitting review of the daily news generated by our government and our elected

ACKNOWLEDGMENTS

leaders. Their report is a must-read—everyone should sign up for their invaluable service.

Then, we would like to thank Roland Lazenby, a gifted friend and writer who opened the door to this book by encouraging us and by walking us through the process of getting our ideas heard. Without Roland, there would be no book, and we thank him. Roland also connected us to Matthew Carnicelli, who became our literary agent in New York. Matthew proved to be a very driven and focused agent. He kicked down a lot of doors and made our job much easier than it otherwise would have been. Matthew too is a great talent and a great friend.

For our editor at Touchstone Fireside, Brett Valley, we have tremendous respect and gratitude. Brett is bright as hell and a terrific editor. He provided wonderful advice and guidance and a magical editing pen. Brett was always there for us—even on the rare occasion when we were beating on each other. He was a pleasure to work with and he made this book a better one.

Personally, I would like to thank my political mentor, State Senator Gene Mahan from Spink, South Dakota, for taking me under his wing a long time ago when I was a young college student. Gene gave me the gift of passion and love for politics. He was all about serving others and he did so with wit and commitment and resolve. Gene had more passion and love for politics than I have ever witnessed before or since. Gene Mahan died far too young and far too long ago now, but his spirit is ageless, his passion timeless.

I would also like to thank my wife, Brenda, for her constant encouragement and faith in me and in this effort. She has always been reliably steady and smart and she has always been there for me. Her talents and insights make me a better person and this book a more focused read.

I would also like to thank my best friend, coauthor, and business partner, Dave "Mudcat" Saunders. Dave is simply the most creative person I have ever met. If life were played out in a foxhole, and often it seems it is, I would want Dave covering my back. He is also a great hunting partner and is funny as hell—and I really like funny as hell.

Finally, I would like to thank my mother, Marie, who raised eight children alone with grace and charm and encouragement. I never saw her complain a day in her life. She instilled in me a belief that we must all work to leave more to this earth than we take away and she repeatedly admonished me that a life serving others was a life well-led. Yet, this humble and deeply religious woman still feared for her own soul. On her deathbed a few years ago she told me she feared she would not get into heaven. I told her that if she did not get in, there was no heaven. So to Marie and to all who persevere, who never lose hope, who overcome great odds and whose spirit is often shaken but not broken, I thank you.

Steve Jarding

I would first like to thank Steve, because anybody who knows me will tell you that without his hard work and focus this book would have never become a reality. Then there's former Virginia House majority leader C. Richard Cranwell, arguably the single most effective legislator in the long and storied history of the Virginia General Assembly. For some weird reason, Dickie took a liking to me over thirty years ago and became my political mentor and big brother. Steve and Dickie have both gotten a lot of stupid questions from me along the way, and I thank them both for actually answering, while saying only half the time, "That was a stupid question." Campaigning is, of course, a team sport, and I would like to thank all of my teammates over the years. Any constructive contribution I may have had wasn't just me.

I would also like to thank my buddy Ben "Cooter" Jones and his precious wife, Alma Viator. Cooter and Alma are the best sounding boards in rural America and have become like family to me. My spiritual mentor, Charlie Painter, isn't comfortable being thanked, so I won't thank him here, but I will say he's the most remarkable person that I have ever met, and nobody has ever had a bigger impact on my life. I must mention "P-Rod," my hunting buddy. As we roam the mountains, he keeps everything, including me, in proper perspective. Then there's Barbara, the best chick that ever lived. The only way to thoroughly cover her many contributions is to say thanks for putting up with all my bullshit.

I wish to make special mention of my daughters, Erin and Abby. Erin, twenty-three, is a cool and beautiful person whose only faults she got genetically from me. And then there's my feisty little four-year-old,

ACKNOWLEDGMENTS

Abby, whose middle name, Grace—meaning "an undeserved gift"—says it all.

And I would especially like to thank my mom, Agnes, who passed away just as this book was going to press. Moms, I've learned, are a special breed. Everybody thinks their mom was the greatest. I don't know if Mom was the greatest, but I do know there was not one who was greater.

Dave "Mudcat" Saunders

To the millions of Americans who have lost hope: *Never* give up. The collective power of your dreams and aspirations can change and better humanity. Keep fighting the fight. You are our inspiration and our compass. Together, we can build a better America and a better world, and we hope the pages that follow will offer a first step in that direction.

Contents

CONTENTS

CONTENTS

CONTENTS

FOXES
IN THE
HENHOUSE

Foreword

BY SENATOR BOB KERREY

In November 1994, Washington, D.C., was hit by a political tidal wave in the form of the midterm election, which dramatically altered the power structure in our nation's capital. Normally the party in power, in this case the Democrats, would suffer some congressional losses, but this was not a normal political year. There was widespread and deep dissatisfaction with the performance of the national Democratic Party, and the national Republican Party capitalized on a scandal involving loans from a House bank to Democratic members of Congress, and on Justice Department investigations of President Clinton's real estate transactions prior to his election. They exploited the unpopularity of Democratic votes for gun control, trade, deficit reduction, and our health-care proposal. Meanwhile, the Republican Party put together a "Contract With America" that promised change that was popular and in some cases overdue.

In that same year, I was a candidate for reelection to my second term in the U.S. Senate representing the state of Nebraska, and I remember that election very well. Steve Jarding helped me win that year in spite of considerable evidence that I should and would lose. He believed that every voter mattered, he believed in establishing our message first, and he knew that politics was a contact sport—particularly in that most difficult year, in what for Democrats can be a difficult state in which to win elections.

Steve Jarding and Dave "Mudcat" Saunders know as much about why candidates win or lose as any two professionals in the country today. They know that when an incumbent either is or appears to be out of touch with the day-to-day challenges of his constituents, victory can be the unlikely wish of an overly delusional person.

Former President Jimmy Carter once answered a question about his successful role in ending wars by getting the combatants to agree to elections. "How do you do it?" he was asked. "Simple," he answered. "I just use the one characteristic that binds all politicians together: their capacity for self-delusion. That delusion is expressed in a common belief that people will vote for them if they just get to know who they are."

When individuals come to power—to elective office—there is something that happens to almost every one of them. The difficulty of the work relative to the people's estimation, the ease with which voters will respond to applause lines and sound bites, and the influence of paid consultants whose job it is to convert human beings into numbers or impersonal jargon all contribute to a coarsening of the representative's attitude toward those he or she is supposed to serve. Jarding and Saunders understand this and know that the most successful candidates understand that elections are about the people who would be served, not about those who serve.

Elected officials too often begin to behave like Mel Brooks in *History of the World: Part I,* when as Louis XVI he is confronted by his staff with the news of the people's great anger. "Sire!" exclaims the aide. "You must do something! The people are revolting!" The king, who is at a trap shoot that uses peasants for clay pigeons, turns and says disdainfully: "I'll say they are."

Furthermore, our distance from voters extends further as we acquire the language of our work. My favorite example of this occurred just after the first debate I had with my opponent in 1994. After the event, I was confident I had scored a resounding victory until my teenage son said to me: "Dad, if you use the phrase 'with all due respect' one more time, I am going to vote against you!"

It does not help for incumbents to lament the fact that Washington, D.C., is the only place where "becoming a professional" is a negative, where learning "how things work" makes one too much of an insider, where accomplishments can be written about as "wasteful spending," where compromise can be denounced as a "selling out," and where helping a friend can be described as a corrupt act or "cronyism." These are political facts of life as certain in their existence as gravity and, like gravity, are just as certain to pull you down if you ignore them.

Among the central challenges for any good and successful political leader is simultaneously learning the details of complicated issues, deciding what you believe the law should say or our course of action should be, and then communicating those complexities in ways your audience can understand. Thoughtful, diligent, and alert men and women find themselves frequently trapped in a moral dilemma that is born of their own efforts. The moral dilemma is that conscience often conflicts with desire to please the audience. No matter how good I am at using the language of the people rather than the language of the Senate, they may not agree with what I believe. Indeed, they may strongly disagree.

Speaker of the House Sam Rayburn was among the most accomplished political leaders of the twentieth century. He was speaking to this moral dilemma when he gave this advice to freshmen members of Congress: "Always remember there are two kinds of people in Washington, D.C.: those who can count and those who lose." It is a lesson too many political people forget. I don't think it's an accident that this is Jarding and Saunders's first lesson for Democrats who hope to win elections.

Jarding and Saunders also talk about the need for candidates to talk to voters "where they live." That is, to find out the fears and insecurities of their constituents and act to address those issues. If this doesn't occur, the public presumes at their peril that politicians are always voting based upon the influence of special interests and money rather than the tug of conscience. This attitude actually encourages the behavior voters condemn. Likewise, the complaint that politicians are paying too much attention to polling data is often muttered by the same citizens who object when they are in the majority offended by the legislator's vote.

Such is the dilemma of those who regularly vote on specific changes in our laws that it is entirely possible to be no more than 51 percent certain you are right one day and 51 percent certain you are wrong on the next. Rare is the issue where certainty approaches 100 percent. Not only is it possible, it is common for a man to vote for and against the same piece of legislation (as we learned in the 2004 presidential campaign), particularly if offending amendments have altered the bill.

Money, technology, and a declining public understanding of the commitment necessary to make democracy work conspire to make matters worse. Although our Constitution places very few requirements on those who seek employment as members of Congress, the harsh reality is that the absence of substantial personal wealth is increasingly seen as a barrier to those without the name recognition so essential for success. Technology has also increased the degree of difficulty of getting one's real message to voters by making every statement—written or spoken—instantaneously and universally available outside the context from which it was originally offered.

In politics, this leads to efforts on the part of candidates and their supporters to very carefully temporize and categorize votes, beliefs, and statements. In successful campaigns it has led to line-by-line research of both the candidate we support and the one we oppose. While this drives the purists crazy, some of it is an essential part of political life. Show me a candidate who claims to always tell the truth and you will have found one who belongs on a street corner, warning us that voices are telling him that the world is about to end.

For Democrats and Republicans these rules lead to cautious statements. Listen to President Bush's and Senator Hillary Clinton's statements on abortion and you might think they believe approximately the same thing. They do not. The first wants abortion to be illegal in most instances and the other wants the opposite. The only thing they agree on is the need to offend as few people as possible with a statement of their beliefs.

That said, beliefs matter. In my opinion the problem Democrats have had lately at the national level is the appearance that we don't have beliefs beyond the desire to appease interest groups that are a part of our "base." Better to let the belief come shining through than hide it under a rhetorical basket.

Still, Jarding and Saunders make very important observations that Democrats have created an opening for the thievery of elections with their opposition to war (You don't support our troops!), opposition to a Constitutional amendment to prevent flag burning (You don't love Old Glory!), their support of civil rights for gays and lesbians (You don't support traditional values!), their opposition to a constitutional amendment supporting prayer in school (You don't support God?), their opposition to the death penalty (You support the criminal not the victim!), and their support of a waiting period before a handgun can be purchased (You want to take away our guns!). Jarding and Saunders argue that political reality suggests Democrats change the way these issues are defined and ultimately debated. My hope—and I believe theirs too—is that Democratic readers will not and do not have to use these observations to abandon their remaining beliefs.

Even more, I hope this "Practitioners' Guide to Politics" will encourage readers to get off the couch and get involved. For the most alarming change I have witnessed over my political lifetime is the shrinking number of citizens willing to commit, to run the risk of speaking their minds on behalf of an issue or candidate, or to continue their efforts through inevitable disappointment, loss, betrayal, and defeat.

Life is hard. Political life is harder still. Jarding and Saunders make the case that the Republicans stole values issues from Democrats and that this theft in part accounts for their success. Perhaps. As I said, they are experienced enough to know such things. As a Democrat, I hope this discovery will lead not to surrender but to a renewed commitment to engage in what must be a perpetual struggle in the arena of vision, ideas, action, and thought, where the great democratic battles occur. *Foxes in the Henhouse* argues for such a commitment.

Introduction

This book was written for the millions of Americans who have been forgotten. For the millions of Americans who have been ignored or taken for granted by elected officials who have lost their way and have no sense of history or responsibility.

Untold millions of people work hard every day, play by the rules, raise their kids the best they can, love and respect their country, and ask only for a fair shake. Increasingly, they are not getting one.

For these forgotten Americans, there are real consequences to an indifferent and uncaring government. Lives are lost, dreams are shattered, hope is starved, and faith is shaken. Parents become disillusioned and distant, children are confused and neglected, families are demeaned and destroyed. Too often this lot in life is inflicted upon them by politicians who wrap themselves alternately in the flag and in religious jargon, all the while taking actions that undermine our nation and defy religious decree.

The truth is, lives are at stake every day, but too many politicians in both political parties seem to have forgotten that politics is about those who would be served, not about those who serve.

America is a great country, but too often of late, we have not been acting like one. Our political leaders increasingly have become puppets and pawns for special interests. In just forty-five years America went from a nation and a people who believed their government was just and good, and indeed was limited only by the extent of our imagination, to one in which our political leaders have brainwashed us to hate our government. In the meantime, our political debate has become self-centered and narrow. Special interests and their checkbooks have taken control of the helm of government and the windfall—for them—has been staggering. In just a few short years, Americans have witnessed the greatest redistribution of wealth from the working class to the richest elites in the history of our nation. Our investment in America's infrastructure is a joke, and shortsighted and cowardly cuts in research and development are a cancer that will cost us dearly. Under the suspect façade of helping industry create jobs, we have cut regulations and piled on tax breaks upon tax breaks, thereby fostering an era of imperial corporate entities. Giving industry a leg up in and of itself is not a bad thing, but when industry does not give back to its workers in return, the relationship is broken. The result is that America's working class has become a disposable commodity as unions are broken, wages are falling, benefits are disappearing, and jobs are exported. And as problematic as these things are, there is a darker side to such indifferent policies. These policies have severely undermined the American family in ways that we have not experienced in three-quarters of a century. A lack of good-paying jobs, minimal if any benefits, lack of health insurance, and the general disregard for our working class fosters insecurity, hopelessness, fear, tension, and turmoil. In short, these policies tear families apart. Ironically, and inexcusably, often the people creating these policies run for office on a pro-family-values platform. It is a sham.

On top of that, because corporate America is given free rein, too often their bottom line takes precedence over any sense of corporate responsibility. One needs to look no further than the toilet that has become our air, land, and water to see the folly of such policy. Never before in our history has the environment been under such an assault. As the polar ice caps melt, hurricanes rage, species disappear, habitat is destroyed, and waters become unswimmable and the fish in them inedible, sold-out politicians increasingly spend their time concocting spurious explanations as opposed to offering sound and honest solutions.

Politicians readily kneel at the altar of greed and pray to the almighty campaign dollar. Too often their souls cannot be saved for their souls were sold long ago. A now favorite campaign tactic is for candidates for office to belittle and demean our government as they attempt to be elected to it. In doing so, they show their ignorance and dangerous contempt for the founding principles of representative democracy. Such bankrupt campaign platforms also conveniently allow politicians to display a debilitating abdication of responsibility. As a consequence, our public policy is routinely designed for immediate gratification instead of long-term interests. This lack of courage, insight, and determination renders it virtually impossible for today's political leaders to leave a positive mark on history. Instead, we are left with politicians defined by indifference, arrogance, sanctimony, and greed.

When this happens, our government fails the people it is supposed to represent. Look no further than the devastation wreaked by Hurricane Katrina in the fall of 2005. A great American city demolished. Hundreds dead and billions of dollars lost. Bodies rotting in the stagnant waters and thousands left stunned and helpless for days on rooftops and in attics. All the while our government and its agencies—filled with incompetent and indifferent cronies selected for service not by the length of their résumé but by their political connectedness, or by the size of their campaign checks—seemed unable or unwilling to respond. It was one of America's darkest moments. It was an embarrassment. An embarrassment to all Americans whose faith in their government was shaken and to America's history as a nation who takes care of its own.

The world took note and shook its collective head in shock. Yet, the response of most of our political leaders was stunning in its indifference. George W. Bush—after the destruction had already been unleashed—rushed his deer-in-the-headlight face and macho hunched-shoulder posture down to New Orleans to announce that FEMA's political appointee and Arabian Horse Association commissioner, credentialed "Brownie," was doing a "heck of a job." Republican Speaker of the House Dennis Hastert, in one of the most callous, insensitive statements ever uttered by a political leader, announced that New Orleans should be bulldozed. The ever out-of-step Senate majority leader Bill Frist, seemingly oblivious to the stark images being chiseled into the memories of all Americans of bodies floating in the streets of New Orleans, bounced into the Senate chamber Howdy Doody–like on the first day of business after Katrina hit, and announced he intended to take up tax cuts for the wealthy as his first order of business. Within weeks of the disaster, the Republican-controlled Congress—so cold, impervious, and insouciant that it seemed it could not help itself—proposed paying for the cost of Katrina, which had lifted a veil and exposed rampant poverty in America, by cutting programs for the poor. And even former first lady and now first mother Barbara Bush got into the act when she stupefied America with her chilling comments that the poor people who had lost everything in the Gulf actually had it pretty good living on cots on the floor of the Houston Astrodome.

Yet, something else happened when the winds and rain from Katrina blew over America. Millions of Americans for the first time in a long time saw that they needed government to work for them and to do a better job. They saw that Ronald Reagan and Newt Gingrich and their gang were wrong. The problem wasn't that government was bad. It was that government was not working for the people it was supposed to represent. People saw that government needed to be better or it could fail them just as it had failed the people of the Gulf Coast.

Out of this disaster comes a tremendous opportunity for Americans to take back their government. It can be a defining moment when Americans say they are mad as hell at this indifferent, greed-coddling band of political impersonators and they are not going to take it anymore.

Ours is the greatest government in the history of humankind—it is time we once again started electing politicians who understand that fact and the daunting responsibility that comes with being so ordained. We own our government—selfish, greedy politicians do not. It is time they learn that government is supposed to work for the people, and when politicians neglect that fact, they can and will be replaced with political leaders who understand that fact.

The power of this nation to do good things is unparalleled in the history of humankind. And indeed, because we have been given much, much is expected. It is time America once again took its rightful place as the beacon of light and hope for the rest of the world. But we cannot do that unless we change the terms of the debate and demand more from our elected officials than the babble and distortions we are currently getting. America deserves far better than that. Too many Americans have lost their voice as politicians lost their nerve.

This book attempts to help give Americans their voice back. In its pages we offer tools to build that voice. We expose many in government who we believe have the wrong idea about what it means to "serve." We argue that the Republicans lost their moral compass when they sold out for electoral success, while Democrats, shell-shocked at losing power, lost their courage and their will to reason and to fight. The result is that millions of Americans are being left behind, millions of opportunities lost, and millions of dreams shattered. The truth is that neither political party is doing a very good job for America right now. It's time for the Democratic Party to find its voice and to find leaders willing to offer solutions and take political risks, and make our government again one of, for, and by the people. We offer the Democrats a blueprint for regaining their courage and will, and then argue that Democrats need to step up and fight for the causes and values that gave Americans hope and opportunity, and have made America the envy of the world.

In doing this, we know we are stepping on some rather large toes. To those individuals and groups we disagree with, we mean nothing personal—but the cause is much bigger than you are. The only thing we take very personally is the need to elect a government that will live up to the promise of this great nation. If we can once again get to that level, the voices of untold millions will be heard, the lives of untold millions will be strengthened, and the dream for a better world will be realized.

The time to act is now.

Steve Jarding
Dave "Mudcat" Saunders

Part I

A LITTLE HISTORY LESSON AND SOME SCANDALOUS FACTS

Chapter 1

HOW IN THE HELL DID THIS HAPPEN?

November 1, 2004. Election eve in the world's greatest democracy . . .

Let's make sure we got this right:

America was in a brutal, nasty war in Iraq, a war that its president, George W. Bush, had convinced Congress and the nation to enter—under false pretenses. Although the threat of "weapons of mass destruction" served as the justification for America's starting the war, no weapons of mass destruction were ever found. America's fighting men and women lacked body armor and sufficient troop numbers. Over 1,100 Americans had been killed in Iraq—*most* of them *after* Bush declared "mission accomplished" there. There was no end in sight. There was no real international coalition helping the United States, and there sure as hell wouldn't be any willing guinea pigs should Bush be reelected. The war was costing the country $200 billion a year. On top of that, the guy who was responsible for 3,000 deaths on American soil on September 11, 2001, Osama bin Laden, was running free and seeing his terrorist empire *grow* exponentially. At one point in the campaign, President Bush inexplicably said he didn't give bin Laden much thought anymore. Polls showed that America's esteem in the world community had *never* been lower and that voters' stomach for the war was tenuous at best.

America's economy was shaky as hell. Unemployment was high—

particularly in states considered swing states. For the first time *ever* since records had been kept, this president had *lost* jobs. Over 3 million Americans had become unemployed under George W. Bush. Jobs that Bush was creating were, for the most part, service industry jobs at one-quarter the pay of the jobs lost—and they offered no benefits. Forty-four million Americans lacked health insurance—4 million of them added since George Bush had taken office. Thirteen percent of Americans, a total of 36 million people, were in poverty. Let's repeat that one—13 percent, or 36 million, of Americans were in poverty, one-third of those children. More than 1.5 million people watched their income fall below the poverty line on W's watch. As a consequence of misguided and suspect tax cuts, the greatest redistribution of wealth from the middle class to the wealthiest Americans in history had taken place in less than four years. There was a projected $7.5 trillion debt, after Bush had inherited a $2 trillion surplus from the Democrat Bill Clinton. More money had been spent in debt under George W. Bush than under any other president in American history. Think of that. But it was actually worse: In his first four years as president, George W. Bush had spent more money in debt than all previous American presidents *combined*. America's deficit spending spree sat at a whopping $412 billion for fiscal year 2004 alone. Interest rates were threatening to explode.

Storm clouds were gathering. This dismal record and all its attendant uncertainty occurred with Bush entrenched in the White House and Republicans firmly in control of both houses of Congress.

Democrats were hungry, and smarter than ever. They shortened their 2004 presidential primary calendar to ensure an early nominee to compete with what would be the incumbent's money advantage. They generated millions of new activists and donors of the Internet variety. They were unified in their disdain for W and careful not to beat the hell out of each other in the primaries. It worked. The Massachusetts senator and war hero John Kerry secured the nomination barely three weeks into the primary campaign season. Fallen Democratic pretenders jumped into his open arms. Kerry started raising money faster than Republican lobbyists pillage Indian gaming funds. Millions and millions rolled in. Kerry didn't even get burned by not taking the federal campaign spending "match!" He was more than competitive with Bush. His online fund-raising surpassed the president's. A million dollars a day poured in! Democrats started these funky 527 groups and raised even more money. Somewhere near $200 million! They were feelin' it, baby. They set up shop in the political swing states. Record numbers of volunteers, donors, and staff flooded Ohio, Pennsylvania, New Hampshire, Iowa, New Mexico, and Florida. Life was good. Democrats were competitive financially! A big hurdle had been jumped.

On top of that, in this time of war, their presidential nominee was no mealymouthed, weak-kneed, pacifistic apologizer. Democrats had gotten themselves an honest-to-God, down-home, authentic-as-Elvis war hero! Even better, John Kerry had medals! Lots of them. Including three Purple Hearts. George Bush thought Purple Hearts were flavored marshmallows in Lucky Charms breakfast cereal. While Kerry had bled for his country—he was wounded three times—Bush's gums bled when he got his teeth cleaned. Kerry earned medals for valor while Bush earned a college athletic letter—for being a cheerleader. In the late 1960s, Kerry did two tours in Vietnam; in the late 1960s, Bush would have been happy to tour Vietnam—so long as the tour bus was air-conditioned and arrived back at the hotel each evening in time for happy hour. Kerry pulled fallen soldiers from the Mekong Delta. The only delta Bush knew of was "Delta Dawn"—Helen Reddy's hit song if you live north of the Mason-Dixon line and Tanya Tucker's if you live south of it—which he listened to by the pool at the club. Kerry chased a Vietcong killer into the jungle; Bush had a killer ride on Air Force One for a date with Tricia Nixon. (Apparently, she wasn't impressed.)

That's right, George Bush avoided the draft, and Dick Cheney "had other priorities" in the sixties. But now that they were the men in charge, safe in their Washington bunkers, war seemed exactly the politically expedient thing to do. Democrats thought Bush's misguided war in Iraq would do something else as well, they thought it would give them an ace in the hole by firing up the dormant "youth" vote, that mass of 40 million Americans aged eighteen to twenty-nine who usually vote in dismal numbers but who were sure to be bebopping to the polls in record numbers this time around. And just to be sure, the Democrats had

Puffy a-rippin' and Eminem a-rappin', parting the political Red Sea for these previously lost electoral souls. Democrats knew they finally had a winner on defense and on patriotism.

To top it off, Kerry picked the superlawyer U.S. Senator John Edwards of North Carolina to be his running mate. Edwards was smart, possessed movie star looks, and had a record of defending the little guy in court unmatched since Atticus Finch strolled to the jury box in Harper Lee's classic Pulitzer Prize–winning novel, *To Kill a Mockingbird.* The Democrats now had the smile to counter Dick Cheney's smirk. They had the lawyer who put the screws to big corporations to counter the callous, unfeeling Halliburton CEO who cashed out after screwing the working people. The planets were aligning.

Even the tenuous 51 to 48 hold Republicans had on the U.S. Senate seemed to be slipping. In Oklahoma they nominated a real nut job, Tom Coburn—they just couldn't help themselves. Six weeks out their senator in Kentucky was branded by certain news media "mentally unfit" to be re-elected. Their nepotistic ways were backfiring in Alaska. Their candidate in South Carolina seemed to open his mouth only to change feet. The times they were a-changin'—just in time for Bob Dylan's autobiography. The sixties were not dead, they were alive! Democrats were on a roll. Democrats couldn't lose . . .

But they did.

November 2, 2004

It is enough to piss a person off . . .

Bush won a second term with 51 percent of the vote and a record nearly 60 million votes to Kerry's 48 percent of the vote and 56 million votes; Bush won the electoral college vote 286 to 252; Bush won thirty-one states, Kerry nineteen.

According to *The Washington Post,* this was the first election in which exit polls showed equal numbers of people, 37 percent, self-identifying as Democrats and Republicans. For decades Democrats had been winning those polls.

Worse, Bush's vote totals improved from his 2000 performance in forty-eight of the fifty states. On top of that, more states now leaned Republican, and in the fastest-growing areas of the country, the outer suburbs of major metropolitan areas, Democrats lost badly. A *Los Angeles Times* study showed that Bush won 97 of the 100 fastest-growing counties in America.

Nationally, George Bush won with groups and in regions he was supposed to win with and in: men, whites, conservatives, churchgoers, the wealthy, rural areas, the South, and the exurbs. Indeed, he swept the South—clean. What was disturbing was that his support within these groups got stronger, not weaker, from 2000 to 2004—even in regions and among groups devastated by his economic calamities.

Bush increased his vote among men from 53 percent in 2000 to 55 percent in 2004; among married voters from 53 percent to 57 percent; among white voters from 54 percent to 58 percent; among conservatives from 81 percent to 84 percent; among white Protestants from 63 percent to 67 percent; among those who attend church at least once a week from 59 percent to 61 percent. Among those earning $75,000 to $100,000, Bush increased his vote from 52 percent in 2000 to 55 percent in 2004, and he received a solid 63 percent of the votes of those earning over $200,000. Among gun owners, Bush won again by a better than two-to-one margin. In America's suburbs, he increased his winning total by 3 percentage points from 2000. In rural America, Bush increased his margin of victory to 59 to the Democrats' 40 percent in 2004, compared with 56 to their 40 percent in 2000. Among working-class whites, who were rocked by his misguided economic policies, Bush won by an amazing 23 points. And, just to make matters worse, exit polls showed that by a 55 to 39 percent margin, working-class, white voters trusted him to do a better job on the economy than Kerry.

Now look at what W did to the normally loyal Democratic base.

Among women voters, Bush increased his vote from 43 to 48 percent from 2000 to 2004. He drew 11 percent of black voters in 2004, up from 8 percent in 2000. He won 23 percent of those voters who self-identified as gay, lesbian, or bisexual. He garnered 25 percent of the Jewish vote, compared with 18 percent in 2000. And he won the Catholic vote in 2004, capturing 52 percent—he lost that vote to Al Gore in 2000 (oh, and by the way, John Kerry was a Catholic). We know Kerry took some heat from the Catholic Church for his position on abortion, but he wasn't trying to get the Pope's vote. Studies show most American Catholics feel as he does on abortion. Had he gone after those voters and showed he was proud to be a Catholic even though he didn't entirely agree with Church doctrine, we believe most Catholics would have respected him and connected with him. But he ignored them.

And the numbers got even worse.

In urban areas, traditionally a Democratic blowout, Bush gained fully 39 percent of the vote—up from 26 percent in 2000. Among Hispanic voters, his percentages were numbing. Bush won 44 percent of the burgeoning Hispanic vote in 2004, up from 31 percent in 2000. That amounted to the greatest share of the Hispanic vote of any Republican candidate for president since exit polling was first employed, in 1972. What about the elderly, voters aged sixty and older, a traditional Democratic coalition partner? Bush *won* among seniors 54 to 46 percent, a seven-point gain from 2000. Among those voters self-identified as "not a high school graduate," another traditionally Democratic group, Bush pulled even with Kerry, garnering 49 percent, up from 39 percent in 2000. And while Kerry did win the youth vote, 54 to 45 percent, up from Gore's winning percentage of 48 to 46 in 2000, the Associated Press reported that fewer than one in ten voters in 2004 were in the eighteen to twenty-four age-group.

Remember, not only did Bush receive these startling numbers but he did so against the best-funded, best-organized, best-prepared Democratic presidential nominee in modern political history.

Despite the greatest get-out-the-vote program ever waged in a dozen or so key swing states, Kerry lost. Despite the Democratic National Committee outpacing the Republican National Committee in fundraising for the first time ever, Kerry lost. Despite record amounts of money raised by a Democratic presidential nominee, Kerry lost. Kerry even had $15 million left over on November 3—after he lost! Explain that one, Senator. Fifteen million dollars might have been just enough to buy 75,000 votes in Ohio. But we digress. Despite a unified party behind him and a seeming universal disdain for Bush among Democrats and significant segments of Independents, Kerry lost. Despite low job approval numbers and high "wrong direction" numbers for Bush, Kerry lost. Despite deplorable numbers of unemployed, staggering poverty rates, and mushrooming numbers of people lacking health care, Kerry lost. Despite more donors, volunteers, and paid staff than any other campaign in American history, Kerry lost. He lost Ohio, Florida, West Virginia, Iowa, New Mexico, Arkansas, and Missouri. He was shut out in the South and nearly blanked in the Midwest. Despite $200 million spent by 527s in these and a handful of other key swing states, Kerry lost them all—except New Hampshire—his neighboring state.

That's $200 million—for New Hampshire. And that is not even factoring in the money spent by Kerry's own campaign.

And Kerry's loss was merely the tip of the iceberg.

Republicans went from fifty-one to fifty-five seats in the Senate.

Democratic Senate majority leader Tom Daschle was beaten by a deer-in-the-headlights, pretty-boy empty suit in South Dakota.

In Alaska, Lisa Murkowski, whose only qualifications were that her old man wanted her to be a senator, won in a walk.

Republicans swept *every* southern Senate seat: In Georgia and Florida they came up big; in Louisiana, they elected a Republican to a U.S. Senate seat for first time *ever;* the psycho Tom Coburn ran away with Oklahoma; the homophobe Jim DeMint cruised in South Carolina; and the Cuckoo's Nest escapee Jim Bunning was handily reelected in Kentucky. The Peter Principle, as it turns out, has reached a zenith in American politics.

To add a block of salt to the wound, the charm of the Democratic vice presidential nominee, John Edwards, seemed to run out; he couldn't even pull his home state, North Carolina, for Kerry (they lost it by a larger margin than did Al Gore four years earlier). On top of that, the Senate seat Edwards gave up to run for president went to the GOP.

And while the state losses are painful, the big-picture losses are stunning. Eighteen of twenty-two Senate seats in the states of the Old Confederacy are now firmly in the hands of the GOP. Throw in the fact that all four U.S. senators from Oklahoma and Kentucky are Republican, and the GOP is coming awfully close to an electoral U.S. Senate trifecta in the South. In the last two election cycles, there have been nine open Senate seats in the South. On November 3, 2004, the GOP was batting nine for nine. Democrats need to get someone up throwing in the bullpen.

Mix the southern red states with those nationally, and a very ominous picture is developing. The red states are getting redder, not just in presidential races but in U.S. Senate races as well. Following the 2004 elections, Republicans held forty-four of the fifty-eight Senate seats in the twenty-nine states that W won in both 2000 and 2004. To put this another way, the Republicans' stranglehold on red states is becoming so great that they are poised to capture a U.S. Senate majority every election cycle without ever having to contend in blue-state Senate contests.

The Republicans didn't stop with wins in the Senate. They slightly increased their hold on the U.S. House of Representatives, picking up 3 seats and moving to a solid 232 to 202 to 1 margin there. They also made the red states redder in this house. All six of the Democratic House seats won by the GOP on November 2, 2004, came in red states. On top of that, the Republicans virtually took over the Texas delegation, beating three long-term Democrats and taking a commanding 20 to 12 margin in the delegation. Funny, it doesn't seem that long ago—because it wasn't— that Democrats like Sam Rayburn, Lloyd Bentsen, and Lyndon Johnson led dominant Democratic delegations from Texas. The wins nationally guaranteed that Republicans would keep control of the U.S. House of Representatives for ten years running. Never before in American history had the GOP held the majority in the House for ten years.

One other topic of note in the 2004 elections. In the eleven states that had same-sex marriage amendments on the ballot—Arkansas, Georgia, Kentucky, Michigan, Mississippi, Montana, North Dakota, Ohio, Oklahoma, Oregon, and Utah—gay marriage proponents were crushed across the board.

Pretty bleak.

So what did Democrats do following the debacle of November 2, 2004?

They went into denial. John Kerry touted the fact that he got more votes than any presidential candidate in American history—except George W. Bush. Democratic National Committee chairman Terry McAuliffe announced that Democrats were so successful in 2004 they would never again be at a money disadvantage with Republicans—except figures for 2005 show that Republican victories in 2004 translated into a windfall at the fund-raising trough, while Democratic fund-raising looked more like a windchill. Party operatives claimed they had the greatest

Democratic get-out-the-vote operation in swing states in American political history (they did)—except the Republicans got more votes in virtually all of them.

Stop it, Democrats. You got your butts kicked. Admit it.

Politics is a bottom-line business. It is all about the win, the actual, count-the-votes win. There are no moral victories in politics. There are no ribbons given for second place—and no power, no policy advancements, no political panaceas. Simply put, to govern, you have to win your political battles.

So what did Republicans do after their commanding wins on November 2, 2004?

They claimed a political mandate. Republican leaders and cheerleaders said, "We are one election cycle away from a veto-proof majority in the Senate"; they said, "We now control the judicial branch of power so thoroughly we will shape judicial precedent for generations, thus solidifying our loyal political base"; they said, "We have unified a national coalition of voters and made significant inroads into the destabilized and uncertain coalition of our opponents, on which we can build even greater electoral successes in future elections"; they said, "We will clamp down on all power in Washington—from lobbyists to the bureaucracy, from the media to the moneyed interests, and use that power to our electoral advantage"; and they said, "You loser Democrats who doubt us, just watch us."

"To hell with you," we say.

These people are drunk on their own power. They believe their own government-subsidized talking heads. They believe there are no consequences for having sold their political souls to faceless, gutless corporate thieves. They have no sense of history or responsibility when it comes to governing the greatest democracy the world has ever known. They believe they have gotten away with their smoke-and-mirrors charade, in which they obfuscate their bankrupt values by wrapping themselves in all that is religious or patriotic. They believe it is acceptable to use this government as their personal playground and ATM machine, stealing from the poor and the working class and pouring billions of dollars into the pockets of the wealthiest and greediest.

They are wrong. They did not win a mandate on November 2, 2004. Republicans—from George W. Bush to any number of Senate,

House, and gubernatorial candidates nationwide—could have been and should have been defeated in 2004. They had weak candidates, an arrogant message, phony patriotic and religious justifications for support, and smug and elitist leadership.

Take nothing away from what they did. But let's be clear, Republicans won in 2004 because Democrats let them win.

It's time for that to stop. Democrats have to regain their footing and their voices. Democrats have to understand that too much is at stake, too many lives will be lost if they continue to lose to these fraudulent pretenders.

Democrats must win some elections.

We know the results of the 2004 elections were bleak for Democrats, but that should not intimidate them; it should embolden them. Enough is enough. It is time to stop the bleeding and win again.

In the pages that follow, we will provide a blueprint, first for how Democrats can regain their voice and their focus, and then for how Democrats can maneuver through some of the thorniest issue areas on the political landscape—from God to guns, from family values to defense and patriotism issues, from fiscal policy to the environment. Along the way, we will fairly unmercifully target those deceitful scoundrels and knaves in the Republican leadership and the elite among their cheerleaders for their often shameless, hypocritical, and soulless words and actions.

We don't like the bastards. So in the pages that follow, we will peel back the curtain at Oz and unmask dozens of Republican leader and cheerleader fools, hypocrites, and charlatans, including the dangerously insecure head case George W. Bush, libido-crazed Bill O'Reilly, the appropriately named Dick "I had other priorities" in the sixties Cheney, the headline-grabbing-in-the-face-of-tragedy Rudy Giuliani, the white-trash opportunist Zigzag Zell Miller, the lightweight bullies disguised as nonpartisans at the National Rifle Association, the man whose life has come full circle from that of a killer of cockroaches to a cockroach himself, Tom DeLay, Pharisees including Jerry Falwell and Pat Robertson, the political prostitutes and genuinely stupid excuses for political commentators Armstrong Williams and Ann Coulter. We will even tell you of the Republican shill who got out of Vietnam because he had an infected hairy cyst on his ass.

We know these guys play for keeps. We know they will stop at nothing in their attempt to gain and retain power. But we do not fear them.

We will tell you how we would have done things differently in 2004 and what Democrats can do differently in 2006 and beyond so they can win again.

Playing to win sounds simple. But for too many Democratic candidates, it has been a difficult and hollow journey. We will offer some basic concepts for how any Democrat can win anywhere in the country, but particularly in areas like the South and the Heartland, where Republicans have been dominating elections for a generation. We advocate playing by the rules—even if the rules are *their* rules—to win.

Democrats have to change the way they practice politics. For instance, they have to learn again how to count. Why Democrats write off parts of congressional districts, regions of states, or regions of the country is beyond us. It is morally wrong to do so. All Americans deserve equal representation. But it is also politically inexplicable. John Kerry conceded the equivalent of twenty-seven states and 227 electoral votes to George Bush. That is 84 percent of the electoral votes Bush needed to win, meaning that he had to get only 43 of the 311 remaining electoral votes in the remaining twenty-three states to become president. What was Kerry thinking? But the senator wasn't alone in our mathematically challenged party. We argue that this is a lesson our party had better learn real fast.

Democrats also have to learn to show some passion. We love the former Senate Democratic leader Tom Daschle, who was defeated for reelection in 2004 by a pretty-boy fool named John Thune. But when, to his face, Daschle was accused by Thune on national television of uttering words that "emboldened the enemy" of the United States, he needed to do more than say he was "disappointed." We argue that had Daschle gone ballistic on Thune, right then and there, Thune would have shat himself, right then and there, and Daschle would have been in a much better position to win reelection. Daschle wasn't the only one who exercised caution and restraint in the face of a blitzkrieg attack on his person, and he sure won't be the last one. We'll talk about that.

Democrats have to learn how to connect with the disconnected voters and how to define themselves *and* their opponents before their opponents have the chance to do it. How in the hell did John Kerry and his campaign allow the draft-dodging, AWOL-loving, Air Force One riding-for-a-date-with-Tricia-Nixon, September 11, 2001, deer-in-the-headlights stunned expression, wimpy shrub, Alfred E. Neuman look-alike George Walker Bush to tear the medals from the chest of an honest-to-God war hero and stomp them beyond recognition? We have some rather strong thoughts on that as well.

Democrats have to learn that when someone attacks your character with a bazooka, you attack his (or hers) with a nuclear weapon. We argue that character assassination is now a conventional weapon in the Republican arsenal. We think Republicans should be careful what they wish for, because when it comes to character assassination, we can blow most of these pretenders off the political face of this earth. In short, we believe we have bigger and better ammunition than they do. We argue that when someone attacks your character or integrity, when someone questions your patriotism, your commitment to humanity, your morals and values, not only do you have a license to fire back but you have a responsibility to fire back. Indeed, voters *expect* you to fire back. We'll go into some detail on this too.

Democrats have to gain a voice and craft an agenda. They have to learn *not* to be such intellectual elitists and to embrace *all* voters, regardless of their cultural or geographic status. They have to relearn the first rule of politics in a representative democracy, that *politics is not about those who serve, it is about those who would be served*. This one is vital to us and, we think, to Democrats' ability to rise up and win again throughout America.

In addition to these basic rules of electoral success, we will argue that Democrats need to figure out how to break through the culture of America. This includes the need to spend time with various cultural groups, from NASCAR to hunting and sporting groups, from high school and college athletics to country and bluegrass music performers and followers. It means spending time in areas where various cultures thrive, and it means offering policy proposals and perspectives to address the needs of people living in these cultures. We'll go into a fair amount of detail on this point, and present a fairly rigorous plan for doing so.

But before we get into the sections of the book that offer a blueprint for Democratic victory, and before we peel the hide off scoundrel Republican leaders and cheerleaders, and before we tackle the major polarizing and often albatrosslike issues sinking Democratic candidates, we will offer a quick historical section that chronicles the heyday of economic and cultural opportunity in rural and southern America, from the New Deal of Franklin D. Roosevelt through the Great Society of Lyndon B. Johnson. It is important that we do this. For among the many propaganda tools utilized by the modern-day Republican Party, perhaps none is more overlooked and potentially more damning than their determination to rewrite American history.

According to the current crop of Republican genetic mutants, the New Deal of FDR was a ruse, Lyndon Johnson and the Great Society did nothing for American society, and not only did Ronald Reagan save the world from the Soviet Union (a very questionable claim) but his redistribution of wealth to the greedy and record deficit spending programs prevented a world economic collapse. We are eager and pleased to respond to such fantasies with voluminous documentation.

In the historical section, we will also expose the cynical and calculated "Southern Strategy" of Republicans like Lee Atwater, who felt that to win the South and the Heartland of America, GOP candidates needed essentially to brainwash and ultimately "culturize" voters against Democrats by getting them to vote against their own economic self-interests, polarizing them on divisive issues such as race, God, gays, and guns.

Finally in the first section, we will offer the damning result of that cynical Southern Strategy—from the arrogance of the Republican-controlled Congress, which results in gutting ethics rules through bureaucratic agencies paying so-called journalists to spew governmental propaganda to scripted press conferences and planted reporters. We will document a government that sold out to the greediest and highest bidders, resulting in disastrous policy, from the consolidation of media ownership through an offensive energy program to a bankruptcy bill that sold out working people to greedy corporate interests. We will assess the Republicans' disastrous trade policies and look at why wage earners are falling further and further behind. And we will examine the arrogance and cynicism that allow George W. Bush to, among other things, pin medals on the chests of individuals who failed their wartime responsibilities.

So, sit back and read and ponder and get pissed off—we are.

Chapter 2

THOSE WERE THE DAYS, MY FRIEND:

THE RISE OF THE SOUTH AND THE HEARTLAND (and the Cynical Strategy That Brought Them Down)

The hangover for Democrats following the devastating 2004 elections is particularly painful because it did not have to happen. Democrats are paying for their sins of neglect, and the price is devastatingly high. John Kerry asked why a Democrat would go south, and the people of that region gave him a bitter answer: If the 102 million people who live in the South and the 60 million people who live in rural America meant little or nothing to Democratic leaders, the Democratic Party would pay the ultimate price—their political lives.

John Kerry and the Democrats in 2004 played mostly on Republican turf. And the "turf" in American presidential politics today can generally be divided into three major categories of issues. First there are the bread-and-butter issues, those that directly affect voters' pocketbooks and quality of life. These include education, health care, jobs, environment, Social Security, pensions, and taxes. Democrats traditionally do pretty well on these issues. (Although we would argue that they have not done well enough taking credit for middle-class tax cuts, nor have they made tax "fairness" a salient-enough issue. As with so many other issues, it seems Democrats in recent times have fought the tax issue on Republican turf, and that is something they must change.)

Then there is the moral category. Too often these issues have been defined only by Republicans and have come to mean abortion, gay rights, prayer in schools, et cetera—the so-called family values issues. These tend to be highly polarizing issues, which divide the electorate and arouse intense feelings on both sides. Democrats need to start defining these issues and quit having to argue with Republican definitions. We believe Democrats can, at a minimum, neutralize the advantage Republicans have had on these issues and, more important, win on them.

The third category of issues is nationalistic, such as rallying around the party in power upon the death of a president, rallying around the party in power during times of great national tragedy—9/11 is the best recent example—or rallying around the party in power when America is engaged in war or international conflict. We know historically how difficult it is to change government in these times. John Kerry, in an attempt to justify his 2004 defeat, actually boasted that he felt he did pretty well in light of the fact that America was at war and wartime presidents historically are almost impossible to defeat. We don't buy that.

The truth is, Democrats have tended to do poorly in recent elections in two of these three categories. Since the Vietnam War, Democrats have lost the trust of the American public on national defense issues. And with the Republican Party's cynical emphasis on polarizing moral issues, Democrats have allowed themselves to be painted as anti-Christian and antifamily and pretty much lost these issues to Republicans too. We will address both of these categories in later chapters and will argue that Democrats have plenty of ammunition to retake defense and patriotism issues as well as family values issues.

In this chapter, we will look at the bread-and-butter issues. Democrats should own these issues and are not getting enough credit for their work on them. They need to remind voters of all they have done for them in this area, including the two greatest periods of government investment in its people in American political history—the New Deal of Franklin Roosevelt and the Great Society of Lyndon Johnson, both Democrats.

No candidate ever really knows which of the three categories of issues will rise to the forefront in the minds of most voters. But a candidate has to be prepared to deal with all three, neutralizing those that do not play to his or her strength and elevating those that do. In difficult economic times, bread-and-butter issues normally take front and center. In wartime, such as the situation we faced in 2004, military and foreign issues tend to dominate. And, regardless of the dominant issues of the day, moral issues are taking a more and more prominent role with a small but significant part of the voting population.

Democrats in 2004 were frustrated because they wanted to talk about the bread-and-butter issues of jobs, health insurance, poverty, and education—areas of strength for them in a sagging economic climate—but could not get anyone to listen to them.

That should not have surprised them. When our Democratic friends told us the 2004 race would be decided on economic issues, we told them they were crazy. The 2004 race was going to be played out on defense and terrorism. America was at war; Osama bin Laden was still on the loose. George W. Bush was going to talk about nothing else, and, as president, he could dictate a lot of what got written on newspaper front pages. We did not disagree that, if we could get to economic issues, Kerry and the Democrats would have a better chance, but we felt that unless Kerry trumped Bush on defense and war issues, he would never get to the bread-and-butter issues. But Kerry did not trump Bush. Our war hero did not trump their draft dodger.

We thought there were opportunities missed. We felt that Kerry should immediately have gone after Bush on the Swift Boat attacks. This was not about just patriotism and war; it was a character attack, and Kerry's stunning silence on the matter was a killer. We had gone so far as to suggest Kerry call Bush out for a debate, hold it in the South, on military matters only—current war issues and the past personal military service of both men—and suggested Kerry should question Bush's leadership if not his manhood if he refused. We also would have hedged our bets and put someone with military credentials on the ticket with Kerry—the war heroes Wesley Clark and Bob Kerrey were at the top of our list (as we said at the time, we did not believe the Democrats could have enough medals on the chests of their nominees). Even Senator Bob Graham would have been a stronger voice, because though he lacked war experience, he provided tough, reasoned, and unwavering insight into the Iraq War by way of his Intelligence Committee credentials. (We also liked his 70 percent job approval numbers in Florida, with its twenty-seven electoral votes.)

Unfortunately, as we saw, not only did Kerry not call Bush out or properly illustrate for voters the blatant choice between a war hero and a draft dodger, but he did not even neutralize the military issue. He bungled it. "I voted for the $87 billion in spending before I voted against it." On top of that, Kerry walked too lightly on the Iraq War and let the Bushies distort his military and defense spending voting record with nary a shrug of the shoulders instead of a full-bore assault on Bush, Cheney, and the other frauds in the administration and their botched military operation in Iraq.

Then there was the category of moral and family values issues. We do not know if the 2004 exit polls are right that 21 percent of the voters who cited moral issues as the main issues which influenced their votes really believed that, but we do know that millions of voters are putting great emphasis on moral issues, and in 2004 Democrats were either silent on them or forced to address them as defined by Republicans. We don't believe that Democrats did a very good job of even reaching out to this group of voters with an alternative vision, much less exposing Republican weaknesses on values issues. Again, if Democrats wanted to move the debate to bread-and-butter issues, ignoring these other salient issues or walking weakly on them was not the way to neutralize them.

The truth is, regardless of your historic success on any issue that matters to voters, they are not going to know what your party did for them if you ignore them, write them off, and don't even campaign for their votes. So, to begin with, don't announce you are writing them off. Instead, travel to their states and regions. Talk to them. Listen to their fears and insecurities. Then find ways to address the issues that are not your best ones while highlighting the issues that are.

Don't make the mistake Democrats did in 2004 by ignoring the issues that were salient to voters and suggesting voters were stupid for not seeing how Democratic issues were the ones that should be influencing them. It happened. We saw it. Democrats repeatedly told voters they were voting against their own economic interests if they voted for Republicans. That may well have been true in part, but it ignored the fact that these voters' reasons for supporting Republicans must have been pretty powerful if they trumped economic self-interest.

Getting voters to focus on economic issues is only half the task. The other half is figuring out what issues these voters are voting on and devising a plan to address and neutralize those issues. Democrats cannot ignore these facts. Voter studies and election surveys indicate that voters in the South and rural America are increasingly voting on issues of patriotism or morals. Evidence suggests that this is partly because these areas tend disproportionately to send their young men and women into military service. Surveys also show that people from these areas attend church services more often and more regularly than do people in other parts of the country. Finally, we contend that moral and patriotism issues are more salient with southern and rural voters because Republicans have spent tens of millions of dollars defining these issues and telling these voters that these were the most important issues while Democrats either remained silent or attempted to debate Republican definitions. Democrats need to redefine these issues and demonstrate that Republicans have not earned the right to claim either for their own. In fact, as we will show, these issues are arguably better for Democrats than they are for Republicans.

For now, we want to address the first part of the equation: Democrats, you must fight hard for your history and for issues that play to your strengths. And you don't have to look far to make the case that you have done a better job on the bread-and-butter issues that affect the lives of most voters and their families. History is a pretty good guide, and Democrats should remind Americans in general, and rural and southern Americans in particular, of what the Democrat Franklin Delano Roosevelt did for them.

The Rise of the South and the Heartland

Something happened in the United States in the 1930s and into the 1940s that radically changed the way Americans viewed *their* government. During this time, American political leaders went from a largely laissez-faire approach to government to one of government activism in creating programs that invested in people. The transformation was largely a by-product of the Great Depression and World War II and its aftermath, but it arguably built the foundation on which the twentieth century came to be known to the world as "America's century."

From the New Deal program of Franklin Roosevelt through the New Frontier program of John F. Kennedy and on into the Great Society program of Lyndon Johnson, American domestic policy increasingly viewed people as assets and sought ways to support them. Millions of Americans remember how Roosevelt helped their families survive and prosper. From education and health care to jobs programs and massive infrastructure initiatives, the federal government was investing directly in its citizens or in programs and policies that bettered their lives. Americans increasingly saw a government that believed people have value instead of one that viewed them as disposable commodities. They also saw a government that was offering opportunity for advancement unlike anything they had witnessed before. And nowhere was this transformation more evident and more successful than in the areas that needed it most—the South and rural America.

FDR's New Deal

Upon taking office in March 1933, Franklin Roosevelt saw that he was inheriting two subdivisions of Americans heading in very different directions. The Industrial Revolution and increased urbanization were creating great opportunity for much of the country, particularly the Northeast and the West. But rural America and most of the South had seemingly been passed by, and for most of the people who lived there, the future seemed hopeless. Lack of infrastructure and overreliance on low-wage, nonmechanized farming, coupled with the South's historic distrust of the federal government, meant that the South and rural America were falling far behind, and the Great Depression only compounded their problems. Roosevelt saw the need to invest in rural America, and in the South particularly, as not just a moral or political matter; rather, he believed America needed to invest in these regions for the vitality and strength of the entire nation.

Things were ugly. By 1938 the South was America's poorest region. Poverty, homelessness, hunger, disturbing levels of disease and hopelessness were epidemic. Roosevelt's own *Report on Economic Conditions of the South* found that per capita income in the region was *one-half* of what it was in the rest of the nation, and the South had the lowest farm income and industrial wages of any region of the country. There was an appalling lack of infrastructure, educational opportunity, and health-care access, and, worse, there seemed to be no interest on the part of political or economic leaders to change. The president called the economic devastation occuring in the South the nation's number one economic problem—a pretty strong comment in light of the fact that he came to office during the depths of the Great Depression. His study concluded, "The low income belt of the South is a belt of sickness, misery, and unnecessary death."

Franklin Roosevelt did something about it, and millions of our parents or grandparents still have vivid memories of the good this Democratic president did. His macroeconomic policies drove wages up and pushed industry south, his litany of so-called alphabet soup programs raised wages and commodity prices, and his commitment to programs designed to build infrastructure and increase mobility further enticed industry to the South and rural areas. Under FDR, agonizingly long workweeks were shortened, minimum wages were set, child labor was abolished, and incomes rose.

While Roosevelt met resistance from many of the established political and economic powers in these regions, he stood up to them, and people in the South and rural America as well as throughout the country saw their incomes and opportunities increase. They responded with their votes. This support became entrenched in the form of a new coalition of Democratic voters that would remain intact for nearly forty years. As long as Democrats got through to voters on largely economic issues, Republicans were shut out of southern and rural elections.

Roosevelt's plan for revitalizing the South and rural America centered upon his belief that the government had to restructure the arcane economies of these regions. To get this done, he pushed through a number of new programs, including the National Industrial Recovery Act. This act was designed to stimulate business investment, curtail unemployment, and increase purchasing power while raising productivity. It established the Public Works Administration, which spent $4 billion on 34,000 construction projects and was responsible for building roads, bridges, dams, highways, sewer systems, and other public works projects. It also set up the Works Progress Administration, which over eight years spent $5 billion and put 8.5 million people back to work building schools, post offices, and other public construction projects. It also had an arts program that put thousands of unemployed artists, writers, musicians, actors, and photographers back to work in every state.

FDR also pushed through the Fair Labor Standards Act, which set a minimum wage; mandated the forty-hour workweek; established the concept of overtime pay; and banned child labor. He created the National Labor Relations Act, which gave workers the right to join unions and unions the right to organize and bargain collectively with employers. And he got worker and plant safety laws passed. Because of all these efforts, average hourly wages mushroomed by 70 percent in the South; the average workweek dropped, particularly in the South, while wages for unskilled laborers almost doubled. Per capita income in the South, which in 1929 had been only $362 annually, or 52 percent of the national average, shot up to 68 percent of the national average by 1946 (Lyndon Johnson's Great Society programs would have a similar effect, pushing it to 92 percent of the national average by 1979).

The Federal Housing Administration was set up to insure home mortgage loans and provide small loans for home construction. Because of Roosevelt's Resettlement Administration, designed to halt rural decay and relocate and rehabilitate the rural poor, coupled with his push to provide better housing, the number of people living in "substandard" housing—housing without running water or some or all plumbing—dropped by one-third in fifteen years. For the first time ever, millions of Americans now lived in homes instead of shacks or shanties.

The Federal Emergency Relief Administration of 1933 did everything from offering literacy classes and vaccinations to millions of America's poor to funding work projects for nearly 5 million households every month. The National Youth Administration provided nearly 5 million jobs for young people, and in 1935 FDR pushed through the Rural Electrification Administration. Prior to this program, only 10 percent of rural areas had electricity. Within six years 41 percent of rural America had electrical power.

Roosevelt also got the Agricultural Adjustment Act passed, designed to limit overproduction in agriculture in order to stabilize prices. This included providing direct subsidies to farmers who did not plant crops. It also refinanced 20 percent of all farm mortgages. This helped put money in the pockets of rural farmers, who for the first time had the resources to automate their operations. It worked. In the South alone from 1935 to 1940, additional income allowed farmers to purchase 100,000 tractors—doubling the number used to farm there. The investment helped mechanize the cotton industry and largely broke the back of the old tenant farmer system. Commodity prices not only stabilized but skyrocketed.

The Civilian Conservation Corps, controlled by the Army, was designed to promote conservation by doing projects such as cleaning up beaches and parks, planting tens of millions of trees in shelter belts in rural America to help prevent erosion of topsoil, and stocking lakes with millions of fish. It employed 2.5 million people during its ten-year existence.

One of FDR's most aggressive projects was the Tennessee Valley Authority, which built twenty dams and the infrastructure that would bring electricity to rural areas in seven states as it controlled floods and created recreational opportunities. The authority itself provided thousands of jobs, and low-cost housing, and it paved the way, with a massive road-building program, to attract industry to the South.

In 1935, FDR set up the Social Security Administration to manage a national pension fund for seniors; an assistance program for dependent mothers, children, and the disabled; and an unemployment insurance system. To restore confidence in banks, he established the Federal Deposit Insurance Corporation, which guaranteed customers that the government would insure their deposits if their banks failed. In 1934 he introduced the Securities and Exchange Commission to protect investors from stock market fraud and prevent insider trading.

With these cornerstone initiatives and dozens of additional programs targeting specific problem areas, Franklin Roosevelt pumped billions of dollars into the weak economies of the South and rural America. These initiatives redesigned the economic foundations of these regions and dramatically reshaped the way Americans viewed their government. Tens of millions of Americans began to see government as an ally, and they knew it was the Democrat Franklin Roosevelt who had forged the partnership.

In 1996 the newsman Daniel Schorr told *The Christian Science Monitor,* "Roosevelt may be a myth . . . today, but sixty years ago that myth looked like hope. In his fireside chats, he turned our Philco radios into shrines, and when he said that America could not afford to live with one-third of a nation ill-housed and ill-fed, we thought he would do something about it. And he did."

The New Deal programs of Franklin Roosevelt forever changed the face of rural and southern America. Some of the programs worked better than others, and many were met with great resistance from status quo politicians and business interests, but it is no secret that FDR became a savior to a generation of Americans. Democrats today need to make sure that people remember it and that Republicans are not allowed to rewrite history, as they have been so prone to do.

JFK and LBJ: The Great Society

While the American economy continued to expand toward the end of World War II and throughout the 1950s, many of the social programs championed by Roosevelt began to slow, particularly in the South and in rural America. And while there appeared to be no turning back to the dark days of pre–New Deal economic policies in these regions, there was stagnation and some regression by the time Lyndon Johnson assumed the presidency upon the assassination of John Kennedy in November 1963.

When Kennedy campaigned for president in 1960, he had been appalled at the pockets of poverty and lack of opportunity in much of rural and southern America. JFK was committed to reversing this American tragedy and rolled out his New Frontier agenda in 1961. He called for a medical program for the elderly, a substantial increase in federal funding for education, a rise in the minimum wage, and an expansion of Social Security. But Kennedy met great resistance from Republicans and some southern Democrats, who were unsure of how big a federal presence they wanted in their states.

All that changed with Kennedy's assassination. The Texan Lyndon Johnson assumed the White House and immediately declared a "war on poverty," adopted most of Kennedy's New Frontier goals, and rolled them into an even more aggressive Great Society program, which included massive assistance for the South and rural America. The Great Society included Medicare; Medicaid; Head Start; VISTA; Job Corps; the 1965 Elementary and Secondary Education Act; bilingual education; work-study, scholarship, and grant programs for college students; food stamps; child nutrition programs; the Wild and Scenic Rivers Act; the National Trail System Act; the Clear Water Quality and Clean Water Restoration Acts; the Corporation for Public Broadcasting; housing acts; Ginnie Mae; the Child Safety Act; the Office of Economic Opportunity; the Civil Rights Act and other civil rights legislation; and a host of additional programs designed to build wealth and give opportunity to people, particularly in LBJ's native South. Johnson believed that government should be the engine for economic prosperity for all Americans, supporting jobs, health care, education, housing, and equality.

In all, LBJ rolled out and the legislature passed over 100 major initiatives in the eighty-ninth and ninetieth Congresses, 1965 through 1968. In part utilizing the national unity that occurred after Kennedy's death, Johnson was able to marshal almost unlimited congressional support for nearly all his Great Society programs.

Not unlike the New Deal programs of Franklin Roosevelt, LBJ's programs opened doors of opportunity for millions of Americans. And his administration should be remembered for this. Democrats, you should proudly remind people of these successes.

We understand why history is not kind to LBJ with regard to Vietnam. He did what he thought was right to win the war, and he clearly made mistakes. When he left office, the war had not been won. Richard Nixon pushed even harder to win in Vietnam, and he too failed. But, Democrats, when you look at Lyndon Johnson only through the lens of Vietnam, you see just part of the president who was LBJ. It is tough for any of us to embrace the failed Vietnam War, even though we as a nation have finally and rightfully begun to embrace the men and women who fought it. But we should not let the cloud of Vietnam obscure the grandly successful domestic programs of Lyndon Johnson. We are proud of President Johnson and his domestic programs.

So-called (and, God knows, Republicans of today are so-called at best) conservatives like to criticize Johnson, calling him a "liberal." But these deficit-driven phonies have lost all license to throw labels at anybody. They are the biggest frauds in ideological history. The best response to an accusation of being liberal that we have heard occurred in Nebraska in 1988, when the former Democratic governor Bob Kerrey was running for the U.S. Senate against the self-proclaimed conservative incumbent Republican senator David Karnes. After Karnes ran a television ad suggesting Kerrey was a "liberal," the former governor was asked by a reporter what he thought of the label. Kerrey's response, "Yeah, so what?" He said that, in light of the out-of-control deficits of the "conservative" Reagan, he was unsure that liberal or conservative labels meant anything anymore. Kerrey went on to crush the "conservative" Karnes by 15 percentage points. The truth is, if the following list of President Lyndon Johnson's accomplishments is "liberalism," we should order a case of it and pass it around.

This is what Lyndon Johnson's Great Society programs did for the American people:

•   Poverty rates in the South fell from over 30 percent in 1962 to 16.2 percent in 1975. From 1963 to 1970, poverty in the United States dropped from 22.2 to 12.6 percent. At no other time has America witnessed such a dramatic reduction in such a short period. And studies show that if Johnson's antipoverty programs had not been in existence, poverty would have remained largely the same.

•   Hunger and malnutrition were dramatically reduced as a consequence of an expanded food stamp program coupled with child nutrition programs. Field Foundation studies from 1967 to 1977 showed that the Great Society war on hunger created "significant change" and was extremely effective in reducing extreme malnutrition in children and adults, and nowhere was this more evident than in the South and rural areas. By 2000 the Food Stamp Program had helped feed over 20 million people in 8 million households. And Johnson's School Breakfast Program had provided over 100 million children a daily breakfast. (By contrast, the sanctimonious, coldhearted Ronald Reagan wanted to cut the School Lunch Program and one time attempted to reduce a vegetable requirement for the program by having catsup declared a vegetable.)

•   As a consequence of Johnson's nutrition programs, coupled with the founding of the Medicaid program, infant mortality rates dropped by one-third from 1965 to 1975. (Today infant mortality rates in the United States have stalled and are the highest among the industrialized nations of the world.)

• Speaking of the Medicaid program, in 1963, studies showed that fully 20 percent of people living below the poverty line had *never* been examined by a doctor (this despite higher incidences of disease and sickness among poor people). In seven years this proportion was reduced to just 8 percent. By the year 2000, 200 million poor Americans had been served by Medicaid. Prior to this program, the only time the poor got access to health care, if they did at all, was after chronic illness had set in.

• LBJ also sponsored legislation to provide cancer and heart centers at hospitals throughout the country to broaden access to care, provided funds to double the number of doctors who graduated from medical school, and committed resources to increase the number of medical specialists as well as to provide for significantly more basic and applied medical research through his National Institutes of Health.

• To help prevent Americans from getting sick from the air they breathed, the water they drank, and the land on which their food was produced, Johnson pushed through a litany of programs, including the Clean Water Restoration Act, the Clear Air Act, the Water Quality Act, the Motor Vehicle Air Pollution Control Act, and the Solid Waste Disposal Act.

• When LBJ took office, virtually no elderly American had health insurance, and there was no real program for health care in any retirement package. In a year and a half, 19 million elderly Americans had health coverage. Since 1965, 85 million Americans have been or are being served by Medicare. This was, and continues to be, an unprecedented success. All of Johnson's health-care initiatives taken together worked beyond anyone's wildest dreams. Indicators such as life expectancies were dramatically increased.

• In ten years the Great Society housing programs reduced the number of people living in substandard housing (with no running water and limited plumbing) in half. Johnson's 1968 Housing Act helped low-income families gain home ownership, and between 1968 and 2000 it worked for over 7 million families. LBJ also started the Ginnie Mae program, which increased the availability of affordable mortgages for poor families.

• John Kennedy's Manpower Development and Training Act, passed in 1962 and continued under LBJ, saw almost immediate results. By 1965, 70 percent of its trainees found jobs in the fields in which they had been trained. Studies showed that, thanks to increased earnings, taxes paid by the graduates would pay for their training in just five years.

- Johnson's 1965 Elementary and Secondary Education Act helped update thousands of public schools by committing federal funds to local school districts for the first time.
- Lyndon Johnson saw the woeful numbers of high school and college graduates (only 41 percent of Americans had a high school degree and fewer than 10 percent had a college degree in 1965) and started scores of scholarship, grant, and work-study programs to help defray the cost of a higher education. From 1965 to 2000, 86 million college loans were provided to 29 million students, and another $14 billion was granted to 6 million students for work-study programs. By 2000 fully 60 percent of full-time undergraduate students received federal financial aid; more than 80 percent of adult Americans had received a high school degree, and nearly one-quarter had finished college. (Voters should be reminded too that Ronald Reagan attempted to zero out the student loan program in all eight budgets he submitted to Congress.)
- Johnson's Head Start program, designed to provide education, nutrition, and parenting assistance for preschool children, was a wild success. By 2000 the program had served 16 million children in virtually every county in America. Studies show that 60 percent of children who participated in Head Start were less likely to be assigned to special education classes, and about one-half of its participants were less likely to be held back a grade—both producing great savings to school districts. Over the years, numerous studies have suggested that Head Start saves the government twice what it costs.

In sum, in the twenty years from John F. Kennedy to Ronald Reagan, poverty rates were cut in half, severe malnutrition was virtually abated, infant mortality rates were down significantly, opportunities for preschool children had increased dramatically, the security blanket for seniors was strengthened substantially, millions of young people had a ticket to college, job-training opportunities were significantly improved, and substandard housing was dramatically eliminated. Democrats need to remind people what their party has done for them. Republicans can try to rewrite history all they want, but tens of millions of Americans benefited from programs Democrats championed.

The New Deal and Great Society are the two greatest initiatives to build wealth among the American people ever undertaken. The numbers of people whose lives were bettered by them is staggering. Remind them of it. Republicans, by contrast, tend to invest in huge, faceless corporate entities and hope that some benefits will trickle down to working Americans after the corporations have had their way with the funds. History shows that this does not work. One needs to look no further than the savings and loan debacle of the 1980s or the more recent scandals at Enron and Halliburton to see that corporate America too often cares only about the bottom line. Greedy corporations too often take the profits and run while the American worker becomes less educated, less healthy, and less secure. It is not a successful formula. And not all Republican leaders have agreed with the concept.

> *Should any political party attempt to abolish Social Security, unemployment insurance, and eliminate labor laws and farm programs, you would not hear of that party again in our political history. There is a tiny splinter group, of course, that believes you can do these things. Among them are [a] few Texas oil millionaires, and an occasional politician or businessman from other areas. Their number is negligible and they are stupid.*
> PRESIDENT DWIGHT D. EISENHOWER
> NOVEMBER 8, 1954

Eisenhower was right. Yet Republicans often try to undo the good Democrats have done, usually attempting to scare voters with trumped-up statistics and threats that some crisis looms and we had better change direction from building wealth in the American people and toward giving to the moneyed interests. George W. Bush tried to do it when he pushed to dismantle the Social Security program. He tried to do it as well with his assault on working Americans through misguided trade and tax policies and through environmental policies designed to appease his corporate polluting harlots.

Ronald Reagan did it too. In the 1980s, for instance, although he received some of his biggest margins of electoral victory there, Reagan virtually turned his back on rural America. At the time of his election in November 1980, the federal government was spending an estimated $10 billion on projects specific to rural America; by 1987 Reagan had cut this to barely $1 billion, and he had gutted general revenue sharing to rural America to zero. His reductions in the farm program alone created a death

march off the family farm. Look at how Reagan cut health care, education, and benefits, how he attacked the American worker again with misguided tax cuts, and how he bullied labor, as best evidenced through his
dismissal of the striking air traffic controllers. Reagan needed the money
to provide his massive tax cuts to the wealthy and to throw at misguided
military weaponry while he virtually ignored the benefits of the men and
women in uniform.

Reagan's cry that there was great waste in domestic programs, meant
to justify belt tightening, proved untrue as well. Studies showed that domestic programs were being run far more efficiently than were government defense programs (defense programs had almost three times more
waste than domestic programs). Studies also showed that the domestic
programs were run as efficiently as similar programs in private industry.

The contention by so-called conservatives that these programs had
dramatically increased the size of government also proved untrue. In fact,
according to the *Statistical Abstract of the United States,* government programs from 1960 to 1980 actually grew more slowly than they did during
the Eisenhower administration. (See Chapter 7 and you will be shocked at
the numbers.)

The same is true of claims by so-called conservatives about taxes paid
by average Americans. In 1960 the average American paid 10.8 percent in
federal and state income taxes combined. By 1980 that figure rose to 12.9
percent, a 2.1 percent increase (2.1 cents per dollar of income, and half of
that came from increases in state income taxes). Yet personal income taxes
paid rose by 3.6 percent in the Eisenhower years. The income tax burden
actually dropped during the heyday of the Great Society programs.

Corporate taxes also fell during this time, and property taxes remained largely the same. In 1961, when John F. Kennedy took office, corporations in America were paying 47 percent of profits. This rate was
lowered during the 1960s and 1970s, and stood at 39 percent of profits by
1980. By contrast, in 1950 this rate was 42 percent, and it had risen to 47
percent by the end of Eisenhower's term. In 1960 property taxes averaged
4.1 percent of the nation's personal income, in 1977 they were still the
same.

By all indicators, the New Deal and the Great Society had worked.
Tens of millions of Americans saw their lives improve through the pro-

grams instituted by Democratic presidents. These investment initiatives are without question two of the great American public policy success stories in the mind of anyone who believes that a representative government should be about helping elevate the lives of the people it is supposed to be serving. And while all of this was happening, government spending was not excessive, taxes were not going up, and deficits were under control. Yet, for all the successes of these economic programs, the seeds of battles over racial civil rights coupled with the Vietnam War going badly were starting to shift the political winds toward much more polarizing and divisive issues. It was in this climate that a cynical, polarizing Republican Southern Strategy began to take root.

The Calculated Dismantling of the South and the Heartland

We are often mystified by how, in a representative democracy, politicians get away with running for office by running down their government. Think about it. In a representative democracy, *we* are the government. We have a responsibility to participate, we need to be involved, we have to keep watch on our representatives and demand the most of them. So if a candidate running for office rips our government, he or she is really ripping us.

And when our candidates for office and our elected officials invited Americans to participate and to ask "what you can do for your country," as John Kennedy did in 1961, Americans responded that there was nothing we could not do as a nation. Polls showed that nearly three-fourths of our citizens believed government was being run by good people and was doing good things.

By contrast, when candidates and elected officials run on a divisive platform, proclaiming that government is bad and does not help people, as Ronald Reagan did in 1980, polls showed that people became confused and, unfortunately, listened. By the time Reagan was elected on a largely negative message about government, barely one-third of Americans believed that government was run by good people who could solve problems. The cynical new president admonished his listeners during his first inaugural address that "government is not the solution to our problem . . .

government is the problem." This was the same Reagan who said, "LBJ declared war on poverty and poverty won." What a pompous, ignorant fool. Ronald Reagan could not hold Lyndon Johnson's jockstrap when it came to providing opportunity to disadvantaged Americans. And that tough guy Reagan never would have had the testosterone to say such things to Johnson's face—LBJ would have had the phony for lunch. Had the Gipper looked into the eyes of the millions of Americans who capitalized on the opportunities presented by the Great Society and New Deal programs, he could not have made such stupid statements. Leaders like Lyndon Johnson understood the challenges of leadership in a free, representative society. By contrast, the vast bulk of Reagan's administration was a sellout and a sham. Reagan gave huge tax breaks to the wealthy and the greedy; Johnson invested in the American people. Reagan sold out to corporate interests and cut regulations that protected workers and consumers; Johnson created the most aggressive programs for protecting our nation's air, water, and land quality in American history. Reagan fought to reclassify catsup as a vegetable in school lunches; Johnson created the School Lunch Program. Reagan may have been "the Great Communicator," but while he was convincing Americans that their government was bad, he was allowing corporate interests to rob it blind.

Where did politicians like Ronald Reagan get their cynicism? What allowed such cynicism to creep into the American mind-set and take hold? What forces came into being that permitted negative and divisive proposals to trump programs of hope and opportunity?

America, meet Strom Thurmond and Harry Dent.

How the Foxes Got into the Henhouse

Before Democrats can embark on a successful national campaign in the South or anywhere in rural America, they must learn everything about their quarry, the Republican foxes. As early fur trappers like Jim Bridger and Liver-Eating Johnston quickly found out, foxes are among the most—if not the most—difficult species to outsmart and catch. And as any family farmer will tell you, a fox can be a devastating thing in a henhouse. Although trapping has become something of a lost profession, America's early pioneers admired the fox as a foil. They talked about it and defined it so well culturally that even modern Americans know more about the fox than about any other wild animal. Ask most anybody about foxes, and you'll hear descriptions such as voracious, swift, brave, sly, relentless, deceptive. Most important, you'll hear the comparison "smart as a fox."

For Democrats to be successful in an arduous campaign to expose the lies and reveal the truth—in other words, turn the Republican Southern Strategy into the Republican Southern Hoax—they must first acknowledge facts. Over the last forty years, Republican foxes have been just plain slicker when it comes to winning elections. Although the "Metropolitan Opera Wing" of the Democratic Party will surely disagree that the Republicans have outfoxed them, election returns don't lie. All you have to do is look at the shift of power over the last forty years.

In seeking a starting point for the Republican Southern Strategy, we went back to 1902 Edgefield, South Carolina, when a somewhat well-to-do southern family celebrated a new addition, a bouncing baby boy named James Strom Thurmond.

As was typical in southern white families of the day, little Strom's beliefs were shaped by a system of religious conservatism. From that would grow his strong belief in states' rights and an absolute loathing of any sort of federal intrusion into the southern way of life. Thurmond merely evolved as a man of the times, a leader born just twenty-six years after the end of the hated Reconstruction (still known by many in the Confederate States as the "Yankee Occupation"). The wounds of the Civil War had yet even to scab over, much less to heal. Unfortunately for all Americans, these wounds would drive Thurmond's political ideals through most of his one hundred years. His first office was county superintendent of education. Three years later he dove headfirst into politics with his election to the statehouse. He added an election as a circuit judge to his résumé before World War II interrupted his rise. After the war he set his sights on the South Carolina governorship and defeated eleven opponents in securing the Democratic nomination. In those days of machine politics and pretty much Democratic Party domination in the South, the Democratic nominee was virtually assured of victory in the general election. The governorship was Thurmond's first platform for influencing national events.

The 1948 Democratic National Convention in Philadelphia was

where the seed of the modern Republican Southern Strategy took root. President Harry S. Truman was sympathetic to civil rights and convinced a young senator from Minnesota, Hubert H. Humphrey, to fire the first shot. On opening night, Humphrey urged the delegates to introduce a civil rights plank to the party's platform. His plank included items such as federal protection against lynching, abolition of poll taxes, and formation of the Fair Employment Practices Commission. Humphrey's speech drew strong applause from many, but a strong volley of opposition from southern delegates began to echo through the hall. In the end his plank prevailed overwhelmingly, and Governor Thurmond and other southern delegates uttered slurs and profanities as they left the convention in protest.

The moment kicked into gear Thurmond's trademark fury. His response was to form an opposition party. Later that July, 6,000 southern Democrats met in Birmingham, Alabama, for the first (and last) nominating convention of the new States' Rights Democratic Party. Pundits quickly dubbed the party the Dixiecrats. Thurmond accepted the nomination for president, and Governor Fielding Wright of Mississippi got the vice presidential nod. An outpouring of accented rhetoric about states' rights, racial separation, and of course the now familiar mantle of the Republican Party—God and patriotism—spurred the delegates onto the campaign trail.

The Dixiecrats were off to the moon, but as they used to say during the early days of NASA's Mercury Program, "No bucks, no Buck Rogers." The splinter group held no appeal for large contributors; like Howard Dean in 2004, they had to depend on small donations. Thurmond's organization finished a weak third in both the popular and the electoral vote. However, they managed to take four southern states (Alabama, Louisiana, Mississippi, and South Carolina), where they were listed on the ballot as Democrats. Truman won the rest of the South, leading pundits at the time to label the Dixiecrats a failed protest movement. History would later show that, instead, the Dixiecrat uprising was the first crack in the Democrats' armor and became the foundation for a strategy that would break their vise grip on the South. Truman was so disgusted with Thurmond that when Thurmond waved to Truman and his vice president, Alben Barkley, as they drove past him at their inauguration, and

Barkley attempted to wave back, the president reportedly grabbed his VP's arm and said, "Don't wave at that [expletive deleted]."

When South Carolina's senior U.S. senator, Burnet Maybank, died from a massive heart attack in 1954, Thurmond, who lost the Democratic nomination to replace Maybank, mounted a massive write-in campaign and was elected, becoming the first U.S. senator ever to win as a write-in candidate. By 1956, *Brown v. Board of Education* (the landmark 1954 Supreme Court decision in which "separate but equal" schools were ruled unconstitutional) drove Thurmond to write the Southern Manifesto, slamming the decision as a "clear abuse of judicial power" that should be "resisted by all legal means." Although many delusional contemporary Republicans claim that race was not the foundation of the Southern Strategy, it should be crystal clear that racism was not only the foundation but the taproot.

While Harry Truman had wanted civil rights served on the table, his successor, Dwight Eisenhower, wanted sanctuary from the issue, especially from the polarizing, hot-button matter of implementing integration. Congress was eventually forced to respond with the Civil Rights Act of 1957. Many southern Democrats gave in to the watered-down version of the act, which did little or nothing for civil rights but did make lynching a federal crime. Yet it was still too much for Thurmond. He responded with the longest one-man filibuster in Senate history, twenty-four hours and eighteen minutes. It didn't work.

After the filibuster, Thurmond's aide and disciple, a twenty-seven-year-old graduate of Presbyterian College named Harry Dent, carried a pail to the senator in case he couldn't make it to the men's room before he had to relieve himself. From carrying Thurmond's piss pail, Dent rose in stature in the arcane world of down-home politics. By 1968 he had established himself as one of the principal architects of the Southern Strategy. *Time* magazine in 1969 reported that liberals referred to Dent as a "southern-fried Rasputin in the Nixon Administration."

By the early sixties, the Kennedy-Johnson civil rights push had left Thurmond hopelessly infuriated. Then his worst fear became a reality— the Civil Rights Act of 1964, unlike the Civil Rights Act of 1957, had meat on the bone. A lot of prodding by Dent and the billfold of the South Carolina textile magnate Roger Milliken persuaded Thurmond that there was political opportunity in his anger. Republicans could now play the race card and peel off white voters in the South. But Thurmond would have to switch parties. He did. And immediately began campaigning throughout the South for his compadre in the Senate and the 1964 Republican presidential nominee, Barry Goldwater. Like Thurmond, Goldwater had voted against the Civil Rights Act of 1964. Thurmond's campaigning, with the help of Dent's political genius plus Milliken and friends' financial support, delivered four southern states (Georgia, Louisiana, Mississippi, and, of course, South Carolina) for Goldwater.

While Dent was the political force behind the Southern Strategy, Milliken was the sugar daddy. A maniacal conservative and billionaire, Roger Milliken reportedly once barred Xerox copiers from his offices and plants because Xerox had put up money for a civil rights documentary. Besides being a segregationist, Milliken was fiercely antiunion. In 1956 he shut down Milliken and Company's Darlington, South Carolina, plant after workers voted to unionize. After a twenty-five-year legal battle, the courts ordered him to pay $5 million in back wages. Unfortunately, 144 of the affected workers had died during the quarter-century-long fight. It seems only the good die young. Milliken was clearly the "patron saint" of the Southern Strategy. Besides bankrolling the development of the strategy in 1968, he heavily supported Republicans and extremist groups in the development of the entire hoax. (He also helped fund Ronald Reagan, Newt Gingrich, the John Birch Society, the Heritage Foundation, and on and on. He was the largest single investor when William F. Buckley kicked off the *National Review*.)

After a twenty-year gestation period, the modern Southern Strategy was born in the summer of 1968. After Richard Nixon promised Thurmond that he wouldn't make the South a "whipping boy," Strom pledged his support of Nixon's candidacy. This was especially important for Nixon because George Wallace and his American Independent Party's segregationist platform were on the ballot. To win, Tricky Dick felt he needed some southern states. That June, Strom and the gang met with Senator John Tower of Texas and other Republicans. Chuck Colson, of Watergate fame, was Nixon's senior adviser at the Atlanta meeting. The policy of forced school integration and the speed with which it would be implemented were much bandied about, but Colson was most interested in how he could use this issue to help get Nixon southern votes. What developed was a strategy based on playing to the southerners' fear of integration as well as using patriotic themes and slogans to capture southern whites, who seemed to have a greater propensity toward patriotism issues and defense spending than did most other Americans. This strategy manifested itself in part in Thurmond's cry of "Freedom of Choice," which in 1968 had to do not with abortions but with white schoolchildren being forced to attend schools with black schoolchildren.

Ironically, contrary to Strom's belief, Nixon didn't like the politics of the Old South, was sold on affirmative action, and often railed against "right-wing bitching." He didn't want to deal with the campaign in the South—he just wanted the votes—so he turned the southern campaign over to Dent and Colson. This was important, because while Nixon likely would have paused at race-baiting issues, Thurmond had no such anxiety. Nixon believed he needed Thurmond so badly that he gave Strom the ability to veto potential vice presidential candidates. The senator exercised that veto against moderates Mark Hatfield of Oregon and William Scranton of Pennsylvania. Thurmond liked Spiro Agnew of Maryland because he thought he was more sympathetic to the Southern Strategy. Nixon, as it turned out, liked Agnew too—albeit for different reasons. In his scandalous tapes, he said that he picked Agnew because "the bastards will never shoot me. They know they'll get Agnew." On election day, Nixon and the Southern Strategy carried South Carolina, Tennessee, Virginia, Florida, and eleven of the twelve electoral votes in North Carolina (Wallace got the other). The Republicans had broken the Democrats' stranglehold on the South, and Tricky Dick was headed off to a date with infamy.

Son of Strom: Lee Atwater and the Wedgies

The modern expansion of the cynical Southern Strategy came at the hands of a guy named Lee Atwater. Atwater wanted to win at all costs, and the Southern Strategy provided him a promising blueprint. The former Democratic National Committee chairman and a fixture of South Carolina politics Don Fowler said of Atwater, "Lee was the guy who introduced hard-core wedge politics into the strategy."

Atwater, without question, was a personality. From the time he was a kid, he drew a crowd. In elementary school, Lee had a buddy who was uncomfortable with the girls. Unbeknownst to his pal, the young Atwater sent invitations for the boy's birthday party to every girl in the class. They showed, and it wasn't even the kid's birthday. A terrible student, he made himself an outstanding rhythm and blues guitarist after hearing James Brown on the radio. His only goal as a kid was to play the guitar. He was well liked by his friends and even some of his opponents. Dick Harpootlian, the former state Democratic Party chairman from South Carolina, who met Atwater while he was at Clemson and Atwater was at Newberry, says of him, "He was a good guy to be around."

After interning for Thurmond, Atwater was hooked on politics. He got heavily involved in the College Republicans and in 1973 served as an assistant to Karl Rove on a campaign that ended in Rove being elected national chairman of the group. (Believe it or not, that campaign was dogged for years by allegations of dirty tricks.)

After traveling across the South with Rove to secure votes, Atwater was named executive director of the organization and, along with Rove, became convinced that if the Republicans could take over campuses, they would be in a position to control power well into the twenty-first century. The College Republicans obviously served both men well, as it did Ralph Reed, who was executive director for the group in the early 1980s. (One strategy note. We believe that for Democrats to win again in the South and rural America, they have to begin rebuilding "Young Democrats" organizations in sororities, fraternities, and on college campuses in general. On most any college campus in America, the Young Republicans organization will be larger and stronger than the Young Democrats organization. This is due in no small part to the national Republican Party's moral and financial support for the Young Republicans groups. Democrats need to recruit better and harder on college campuses, and they need to give campus groups adequate financial backing to make them viable. These groups then need to show students a good time while they show them that Democrats better represent the issues affecting young Americans.)

After working with Dent's consulting firm, Atwater ran Ronald Reagan's South Carolina campaign in 1980. This is when his wedged, dirty-trick campaigning began; it continued until he had gained the title

"Darth Vader of the Republican Party." That year he was advising Floyd Spence, who was running for Congress in South Carolina against Tom Turnipseed. Atwater sent a letter from Strom Thurmond throughout the congressional district saying that Turnipseed's election would give America to the "liberals and communists." At the last minute, he sent out a direct-mail piece from a prefabricated independent pollster to white voters in the suburbs saying that Turnipseed was "a member of the NAACP." To top it off, he planted a reporter in a press conference to ask Turnipseed about his mental problems. Turnipseed, as a child, had received shock treatments for chronic depression. Atwater later bragged about planting the reporter, claiming his opponent had been "hooked up to jumper cables." Later in his life, Atwater claimed, "While I didn't invent negative politics, I am one of its most ardent practitioners."

In the 1980s, he was also instrumental in introducing wedge terms such as "welfare queen," a phrase implying that many of America's tax dollars were going to blacks who got paid for doing nothing. He painted African Americans as lobster-eating food stamp recipients who were making a mockery of the welfare system. Lost in this trickery were the facts, including the fact that most welfare recipients were white. He used sound bites like "no-show jobs" in reference to federal jobs programs—ignoring the fact that it was Richard Nixon who used jobs programs for political purposes. Before Republicans became masters of using the greed of "tax cuts," Atwater was the unabashed master of using fear. After serving Reagan and doing a stint with a top Republican consulting firm in Washington, D.C., Atwater became the national chair for George H. W. Bush's 1988 presidential campaign. The vice president quickly assigned his son W to Atwater. The dirty tricks continued through the 1988 campaign with his most famous of all, Willie Horton. Atwater introduced Horton at a point when the Democrat, Michael Dukakis, was holding a 17-point lead in the national polls. Horton, a convicted murderer sentenced to life, was on furlough from a Massachusetts prison when he committed a rape. Atwater, through earned and paid media attention, was determined to transform Horton into, as he would say, "Dukakis's running mate." History says it worked. The elder Bush rewarded Atwater by making him chairman of the Republican National Committee.

The one glaring ironic truth of the polarizing evils of the Southern Strategy is the remorse and repentance of most of the strategy's major architects and builders. Their consciences apparently couldn't rest. Atwater's mentor, Harry Dent, pleaded guilty to aiding and abetting an illegal campaign fund that in 1970 gave more than $3 million to Republican congressional campaigns. Although the judge said Dent was an "innocent victim" and gave him a slap on the hand, Dent dropped politics and became a missionary, traveling the world spreading the Gospel. South Caroline Democrat Fowler says of him, "Harry Dent did nothing I know of in the last thirty years that would lead me to believe his remorse and turn to God was anything but totally sincere."

After being Nixon's chief counsel from 1969 to 1973, Chuck Colson pleaded "no contest" to his role in the break-in of Daniel Ellsberg's psychiatrist's office in September 1971 and was sentenced to seven months in prison. Before the plea, Colson announced he had become an "evangelical Christian." Many members of the media attacked him at the time for using the conversion to get a reduced sentence. However, after his release from prison, Colson founded Prison Fellowship, which is still going strong.

And then there was the sad end for Lee Atwater. Upon learning of his brain tumor in 1990, which resulted in his death on March 29, 1991, Lee summoned Harry Dent for spiritual guidance. Atwater, too, turned to God. Before his death, he sent letters asking for forgiveness to anybody he felt he had wronged. To Tom Turnipseed, the guy he "hooked up to jumper cables," he wrote, "My illness has taught me something about the nature of humanity, love, brotherhood, and relationships that I never understood, and probably never would have. So from that standpoint, there is some truth and good in everything." To many Democrats who despised Atwater, his conversion was simply "cutting a deal with God." Mary Matalin, Atwater's chief of staff at the Republican National Committee, contends, "Even before he got sick, Lee would ask questions about faith. In any event, 'cutting a deal with God' and a true conversion are certainly not mutually exclusive." The Democrat Dick Harpootlian confirms, "I only saw Lee one time after he got sick, but I have no doubts. He was a changed man."

Apparently these men who concocted the Southern Strategy believed the truth would set them free. Unfortunately for the country, their strategy still haunts American politics. Democrats need to learn how to use truth to free America and the South from the divisive lies of the Southern Strategy. It's time.

Chapter 3

THE RESULT: FOXES IN THE HENHOUSE

The bait-and-switch strategies of Republicans over the past forty years, which have emphasized single polarizing issues at the expense of economic and social ones, have been devastating to rural America. The political gambit transformed people previously united and transfixed on issues of opportunity, hope, and attainment into people divided very often by race, values, hatred, and stereotypes. This polarization has ultimately helped institutionalize poverty while it artificially deflated wages, deemphasized educational attainment, and bred a mind-set of hopelessness through much of rural America.

And although people like Harry Dent and his disciples, as well as a host of ambitious Republican politicians, must take responsibility for the debilitating results of this strategy, Democrats, who too often sat back and covered for their own cultural and political inadequacies by blaming the "fools" in rural America who were voting against their own economic interests, must admit their role as well. These rural "fools" may have been voting against their own best economic interests, but they also had a litany of cultural and value-laden interests the power of which fools in the Democratic Party failed to see or respect.

We should also note that we are not suggesting Dent, Atwater, or any of the political leaders who gorged themselves on their divisive strategies did so and continue to do so with malicious intentions. But while the intentions may not have been malicious, the results clearly have been.

There is a price to pay for buying into the politics of division. When

Republicans found they could win in rural America on the strength of single polarizing issues, with no pressure to deliver tangible goods in return, they had stumbled onto a powerful political strategy—victory with very little pain or payback. When Democrats failed to appreciate and thus respect the power of the culture and values that underscored these issues, belittling or ignoring what they did not understand, they abandoned rural America. The result was that rural Americans were rendered electorally impotent. Republicans were communicating with them but taking them for granted, and Democrats were ignoring them.

Rural America has paid a devastating price for this transformation. From their children to their seniors, from their jobs to their educational opportunities, and from transportation to health care, rural America has suffered and continues to suffer tremendously under this dead-end electoral dilemma. The numbers are shocking. And because rural America traditionally was a reliable breeding ground for some of the strongest values of family, faith, and work ethic, the loss to the nation is as great as it is to rural America.

The Numbers

There are 2,052 counties that make up rural America. Fully 75 percent of our land is in rural America, and 59 million people, or 21 percent of the population, live there. These numbers are actually deceptively low because in 2003 the Census Bureau changed its definition of "rural," now defining rural areas very narrowly as open country and small-town areas, whereas "urban" is now defined as a core of at least 50,000 people—but for geographic purposes, the urban lines include fringe counties that meet various criteria for workers commuting into cities. The result is that 298 counties with 10.3 million people that were classified as rural are now considered urban, and 45 counties with 3 million people that had been classified as urban are now considered rural. That is a net of 253 counties and 7.3 million people who are now reclassified as "urban." So the 59 million figure could just as easily be more than 66 million.

Regardless of the formula the government uses to divide its citizens into rural and urban classes, rural America is where a significant portion of the American population lives, works, and raises families. And these people are taking a hit. Lack of jobs, educational opportunities, infrastructure, and health-care providers and facilities, coupled with a substantial out-migration of young people and college-educated workers and poor educational attainment for those who remain, has caused rural America to become stagnant in many ways. On population growth alone, rural America is mired in a torpid pond. From 2000 to 2003, when the urban population grew by almost 4.0 percent, small-town America grew by only 1.6 percent and rural counties showed virtually no growth. In fact, 60 percent of all rural counties *lost* population during this period. Census Bureau projections suggest that this trend will continue.

On top of these problems, much of the loss in population comes from the segment most essential to community growth and vitality—children. While the number of children in America increased by 34 percent from 1950 to 2000, the number of children in rural America *dropped* by 37 percent. In 1950, 29 percent of all young people lived in rural America. By 2000 the percentage had fallen to 17.

But the numbers keep getting worse for rural America, and our political leaders don't seem to care—indeed, the more rural America voted "red" in the past couple of generations, the worse it seemed to get. Even though George W. Bush won rural America by a 59 to 40 percent margin in 2004; even though rural women voted for him by a 62 to 38 percent margin; even though married people in rural America voted for him by a 65 to 34 percent margin; even though blue-collar workers in rural America voted for him by a 63 to 37 percent margin; even though people earning under $30,000 in rural America voted for him by a 52 to 47 percent margin; and even though the South and much of rural America are increasingly sending Republicans to the U.S. Congress, Bush and the Republicans have done little for rural America.

Take a look at what has happened to rural America in some key demographic categories.

Poverty

Every year since the government began keeping records in the 1960s, rural poverty rates have exceeded urban rates. But that is not to say there have not been successes. Democratic presidents, like Lyndon Johnson and Bill Clinton, had great success in reducing poverty rates generally and in rural America particularly. Republican presidents have not fared so well. It's hard to believe this is an accident.

George W. Bush and the current Republican-held Congress, for instance, have been a disaster with regard to reducing rural poverty. While Clinton policies had lowered the poverty rate from 17.2 percent in 1993 to 11.3 percent in 2000, Bush, the Republican-controlled Congress, and their "greedy first" policies reversed the trend. Nearly 2 million more people fell below the poverty line in Bush's first five years in office. (Poverty is officially defined by the United States Department of Agriculture as "income less than that deemed sufficient to purchase basic needs of food, shelter, clothing, and other essential goods and services.")

By 2003, over 14 percent of the rural population was poor, compared with 11.6 percent of the urban population. The rural poverty rate for African Americans stood at 33 percent, for Native Americans at 35 percent, and for Hispanics at 27 percent. And fully 36 percent of all the rural poor were children. In 2002 an embarrassing 20 percent of all children living in rural areas were poor, and over one-half of all rural poor children lived in the South. These are really ugly numbers.

Republican diversionary tactics and divisive single issues, coupled with Democratic confusion and near silence on all matters cultural, institutionalized poverty and all the problems associated with it—low education rates, poor health care, and low-wage jobs—in rural America. Study after study points out that childhood poverty leads to learning and discipline problems in school, much greater incidence of teenage parenting, more criminal activity, and far less earning power and greater chances of unemployment when the child grows up. In short, poverty became a multigenerational fact of life. The numbers bear it out.

According to the Department of Agriculture (USDA), of the 386 counties in America considered "persistently poor" (defined as having a total population of 20 percent or more who were poor over a thirty-year period), 340—an astonishing 88 percent—are found in rural America. Fully 14 percent of all rural citizens live in these counties. And among the 340 rural persistent-poverty counties, a numbing 280, or 82 percent, are in the South, with another 60 in the West and Midwest; *none* are in the Northeast. Over 17 percent of all people who live in the South are poor, and over 25 percent live in persistent-poverty counties. And the more rural the county, the greater the concentration of the poor. According to the USDA, almost 28 percent of the people in "completely rural" counties (those not adjacent to urban counties) live in counties marked by persistent poverty.

None of this has snuck up on us. The numbers have been getting increasingly bleak for a generation. But when politicians are allowed to put their own ambitions first and to develop a cynical agenda that obfuscates reality, and when they are allowed to believe service is about them and not about the people who would be served, and are allowed to feel no pain for their neglect, we have a recipe for social and cultural disaster.

And it is not just with poverty that rural America is being hurt.

Education

There are, without question, many reasons for persistent poverty and poor economic opportunities. But perhaps none is as great a factor as educational attainment.

In rural America, education and educational opportunities are a chronic problem. Too often when young people from rural America attain a college degree, they do not return to rural America, because of the lack of jobs and economic opportunity. As a consequence, less than one-fifth of the twenty-five- to twenty-nine-year-olds residing in rural America have a college degree, compared with over one-third of people living in urban areas. The outmigration of college-educated workers becomes a disincentive to business to locate in rural America, and the remaining undereducated workforce results in an economic culture of low-wage jobs.

The rural crisis in education is nowhere more present than in the South, which is home to one-half of America's rural adults who do not have a high school degree. In fact, in all of rural America, nearly one in four adults age twenty-five and older did not receive a high school degree, and another one in three has only a high school degree. That's six out of ten adults in rural America who have received no more than a high school degree. On top of that, only 15 percent of rural adults have a four-year college degree, compared with nearly 30 percent in urban areas.

These low education rates translate into high poverty rates, high unemployment rates, and low wages for those who do find work. Rural unemployment rates for workers age twenty-five and older are typically five times higher for those without a high school diploma than for college graduates. What would be the value of a college degree for rural Americans? The pay of college graduates in rural America is more than double that for those who have not completed high school. A commitment to get our education rates up in rural America will eliminate many of the problems faced by people who live there. (Although, when compared with college graduates in urban America, college graduates in rural America earn on average 12 percent less—another incentive to head to the city. So with higher educational attainment must come incentives for businesses to locate in rural America so that college graduates have reason to return home.)

It is also no accident that the lower one's educational level, the greater one's chance of landing below the poverty line. In fact, the 25 percent of rural counties with the lowest high school completion rates include fully 66 percent of all persistent-poverty counties.

The educational problems in rural America also begin at the earliest of ages. According to a study on early childhood education by the Population Reference Bureau released in January 2005, rural children were beginning grade school well behind their urban counterparts in reading and math skills. This is likely because of underfunded schools, inadequately trained teachers, and a general lack of community commitment and services. In addition, because rural parents have the least amount of education, emphasis on and appreciation of educational attainment are often lacking. If Mom and Dad seem not to give a damn about education and had little of it themselves, their children are less likely to see the importance of a good education—even at a very early age.

Rural America is getting no help from George W. Bush and the Republican-controlled Congress. Bush's fiscal year 2006 budget proposed *cutting* education funding for the first time in over a decade, and the cuts hit rural America hardest. According to the National Education Association, Bush's cuts to formula grants like education technology funding, the Safe and Drug-Free Schools Program, and the 50 percent reduction under the Innovative Block Grant in Bush's "No Child Left Behind" program leave "most rural districts across the country with a net loss in federal education funding," while his mandates under the No Child Left Behind Program are increasing. The association estimated that Bush's proposal would severely hamstring over 800 school districts serving rural populations. Not exactly the way to turn things around, Mr. President.

On top of that, Bush's fiscal year 2006 budget proposed zeroing out the $1.3 billion Perkins Vocational Education Program, which gives vital job training to tens of thousands of rural students in areas that offer higher pay and very often allows them to stay in rural communities.

Doesn't sound to us like a president committed to rural America. But Bush's lack of commitment to rural America doesn't end with education.

Health Care

Poor health care is another devastating link in the poverty chain, and in rural America, the state of health care is bleak. Health-care providers and patients in rural America face a litany of problems not encountered in urban America, including isolation, economic disparity, lack of access, and diminished quality of care. Look at what a study conducted by the Office of Rural Health Policy found in 2004:

• Approximately 59 million people, or 21 percent of the population, live in rural America, yet only about 10 percent of all physicians practice there. The Department of Health and Human Services defines a population as being adequately served when the ratio of providers to patients is 1 to 2,000. Yet in the most rural American counties the ratio is often more than twice that, and the average throughout rural America is 1 provider for every 3,500 patients.

• There are 910 Health Professional Shortage Areas—geographic areas with a critical shortage of health-care providers—in urban America while there are an astounding 2,157 in rural America. About 40 percent of all rural residents live in these areas, compared with only 12 percent of the urban population.

- Between 57 and 90 percent of all first responders in rural areas are volunteers.
- More than 470 rural hospitals have closed in the past twenty-five years.
- Rural hospitals and physicians historically receive dramatically less for services than do their urban counterparts.
- Fully 20 percent of rural counties lack any mental health services, compared with only 5 percent of urban counties. In 1999, of the 1,669 Mental Health Professional Shortage Areas, 87 percent were in rural areas, affecting over 30 million people.
- People who live in rural America are far less likely to have employer-provided health-care coverage or prescription drug coverage, and the rural poor are more likely not to be covered by Medicaid benefits than are people in urban areas.
- There are 50 percent more dentists per 100,000 people in urban America than in rural America.

And it doesn't help when George W. Bush and the Republicans in Congress do things like proposing to zero-fund the Critical Access Hospital designation for 700 rural hospitals, a move that would threaten many with financial ruin. The designation, established in 1997, allows for small rural hospitals to be reimbursed by Medicare at higher rates than other hospitals. It was literally the difference between keeping the doors open and shutting down for most of these hospitals. Sure enough, in his fiscal year 2006 budget, Bush proposed *zeroing out* the *entire* Rural Hospital Flexibility Grant Program, which houses the Critical Access Hospital Program.

On top of that, Bush's 2006 budget proposed cutting the Rural Health Outreach Grant Program by 75 percent. That program is designed to get rural providers to work together to build better systems of care. Could our president be thinking that he can make these unconscionable cuts because he has these voters anyway?

But the president didn't stop there. Bush proposed zeroing out the Small Hospital Improvement Program, which was created to assist rural hospitals with fewer than fifty beds to upgrade their medical technology infrastructure. There's that "Compassionate Conservative" coming through. He also proposed zeroing out the Community Access Program, which provided grants to increase access to health care to the uninsured and the underinsured, again hitting rural America particularly hard. In short, those who have the greatest need got hurt the most.

Health care and health-care availability in rural America were on life support, and George Bush and the Republicans in Congress have pulled the plug.

But at least rural Americans have plenty of good-paying jobs to purchase what health care is available, right? Wrong.

Jobs and Economic Opportunity

Today over 25 million wage and salary workers live in rural America. But work is increasingly hard to come by in these areas, and high-wage jobs are becoming as hard to find as compassion in the hearts of Republican leaders in Congress. Unemployment in rural areas tends to be higher than in other parts of the country as well. By 2003 unemployment in rural America had hit 5.8 percent, the highest level since 1994, and in the South and Midwest, there was actually a net loss of jobs in the past several years. On top of that, the average weekly wage for rural Americans stood at $555, compared with $699 for workers in urban areas for the same amount of work. Median household income in rural areas lags considerably behind urban income. In 2003 the median household income in rural America was $35,112, compared with $46,060 in urban America. But in the last decade, the growth in earning power of workers in rural America was less than half what it was for their urban counterparts, and the actual earnings of workers in rural America fell to just 66 percent of the earnings of urban workers. In fact, 40 percent of families in rural America are considered "working poor," which means they are teetering on the edge of poverty but often cannot obtain public support because their income is above the poverty level.

Some politicians attempt to justify the plight of rural Americans by citing statistics which show that federal social program payments to rural Americans on average are higher than they are to urban Americans. In 2001, for example, these politicians would tell you, annual per capita federal payments for things such as Social Security, unemployment insurance, Medicare, and food stamps to rural Americans averaged $4,375, while transfers to urban Americans averaged $3,798. So rural America really is being looked after by these corpulent caldrons of compassion. Nice try.

The truth is people in rural America are getting more social program funds because unemployment is higher, and, if they have jobs, they too often are low wage. Furthermore, rural society is aging so much more rapidly than urban America that greater federal funds are needed. The Republican who tells people in rural America they should be grateful for the high transfers is like the well-fed fat person telling starving people they should feel lucky because their lack of food will allow them to lose weight.

Part of the problem for rural America is disastrous trade practices, which have cost hundreds of thousands of jobs. In the textile industry alone, a vital employer, particularly in the southeastern United States, nearly 1 million jobs have been lost in the past decade. Economic growth is lagging in 60 percent of all rural counties. Many of the jobs that remain are minimum-wage jobs with no benefits. In fact, a job in rural America is twice as likely to be a minimum-wage job with no benefits as is a job in urban America. The minimum wage was last raised in September 1997, so today 11 percent of rural workers earn $5.15 (the federal minimum wage) to $6.14 an hour, although the proportions in southern states are much higher—18.0 percent in Louisiana, 17.1 percent in Arkansas, and 16.7 percent in Mississippi. Critics of raising the minimum wage contend that a significant share of the beneficiaries of an increased wage are not the poor but rather part-time teenage workers. A study by the sociologists Leslie Whitener and Timothy Parker suggests that in rural America that would not be the case: "Our analysis suggests that the minimum wage increase in rural areas would primarily affect adults and unmarried women. Most of the likely beneficiaries are women (63 percent), whites (85 percent), people 20 and older (77 percent), and people who are not married (66 percent)." The study concluded, "Family income and size data suggest that a large proportion of those who would benefit from the minimum wage increase are likely to be poor."

Another problem is that, without economic opportunity, when

young people leave home in rural America they do not return. Indeed, the number of rural counties losing population rose from 600 in 1990 to well over 1,000 in 2004. That constitutes over one-half of all rural counties in America. This loss of population was felt in every region of the country but was particularly evident in Great Plains states.

It is a vicious circle. First, the people living in rural America do not have the education to get higher-paying jobs. Then, because of an under-educated workforce, high-paying jobs leave rural America. Now there are no high-paying jobs for rural workers to get, but they do not have the education levels to qualify them for jobs outside rural America. So they are stuck. And when they are stuck, the other damning consequences of trying to survive on low wages and no benefits begin to tear at the fabric of the family unit and at the self-confidence and self-esteem of the workers. That is in no small way why hope is low and suicide rates are high—in fact, suicide rates today are higher in rural America than they are in urban America. Hope doesn't die easy in rural America, but when it dies, it dies hard.

But practically, what do rural people do when jobs are not available to them in their communities? They commute—a lot more than you might think.

According to the Population Reference Bureau, almost one-third of all rural workers commute to a job that is over twenty minutes from their homes. This is a particular problem for the estimated 30 percent of rural resident workers who commute to work in a vehicle borrowed from a family member or friend. It is also a problem in that over half of all rural counties have no public transportation system, and in most of the counties that do, the service is limited and often stops at the county line (only one out of four rural transit systems operate in multiple counties), which is of little or no benefit for the over 30 percent of rural workers who work outside the county in which they live. Part of the problem is that less than 10 percent of what the government spends on public transportation goes to rural counties.

In the last decade alone, rural traffic on roads and highways increased by 30 percent. This creates another problem for rural families: Automobile maintenance costs and bloated gas prices become a major expense. In fact, over 1.6 million households in rural America cannot afford to own a vehicle. The rate of carlessness is twice as high in rural counties as it is in urban areas. Talk about isolation.

How might government officials help with this dilemma? The Rural Families Data Center recommends that incentives be offered to build affordable housing closer to job growth areas, provide the assistance needed for day-care services, and change credit requirements so that lower-income families have an easier time obtaining automobile loans. It wouldn't hurt to make more funds available for rural public transportation either.

Doesn't sound all that difficult to us. Apparently, the Republicans just did not think to do any of this for their red-state supporters. Perhaps they are too busy writing all of those tax breaks for the greedy.

On top of the problems with public transportation and long distances to work, stores, schools, and health-care facilities, rural Americans who wish to travel out of their communities by bus or plane are pretty much up the proverbial river without a paddle. The Republicans led the charge to deregulate the airline industry in 1978, and the great snake oil salesman to rural America Ronald Reagan deregulated the bus industry in 1982. On top of that, the Gipper led the charge to transfer the responsibility, and with it much of the expense, for transportation to state and local governments. The problem was that states could not afford the costs.

Bus and plane service pulled out of the less profitable rural communities. In 1982, before deregulation, bus service was available to 15,000 rural communities. After deregulation, that dropped to fewer than 4,300. And just try to catch a plane out of anywhere in rural America. If they can afford air travel, which is unlikely, rural Americans have to expect bizarre routes, routine stopovers, and an inordinate amount of downtime waiting to catch a plane, usually a puddle jumper. And the decline in air service has not stalled. From 2000 to 2003, flight service to rural America continued to drop, falling almost 20 percent.

But Republicans weren't finished screwing rural Americans. In the transportation trifecta, cuts in national train service, mainly in Amtrak funding, have hit rural America hardest. Today 60 percent of rural residents are not even near train service areas, and rail service today is available in only 200 rural locations. The inability to move in and out of rural America by plane, train, bus, or automobile also becomes a great disincentive for industry to locate there.

So if industry is not locating in rural America, and indeed has been pulling out of rural America, and government is providing little by way of incentives to move good-paying jobs to more rural areas, what jobs are available to the people who live there?

A startling 44 percent of all jobs in rural America fall into two sectors: government or the service industry. That is, rural Americans are teaching in public schools; working for the state, local, or federal government; or making one another's meals, selling one another consumer products at minimum wage, picking up one another's garbage, or cleaning one another's houses. Not much else. By contrast, in the higher-paying producer services sector, rural America has fallen well behind its urban counterpart. Only 11 percent of total earnings in rural America come from jobs in this sector, like telecommunications or energy, compared with almost 30 percent of the total earnings in urban America.

Indeed, the old stereotype that rural America is dominated by farms and agricultural interests is a thing of the past. With the consolidation of farming interests, the death march of family farmers under Republican administrations from Reagan to Bush II, and policies shifting massive farm payments predominantly to Republican-friendly corporate interests as opposed to family farmers, less than 5 percent of rural workers today work on farms. An unfortunate offshoot of the consolidation of agricultural interests is that, as farms dried up, so did the large farm families that once occupied much of rural America.

What too many Republican leaders do not understand is that these family farm "factories," if you will, gave America far more than just the food we ate. They were tremendous breeding grounds for family values, a strong work ethic, and a deep appreciation for the importance of taking care of the land on which we live and sustain ourselves. Because of the disastrous farm policies of the past twenty-five years of a predominantly Republican-controlled Congress and White House, the farm family, which was for generations considered the backbone of America, is gone. According to the 2000 census, average family size is now larger in urban areas than it is in rural America.

One problem that government could correct that would help rural America greatly is the manner in which it distributes federal funds. Rural America receives decent federal funds—for things such as Social Security, food stamps, and unemployment insurance—but what it needs are funds that build communities and attract jobs—funds for infrastructure and technology assistance.

According to the National Rural Network, in rural areas 71 percent of the federal funds are income security funds. In urban America, only 48 percent of such funds are these types. By contrast, then, urban America is getting 23 percent more funds than rural America for things such as road construction, telecommunications, water and sewage systems, and business incentives. On top of this, rural America is on the short end when it comes to competing for funds for defense and space programs, as well as for law enforcement, energy, and higher education and research programs. According to the National Rural Network, the federal government now returns $6,131 per capita to urban areas, while returning only $6,020 to rural areas, resulting in a more than $6.5 billion annual disadvantage to rural areas. That's a big deal.

And when you add them up over years, the numbers are glaring. Again according to the National Rural Network, from 1994 to 2001, the federal government spent two to five times as much, per capita, on urban community development over rural community development and only one-third as much on community resources in rural areas, for an annual $16.5 billion rural disadvantage. Over seven years, that is more than $115 billion. Rural America could have used that.

But George W. Bush is changing that, right?

Yeah, right. Look at Bush's fiscal year 2005 and 2006 budget numbers for key programs for rural America.

Budget Allocations for Programs Important to Rural America

PROGRAM	FY 2005 FINAL*	FY 2006 BUDGET*
COMMUNITY DEVELOPMENT		
Community Development Block Grant Funds	$4,150.03	$0.00
Community Development Funds	$5,610.00	$3,710.00
USDA Rural Community Advancement Program	$716.05	$521.69

ECONOMIC DEVELOPMENT

Economic Development Administration	$257.42	$26.58
Small Business Administration MicroLoan Program	$15.00	$0.00
Workforce Adult Training	$891.00	$866.00
Workforce Youth Training	$996.00	$950.00
Workforce Dislocated Workers	$1,500.00	$1,350.00

EDUCATION

Rural Education	$56,576.60	$56,047.80
Perkins Vocational Education Program	$130.00	$0.00
Rural Education Achievement Program	$300.00	$167.00

HEALTH AND HUMAN SERVICES

Rural Hospital Grant Program	$39.50	$0.00
Rural Health Outreach/Network	$39.60	$11.00
Small Hospital Improvement Program	$15.00	$0.00
Community Health Access Program	$83.60	$0.00
HHS Community Services Block Grant Rural Infrastructure	$679.30	$0.00

NATURAL RESOURCES

USDA Resource Conservation and Development	$51.64	$25.60
Clean Water State Revolving Fund	$1,100.00	$750.00

UTILITIES

USDA Rural Utilities Service Electric Loans	$3,320.00	$2,520.00
USDA Rural Utilities Service Water and Waste Disposal Programs	$462.00	$377.00
USDA Rural Utilities Service Rural Telephone Bank	$175.00	$0.00

*All dollar figures are in millions.

(continued)

USDA Rural Utilities Service Rural Broadband	$11.72	$9.97
Access Loan and Loan Guarantee Program	$550.00	$358.88
MISCELLANEOUS		
Essential Air Service	$102.00	$50.00
Department of Homeland Security State Homeland Security Program	$1,100	$820

These numbers are alarming and inexcusable. These are not just cuts, they are life-altering policy shifts that will further devastate rural America. George W. Bush and his Republican mimics in the Congress are punishing rural America, and they need to be stopped.

According to the American Public Works Association, Bush's fiscal year 2006 budget cuts in the Community Development Block Grant Program would cost rural America at least one-third of its federal economic and community development resources, with the result being a major shift of development costs to state and local resources—most of which cannot absorb the costs. Under Bush's plan to eliminate the Community Development Block Grant Program, rural communities lose over $1 billion in funding that assists local governments in community development activities. The association contends that "this especially impacts rural communities with limited tax bases, leaving many small jurisdictions without resources for vital projects modernizing their infrastructure and developing their economies."

The association also derides Bush's effort to cut the Essential Air Service Program in half, noting that the cuts would prevent many small rural airports from providing connection service at all. And the group notes that the cuts in the Rural Utilities Service Water/Sewer Programs and the Empowerment Zone/Enterprise Communities programs "will substantially impact rural communities' ability to maintain and improve their public infrastructure." Bush even wants to cut the Rural Utilities Service loan program, which helps finance electrical infrastructure in 75 percent of the nation. This program has helped create an efficient rural electrification system, ensuring that rural Americans have access to safe, reliable supplies of power. And it is a *loan* program that is *paid back—with interest.*

Bush's proposal to zero-fund the Small Business Administration's MicroLoan Program is yet another slap in the face to rural America. Nearly 75 percent of all job growth in rural communities in the Midwest and Great Plains comes from microbusinesses (businesses with five or fewer employees). According to the Center for Rural Affairs, "The niche that the MicroLoan Program serves is significant in rural areas and necessary for rural economic development, and would not be served by other small business credit programs." The center also took issue with Bush's plan to cut in half the Resource Conservation and Development (RC&D) Program, which has been a success story for twenty years and which focuses on natural resource conservation and rural economic and community development in multicounty areas. According to the center, the Bush proposal "would terminate all federal support to 189 RC&D Councils, with at least one such RC&D in each state." Most all of these councils are rural.

Funny, we didn't see Mr. Bush mentioning these pending cuts as he rolled through rural America in the fall of 2004. Conning voters with phony macho calls to patriotism apparently left little time to let them know that, were he to be reelected, he would screw them royally.

The purpose of the Rural Community Advancement Program (RCAP) is to provide critical infrastructure, including water, sewer, and advanced telecommunications, as well as business development in rural communities. According to the National Association of Counties, Bush's plan to cut this program by almost one-third would eliminate "several important programs" at a time when the programs and funds are needed to "upgrade aging critical infrastructure" at the local level. The association argues that "cutting RCAP by $195 million seriously impairs their ability to obtain the necessary capital for these improvements and places rural communities at a disadvantage in today's global marketplace." The organization also warns that Bush's proposal to zero-fund the rural broadband telecommunications grant and Distance Learning and Telemedicine loans would cripple the capacity to provide needed services to rural Americans as well as needed learning tools to rural young people. In addition, the group took strong issue with Bush's plan to virtually eliminate the Economic Development Administration (EDA), noting that "without the vital funding the EDA grants provide, many small and rural communities will be unable to continue to address the economic development issues of their region, stalling their business expansion, planning and revitalization efforts."

And it is not just jobs. Look at the cuts in the Clean Water State Revolving Fund. That program provides low-interest loans for water and sewer infrastructure. It also funds alternative projects to reduce pollution in water and sewer systems and streams. It is estimated that to repair water and sewer systems in the United States, $54 billion would be needed. Bush's proposal cuts a $1.1 billion program (already embarrassing) to $750 million. On top of that, he proposed cutting the grants available to local governments by almost 40 percent.

What's up with that? What could Bush possibly be thinking?

The truth is, this has nothing to do with thinking. W just doesn't care. That's why he proposed cutting funds for job training programs, which train adults and youths and displaced workers for new jobs.

This budget is embarrassing and offensive to rural America. But Bush and the Republicans clearly do not care. They think they own rural America. They think they can cry gay marriage, abortion, flag, apple pie, and motherhood, and the "fools" in rural America will roll over and vote for them. They think they can divert attention from their greedy tax giveaways and disastrous economic record by playing a nationalistic card on their Iraq War and the "losers" in rural America will give them carte blanche. Republicans believe they own rural Americans, and they can neglect their kids, deny their schools, ignore their infrastructure, obliterate their health care, eliminate their air service and transportation, deceive their elderly, and hoodwink them with low-paying, no-benefit-providing jobs. Because the Republicans think all they have to do is show up with their macho smirks, tell the "hicks" in rural America to suck it up for the ole Red, White, and Blue, scare them into believing the moral sky is falling because a couple of gay guys want equal protection and equal rights in Massachusetts, lie about the Democrats not being their real friends, and the rural voters will vote Republican every time.

So if the government is screwing rural America when it comes to pumping in federal assistance at a rate comparable to that of urban America, and if the government is offering few if any incentives for industry to relocate or expand in rural America, and if industry is indeed ignoring rural areas, what are the growth industries in rural America?

Casinos and prisons.

There are now casinos in 140 rural counties in twenty-three states. Gambling is a vice that preys primarily on poor people, and its payroll tends to keep its employees poor, but it's a job.

Also, in the 1990s America witnessed a boom in the construction of new prisons, and where do you think most of them went?

Over 50 percent of all new prisons constructed in the 1990s were built in rural locations—245 to be exact—a very disproportionate number considering that only 21 percent of Americans live in rural areas. But urban America doesn't want prisons. They cause adjacent property values to fall, and they scare residents who live near them. The solution was to build prisons in rural areas, where a lack of good-paying jobs trumped fears of reduced property values and citizen safety. In fact, rural communities increasingly found themselves bidding on the prisons with other rural areas (generally making significant sewer, water, and building concessions) as a way to create jobs, on average 300 per prison. On top of that, political leaders tried to sell desperate rural communities on the fact that prison populations are counted in the overall population of a county, meaning that when the government doled out funds to counties, the higher population would translate to increased government largesse.

What a way to "grow" your community.

And if people in rural America could not land jobs at a casino or a prison, and their service-sector jobs did not pay them enough on which to live and support their families, what did they do?

They went out and got a second job.

By 2003, almost 2 million people in rural America held down two or more jobs. In fact, 6 percent of all people who work in rural America hold two or more jobs, and in the Heartland states of Kansas, Nebraska, North Dakota, and Utah, over 10 percent of all workers hold two or more jobs. It seems that in many of the midwestern states, when corporations bought up all the farmland and then hired the original owners, the farmers, to farm the land for them, they did not pay the original owners enough to support their families, so the "employee" farmers had to moonlight.

Thank you, Mr. President. Let's see, increasingly rural people need to work two jobs, which means they have less time to see their kids and spouses, less time to do things as a family, less time to enjoy a quality life— this must be all that pro-family-values stuff that you and the Republicans are always talking about.

Quality of Life

George W. Bush and the Republicans like to suggest that things in the South and in rural America are better than they really are. For instance, the Bush administration took great pride in announcing that one of the best examples of how their policies strengthened the economy was that home ownership was on the rise. Let's look at what they did for home ownership for their solid red-state supporters through the South and in all of rural America.

At first glance Bush is right, home ownership is up—even in rural America. Can you say, "All I want is a double-wide trailer with polyester curtains and a redwood deck"? 'Cause that's the housing rural America got as a gift from George W. Bush and the Republicans in Congress.

According to the Population Reference Bureau, mobile home construction in the United States has boomed, increasing by 20 percent in the 1990s alone, and growing even faster since then. And where are they being built?

In rural America.

According to the Office of Management and Budget and the Census Bureau, nearly 20 percent of all housing now in rural America is "manufactured housing"—that's mobile homes to Bubba. This compares with only 6 percent in metropolitan areas. And while we have no problem with mobile homes, and God knows have no problem with people who live in them, we do have a problem when Bush stands up and says this housing is evidence that he is helping people achieve the American dream of home ownership, thus strengthening the economy.

Not that W would have any idea, but there are a couple of problems with that tight little theory. First, manufactured homes are still bought primarily by low-income families—these are the only homes they can afford. Studies suggest that 70 percent of mobile home buyers have annual incomes of under $40,000, and their mean income is just under $29,000. By contrast, the mean income for other homeowners is $66,000. Second, the average-sized mobile home is just under 1,600 square feet, while the average-sized conventional home is just over 2,300 square feet, or roughly one-half larger. So, owners of manufactured homes were getting their own homes, just a lot less of them.

Third, according to the 2000 census, the average mobile home was valued at $31,000, while the value of the average conventional home was $119,000—suggesting that mobile homes do not retain their value nearly as well as conventional homes. Indeed, studies show that a typical mobile home doesn't hold its value at all. It *depreciates* to one-half of its original price in as little as three years, and the resale market for trailers is extremely bleak. Fourth, buyers of mobile homes typically pay much higher interest rates for loans—as much as 5 percent higher—often because the buyers must use personal property loans because these loans do not require up-front costs, which they often cannot afford. And when they *are* able to get mortgages, buyers often stretch payments over thirty years with the idea that they will have smaller monthly payments. But in doing so, the buyers simply buy themselves thirty years of debt with nothing to show for it as their trailers' values depreciate to nothing long before the note is paid off. Maybe if King George had not jumped into bed with all of the banking interests, he could have forced them to stop these unfair lending practices.

Fifth, and perhaps the most damning statistic of all, according to the Population Reference Bureau, at least 50 percent of all mobile home owners do not own the land on which their homes sit—and that number is probably low. And having to rent the land, usually in a trailer park, is like having a hidden second mortgage, except that in this case you make a payment each month to some landlord but you get no equity for it. On top of that, the resale value of your mobile home drops dramatically when you do not own the land upon which it sits. Finally, when many of these mobile homes are built in rural areas, there are no public water or sewage systems for them to connect to, creating additional expenses for the new "home" owner.

For millions of rural Americans, owning their own piece of the "American dream" is the least of their daily problems. According to the

Department of Agriculture, nearly 12 percent of all rural households lack enough food, and almost 20 percent of all rural children live in households unable to feed themselves. Moreover, 16 percent of households with children are "food insecure" at some time during the year. Food insecurity is defined as not always having access to enough food for active, healthy living for all household members because of lack of money or other resources. And the USDA indicates in a recent study that 81 percent of rural families reported that at times during the year they had to rely on only a few kinds of low-cost food because they were running out of money, 52 percent of families reported that at times they could not afford to feed their children balanced meals, and 25 percent of families reported that at times their children were not eating enough because the family could not afford enough food. Food insecurity is fourteen times more prevalent in homes with annual incomes below 185 percent of the poverty line than in households with incomes above that line.

That's George Bush's rural *America,* not some rural Third World nation.

Additionally, 20 percent of rural America's poor children live in a household without a telephone, and 8 percent live in a household that does not own a vehicle. It's tough to call a doctor in an emergency or rush your kid to an emergency room when you don't have a phone to dial or a car to get you there.

Now look at some of the other problems facing our greatest natural resource—our children.

Children

For all of the damage done to people in the South and in rural America by Republican smoke-and-mirror diversions from economic and quality of life issues to selfish, politicized, mostly irrelevant single issues, no group of people has been hit harder than the children who live in these areas. Lack of governmental investment, high unemployment, low-wage jobs, limited day care, scarcity of food, poor health care, lack of educational opportunities, and little mobility all contribute to an environment where the least among us are hurt the most.

Twenty-one percent of all children living in rural America live in poverty. Another 14 percent live in what the USDA describes as a "near-poor" state. That's 35 percent of the 12.5 million children in rural America either living with poverty or teetering on the edge of it. And remember that poverty is defined as having income less than that deemed sufficient to purchase basic needs of food, shelter, clothing, and other essential goods and services. There are no frills here. These kids are not getting enough food, clothing, shelter, or health care to grow into healthy adults. And let's be clear. These kids are not poor because their parents are sitting in La-Z-Boys all day long eating Twinkies and watching *Judge Judy*. Fully 70 percent of our poorest children live in households where someone works. No, the truth is, rural America is working, we are just not paying them worth a damn for the work they do.

That has got to stop. Republicans have neglected this gigantic problem, and they need to pay for their sins of omission.

The numbers are nothing short of offensive. Over 750, or 37 percent, of the 2,052 rural counties have poverty rates higher than 21 percent. The more rural the county, the higher the poverty rate. In rural counties adjacent to urban counties, the poverty rate averages 18 percent. In rural counties not adjacent to urban counties, the rate mushrooms to 23 percent. The South has the highest percentage of children classified as poor. And the numbers become staggering when we factor in children of families with incomes below 200 percent of the poverty line. While these families are not considered poor, they clearly are not far from the poverty cliff. And when we combine families in poverty, the near poor, and those whose income is less than 200 percent of the poverty line, they include a shocking 47 percent of all rural children, compared with 36 percent of urban children. According to the 2000 census, forty-eight of the fifty counties with the highest poverty rates are located in rural America.

And if Republicans are not taking care of children throughout rural America, let's see if they are at least taking care of their reddest of red-state supporters. Let's look at child poverty rates in the solidly red eleven states of the Old Confederacy. As you will see, the rates are horrific throughout these states but particularly for the reddest of the red families, rural families:

Percentage of Children in Poverty in the Old Confederacy

STATE	URBAN %	RURAL %
Alabama	20.2	27.5
Arkansas	19.5	25.0
Florida	17.2	24.0
Georgia	15.2	26.0
Louisiana	24.8	34.6
Mississippi	21.5	31.5
North Carolina	14.3	22.0
South Carolina	17.1	29.6
Tennessee	17.3	20.5
Texas	19.8	24.1
Virginia	11.3	19.5

That's an average rural poverty rate of 25.9 percent. Nearly 26 percent of all the rural children who live in these states fall below the poverty line. Mr. President and all your Republican cheerleaders, take a bow—it's your show.

Now let's look at the additional seventeen states that John Kerry conceded to W and see how Bush and the Republicans have been helping take care of the children of the parents who voted for them:

Percentage of Children in Poverty in the Additional Red States

STATE	URBAN %	RURAL %
Alaska	9.9	17.1
Arizona	17.7	38.9
Colorado	10.6	17.0
Idaho	12.8	18.0
Indiana	12.3	12.4
Kansas	10.3	14.3
Kentucky	15.6	30.4
Missouri	13.9	22.4
Montana	16.2	24.2
Nebraska	11.1	14.4

Nevada	14.2	14.1
North Dakota	10.2	19.2
Oklahoma	17.8	24.9
South Dakota	10.9	29.0
Utah	9.3	16.6
West Virginia	20.7	29.8
Wyoming	14.4	15.7

That's an average 21.1 percent of all rural children falling below the poverty line in these additional states and an average 23.8 percent for all rural children in the 27 states Kerry conceded to Bush. (Early on, Kerry had a political operation in Florida, but by summer he was pulling his resources there out and shifting them to more competitive states.) These rates are embarrassing and unconscionable.

While poverty in rural America is a national disgrace, problems for the near poor can be equally trying. One of the most telling measures of the damage of low-wage jobs and lack of economic opportunity is working families' ability to get health insurance. Over half of all rural working families have employers who do not offer health insurance. Twenty-two percent of children living in rural areas are not covered by health insurance, compared with 12 percent in urban areas. That means 22 percent of our rural children are not going to a doctor when they need to. It means that for 22 percent of our rural children, acute medical problems often evolve into chronic medical problems because of an inability to see a health-care professional. That means our policies are failing our children.

According to the Rural Families Data Center, mortality rates for children living in rural areas are 40 percent higher than for children in urban areas of the country. These results stem from the higher poverty rates in rural America as well as lower education rates and lack of medical specialists and facilities.

And what about adequate and affordable day care for our nation's rural children?

That's lacking as well. The families of only about 25 percent of rural children who seek day care find it in center-based group care facilities. The reason? Too many rural people cannot afford it, so it just doesn't exist.

Full-day child care generally costs between $4,000 and $10,000 a year. But 25 percent of all families with children earn less than $25,000 a year. And the government offers little help. National figures show that only about 14 percent of children eligible under federal law get any assistance with child care. Part of the problem is that, in twenty states, if families earn more than $25,000 a year, they do not qualify for any day-care assistance.

So what do rural families do? Too often they have to turn to family, friends, or relatives. But that care is often questionable. One study found that 20 percent of children in rural Nebraska had three or more caregivers a week. Also, with more informal arrangements for day care, regulation is virtually nonexistent, and studies show that caregivers tend to be less educated, less likely to have specialized training, and more likely to have higher numbers of children under their care. In sum, day care is routinely pretty lousy for America's rural children.

Something is not right here. At least the Republicans are not discriminating based on age. They are treating our senior citizens just as poorly.

The Elderly

It should come as no surprise that if Republican policies are not taking care of the youngest among us, they would be neglecting the oldest among us as well.

Twenty percent of the population in rural America today is classified as elderly—age sixty or older. This compares with 15 percent of the urban population. On top of this, because of the outmigration of rural young people and an actual inmigration of elderly from cities to rural America, the elderly population in rural America is rising at a much faster pace than it is in urban America. Much of the elderly population is concentrated in the South, although there are a substantial number of rural elderly in the Midwest as well.

Nearly 15 percent of all elderly people in rural America are poor, compared with under 10 percent of the elderly in urban America. And as with other age groups of rural Americans, the more remote the area, the higher the poverty rate among its elderly. On average, the rural elderly have lower incomes than their urban counterparts, and fully one-half of the elderly in rural areas are considered low income, which the government defines as having income below 200 percent of the federal poverty level. This compares with 37.9 percent of the elderly living in urban areas.

Government statistics show that the rural elderly are less likely to have supplemental, private health insurance and instead are much more dependent on Medicare and Medicaid coverage. Government figures also show that prescription drug coverage is lacking for rural Medicare beneficiaries to a much larger degree than it is for the urban elderly. On top of that, a damning 40 percent of rural elderly live in Health Professional Shortage Areas, compared with only 12 percent of the elderly in urban America.

Finally, federal studies have shown for some time that the more rural the elderly, the greater their tooth loss. And by the turn of the century, the proportion of lower-income elderly living in rural America who had lost all of their teeth reached 50 percent.

The GOP Is Not Even Taking Care of Its Own

Perhaps the best evidence of how much the Republicans are taking rural America for granted, particularly in the South, is not how their policies are screwing rural Americans but how they are rewarding the members of their party who are winning elections to Congress from these areas. Look at the number of House and Senate committee chairmanships from the South in the period 1955–2001. It is striking that, as southern states became redder electorally and sent more Republicans to Congress, they did not appear to reap a corresponding rise to powerful positions in Congress.

Southern Committee Chairs in Congress, 1955–2001		
YEAR	NUMBER IN HOUSE	NUMBER IN SENATE
1955	12	8
1967	10	9
1971	8	9
1975	9	6

Southern Committee Chairs in Congress, 1955-2001 *(continued)*

YEAR	NUMBER IN HOUSE	NUMBER IN SENATE
1979	5	4
1981	6	3
1983	7	3
1985	8	2
1987	7	7
1989	8	6
1991	8	6
1993	6	6
1995	4	2
1997	3	4
1999	6	4
2001	3	1

Looks pretty lousy to us. It seems the more the South voted Republican, the more national Republicans took the South for granted.

The Bottom Line

Residents of rural and southern America—their children, their elderly, their workers, and their families—are paying a heavy price for Republican neglect. Democrats have to connect again with these voters, their culture, and their values. Democrats have to become the voice for these forgotten Americans.

From education to health care, from jobs to transportation, from children to seniors, the 59 million people who live in rural America and the 102 million people who live in the South have been getting the short end of the economic stick and have been taken for granted by George W. Bush and the Republicans for whom they have been voting. These pious pretenders are truly the foxes in the henhouse, and in their voracious desire to steal from the poor and give to the rich, they have hit the South and rural America the hardest.

And Democrats have to take their share of responsibility for failing to understand the importance of values and culture to this group and then blaming the people of rural America when the Democratic political agenda began to fail there.

The bottom line is this: It is immoral that Republicans continue to steal from the people of rural and southern America while they shower the wealthiest in this country with untold riches. It happened because of arrogance. If the Republicans who have overseen this death march out of rural America felt there would be any political consequences for their actions and inactions, they would have capitulated in a heartbeat. But these scoundrels do not believe there will be consequences. So they continue to turn away while millions suffer and a vital region of our country slowly withers away.

Part II

THE ROAD TO POLITICAL RECOVERY

Chapter 4

GETTING TO KNOW THE CULTURE OF RURAL AMERICA

The road to political recovery begins with an attempt to understand rural culture. For far too long, national Democrats have approached rural culture with an upturned nose and a closed mind. We believe that if Democrats are going to succeed in turning those red states to blue, they must make a concerted effort to understand the rural American and the "Bubba," and the things that rural Americans hold near and dear to their hearts. A good place to start is with certain strong interests shared by rural culture such as NASCAR, music, college football, and hunting and fishing. Using Mark Warner's successful campaign for governor of Virginia in 2001 as an example, we'll show you the ways we used this culture to introduce Warner into rural areas and sell him to the voters. But before we begin it is absolutely essential to look at rural "Bubbas" and see what makes them tick. Before Democrats start to reach out to Bubba, they need to know exactly who Bubba is.

As it is quite evident that, when it comes to Southern white males and females, the "big tent" of our national Democratic Party has evolved into a "pup tent," it seems only prudent to give our once-great inclusive party a reintroduction to a fellow they haven't taken the time to talk to in the last forty years. National Democrats, his name is *Bubba*. Make no mistake about it: If we're ever going to regain Democratic control of America, we need to get to be buddies with Bubba once again. In the likely event you're one of the mathematically challenged members of our party, the lack of room for Bubba in our "pup tent" is why we've been getting our asses kicked in the South and the Heartland.

Although any pollster will tell you the Democrats have lost the majority of white males in rural America, the first thing one must learn about Bubba is that he is not just a white male. Bubba stands for a blue-collar outlook that transcends gender, color, economic, and geographic bounds. Bubba-spirited females are common throughout America, and as Jesse Jackson will tell you, in the rural South black Bubbas are also very common. Economically, we know a ton of rich Bubbas. Geographically, Bubbas are dominantly abundant in America's rural areas, but it must be pointed out that they live everywhere, not just in the countryside. Beginning with the Industrial Revolution and especially today, economic opportunities are rare in rural America. As a result, Bubbas have been forced to migrate to the cities, suburbs, and exurbs of America. Unbelievably, the Democrats have not figured this one out, and fail to understand that a political strategy aimed at rural America hits many geographically misplaced Bubbas right in the heart. The greatest misconception is that Bubba is a redneck. It is essential in electoral politics to understand that not all Bubbas are rednecks.

Democratic elitists have stereotyped Bubbas to the point many think all Bubbas are rednecks, but this is far from the truth. Bubba is easily distinguishable from a redneck. In fact, there are few commonalities between the two. Bubbas and rednecks have been equally hard hit on the economic front, each despise government intrusion into their day-to-day culture and lives, and overwhelming numbers of both pull for Dale Earnhardt Jr. Once Bubba trusts a Democrat enough to listen, the economic argument is easy to win. As far as "government intrusion" is concerned, while Democrats have allowed the Republicans to falsely paint us as "government intruders," the Terri Schiavo incident suggested with certainty just the opposite. Bubba needs to be reminded of the Schiavo spectacle and Democrats need to be the ones doing the reminding. As for the issue of Dale Jr., we don't have an answer, because like Bubba and the rednecks, we love racing, too.

But the differences between Bubba and the redneck are many. In the world of campaigning, the most important is that Bubba is registered to vote. On the other hand, rednecks can't or don't vote. They can't vote for any number of reasons—domestic violence, auto theft, every kind of auto part theft, breaking and entering, entering and breaking, shooting deer at night, selling bear parts in the Far East, 200 bad checks all less than ten dollars each, meth sales, and of course, another several thousand or so alcohol-related crimes. And then most rednecks who can vote, don't. They're simply too ignorant to care.

Whether he goes to church or not, Bubba has an ingrained belief in the power of the Almighty. Churchgoing Bubbas (and there are many) keep God in their hearts, not on their sleeves, while churchgoing rednecks wear rhinestone crosses, ask you constantly if you know Jesus, and of course, bumper-sticker their vehicles with displays of spiritual self-righteousness. Many even put "Christian" into the names of their businesses. Naturally, Bubba won't do business with them, so the only people who end up getting screwed by rednecks are other rednecks. Bubba prays often and kneels when he prays, asking, "God, show me the way." The redneck seldom prays but always deals when he prays, "God, if you'll get me out of jail, I swear I won't hit her nearly as hard next time." Bubba's faith manifests itself in strong family values and bonds.

Although Bubba takes one week of his two-week vacation to hunt deer, he always spends a week with his family in the summer. Rednecks hunt both weeks. And while Bubba may stop at the local beer joint for a beer or two on payday, he'll bring home the grocery and rent money. Rednecks stay until closing time. When his kid is having trouble in school, Bubba says, "You better cut out this nonsense or I'll fix it and you ain't gonna like it." A redneck's kid falls behind, and he says, "Quit. You've already wasted too much damned time. Get yourself a job."

Although the word "environmentalist" conjures up thoughts of "tree huggers," Bubba feels strongly about resource conservation, air and water quality, and won't litter. While Bubba throws his own beer cans in the back of his pickup, a redneck throws his out the window. Rednecks litter their own yards and fishing holes with car parts and beer cans. When litter lands on Bubba's land, Bubba is none too happy. Dump anything in Bubba's fishing hole or hunting spot, he'll let you know about it. This is not to say that Bubba is a bully. He's not, but rednecks try his patience. One of the redneck's most obnoxious traits is his need to have the last word, especially in cultural and political discussions. A great example of this white trash "last word" phenomenon unfolded before our very eyes at the 2003 Brickyard 400 at Indianapolis. Freddie Hutchins, our trusted twenty-four-year-old assistant whom we consider our kid, made the mistake of parking our generic-looking rental car among about 10,000 other generic-looking rental cars. As we waited for the other 9,999 rental cars to leave so we could find our car, we stumbled upon a camping area. There were two middle-aged redneck women grilling about three campers apart. As NASCAR colors and drivers' numbers abound in the camping areas, one of the women was a drunken Jeff Gordon fan, and the other woman a drunken Dale Jr. fan. As is always the case with rednecks, there were beer cans, bean cans, Vienna sausage cans, broken Coleman lanterns, and other trash strewn around both campsites. The women, who unfortunately for us and other passersby were scantily attired, would not leave each other alone. They pitched insults unmercifully at the other's NASCAR driver, each striving to come up with the perfect verbal abuse. Finally, the Earnhardt woman screamed, "Don't you ever call Junior an asshole again!!" As was her nature, the other woman had to get the last one in. She came back with, "Not only is Junior an asshole, but his Daddy was an asshole before him!!!" We watched, somewhat mystified and somewhat amused, as the parties got physical—an event that can only be described as a cat-fight-style "Thrilla in Manila."

Although he may disagree with another's beliefs, Bubba is tolerant of other people's opinions, while a redneck only tolerates another redneck. However, as in the case of the redneck women at the NASCAR race, they often don't even tolerate each other. In the South, when Bubba sees a Confederate flag, he thinks of "Southern Pride and Valor," while a redneck thinks of "White Pride."

As far as gay rights are concerned, Bubba may not totally understand it, but as long as nobody bothers Bubba, Bubba's spirit of individual liberties says, "It's their mouth, they can haul coal in it if they want to." In fact, Democrats could help neutralize the Republican-built wedge issue of gay marriage if they would simply declare it a "states' rights" issue. Bubba would forget it. Of course, rednecks will be rednecks, so if you're gay, don't expect a lot of tolerance from rednecks anytime soon.

As far as getting Bubba back into the "big tent," it's simple, but it's not easy. Convincing the liberal intellectual wing of our party who spout "tolerance" to actually have some toward Bubba is a formidable task. However, as losses mount, who knows? The truth is Bubba has been voting for Republicans. But rural America's institutional memory is still clearly imprinted with Democratic New Deal politics. Get through the culture with true tolerance, give Bubba a cause, and he *will* pull the "D" lever. In many areas of rural America it has become culturally and socially unacceptable to be a Democrat so it may be a while before he tells anybody . . . but he will pull the "D" lever. Stick your nose up at Bubba, give him no causes, and he'll vote for the Republican for cultural and social reasons alone.

For a long time now, Bubba's been told by everybody from Rush Limbaugh to Charlton Heston that Democrats are nothing but a bunch of antigun, anti-God, tax-and-spend wimps. Democrats need to show Bubba they aren't, because we assure you, Bubba doesn't want criminals to have guns any more than Democrats do. Concerning God, we have met Democrats who believe in strict interpretation of "Freedom of Religion" (as do we), but neither of us has met a Democrat we could say was "anti-God." As far as "tax-and-spend Democrats," those who are not dead have for the most part been replaced by "cut tax for the greedy and spend" Republicans, whose deficits are merely a tax on the kids and the yet-to-be-born. Remarkably, the Democrats have sat back for years, let these lies be told, and lament, "How could anybody believe this?" We don't know exactly "how," but we can say conclusively that the majority of Bubbas have bought it. Our question to the Democrats is "why" haven't we fought back by tearing down the cultural wall of straw and getting to the message Bubba craves?

We believe the first step in the process is to tear down the wall of intolerance and the stereotyping of rural Americans. This can only be achieved if we strive to understand and accept Bubba for what he is—respectful of his own culture, moral, free, proud, and last, but definitely not least, no dummy. Once Democrats get to know Bubba and how his views intersect with Democratic aims, it will be much easier for them to break into rural America.

Goin' to the Races

If you want to find a way to get through to the culture of rural America, there is no better place to start than the world of NASCAR. We went right to the heart of NASCAR in several campaigns, most notably Mark Warner's successful bid for governor of Virginia. We've even been credited with coining the term "NASCAR Dad." We didn't. We don't even know what the term means.

What we do know is that if the person who *did* coin the term was trying to say, in the form of a "neologism," that the Democrats desperately need to find a buzz phrase that their candidates could use to craft a solid message and pitch it to white males, he or she was aiming in the right direction.

Currently, there are 75 million NASCAR fans, 40 percent of which have children under eighteen. Sixty percent of NASCAR parents are male, while 40 percent are female. Using elementary arithmetic, there are about 18 million "NASCAR Dads." In a national campaign, why would a Democrat just single out 18 million fans when for virtually the same amount of resources that candidate could go after all 75 million? In the Mark Warner campaign, the "neologism" we *really* used was "NASCAR Fans."

We knew linking NASCAR to candidate Mark Warner would generate a lot of free media. We were aware of and had been mesmerized by the numbers, profiles, demographics, and most important, the buying habits of NASCAR fans. Our fascination with the numbers was well founded. One-quarter of the country are NASCAR fans and NASCAR is the number two–rated sport on television. NASCAR Nextel Cup races were the number one sporting event on network television twelve of twenty-six weekends in 2004. Attendance at races all over the country, including the short tracks in the nooks and crannies of rural America, is phenomenal, with seventeen of the twenty highest-attended sporting events in the United States being NASCAR events. The "brand loyalty" of the NASCAR fan is also phenomenal. When Bill France Sr. started NASCAR in 1948, he candidly and often told NASCAR fans that if the sport were to succeed, the fans must buy the products they see at the track. In other words, support the people who support our sport. The late legend's words are still echoing through the world of NASCAR. Madison Avenue will tell you when there is a choice to be made in product purchase, a NASCAR fan is three times more likely to buy the product he has seen at the track. By the time of Mark Warner's campaign, our belief in the fertile ground of NASCAR had evolved into disbelief that Democrats had never before turned over the NASCAR rock. So we turned over that rock.

We quickly got in touch with our good friend Eddie Wood of the Wood Brothers Racing family. For those readers who have been living in a world devoid of any link with southern culture, the Wood Brothers and their famous "21" car are considered legends in the annals of NASCAR. An affiliation with the Woods was a huge boost to Warner's rural strategy; their name is deemed sacred in much of the backwoods and fields of rural Virginia. Besides being the oldest continuously operating race team in NASCAR, the Wood Brothers Fords or Mercuries over the years have featured a roster of drivers that reads like a who's who of American racing—A. J. Foyt, Marvin Panch, Parnelli Jones, Tiny Lund, Curtis Turner, Dan Gurney, Cale Yarborough, Donnie Allison, Neil Bonnett, Dale Jarrett, Michael Waltrip, Elliott Sadler, Ricky Rudd, and David Pearson, who along with Richard Petty dominated NASCAR in the sixties and the seventies. Besides visiting victory lane at the Daytona 500 four times, the Wood Brothers were the race team that added the innovation of the orchestrated pit stop.

Eddie Wood is one of the real characters of NASCAR, and the following story is one that convinced us Eddie was ready for politics. Several years ago, a good friend who owned a country store sent Eddie a sealed paint can for Christmas. Because Eddie anticipated a prank, he waited six months to open the can. Inside was a dead lobster. Not to be outdone, Eddie and the gang filled up the can with the freshest pile of cow manure he could find. They resealed it and sent it back. Upon receiving the can, Eddie's buddy definitely knew something was going on, and instead of opening the can, he placed it on a shelf near the stove in his store. One cold winter day, the stove was blasting and the paint can began to heat up. The highly gaseous contents of the can expanded to the point there was a loud explosion in the store. Thankfully, nobody was injured by the explosion of cow manure, but the incident suggested that Eddie would be perfect for the world of politics. After all, where else is there more shit flying than the world of politics?

With Eddie on board, we started to work on Warner's NASCAR plan. The stars lined up just right for the campaign. In view of the simple fact the campaign was in Virginia, it was obvious we needed to use the Wood name in every way we could. Enter the third generation of Wood Brothers, Eddie's son Jon Wood. From the time he started winning go-kart championships as a kid, it was evident that Jon was blessed with the tools and psyche needed to be a top-flight driver. Jon as a nineteen-year-old racer was simply a piece of work and still is today. Eddie has always said, "Race car drivers either have something we're missing, or they're missing something we have." And Jon definitely fits the mold of his daddy's description. Jon will one day become a NASCAR superstar. Write it down.

The decision had already been made that it was time for Jon to leave the world of NASCAR's Late Model racing and head to one of NASCAR's three major series. NASCAR's Craftsman Truck Series was running the Advance Auto Parts 250 on April 7, 2001, at Martinsville Speedway, Virginia, so we went looking for a truck Warner could sponsor and Jon could drive. In mid-March, we found the ride we were looking for. A good ol' Georgia boy and one hell of a racer named Billy Ballew was looking for sponsorship for his No. 15 Ford F-150. By the time we got the deal put together for Martinsville, there were only ten days until the race. As is the usual intention in racing, we wanted to run strong, so Billy quickly got us a motor from famed Georgia engine builder Ernie Elliot, brother of former NASCAR great Bill Elliot. We decked the truck out in the old-time Wood Brothers paint scheme of white body and red roof. The red and blue "Warner 2001" decals looked fabulous and were easily read on the white body. On the quarter panels, we placed our "Sportsmen for Warner" logo, complete with gun and rod.

When we announced that Warner was going racing, our prediction of tons of "free media" became reality. With the "free media" came the questions from the detractors of the "politically correct" wing of the Democratic Party. Aren't you worried about offending our core constituencies because NASCAR is a sport dominated by white males? No. We did not look at NASCAR that way. But we did know that due to its southern roots, NASCAR has at times been unfairly maligned and stereotyped by many on the left as a sport not interested in diversity. This mis-conception, based on the ignorance of the intellectually elite, could not be further from the truth. NASCAR and its teams have spent millions and millions of dollars to expand its fan base to all Americans. NASCAR's well-funded Drive for Diversity program reads like this: *"NASCAR sup-ports the Drive for Diversity program aimed at developing diverse and female drivers and crew members. The program goals are to: Recruit and develop a feeder system for diverse and female drivers and pit crew members. . . . Mentor partici-pants. . . . Create a pipeline of talented drivers and crew members by starting in lower divisions aiming at progressing participants up the NASCAR ladder as per-formance dictates. NASCAR believes this program will greatly enhance the skill level and probability of success for the growing number of experienced minority and female drivers and crew members competing on tracks around the country."*

Ongoing NASCAR programs like the Urban Youth Racing School, the Supplier Diversity Program, the NASCAR Diversity Internship Pro-gram, and the sport's celebration of Black History Month have drawn rave reviews as well as support from the NAACP, the National Urban League, and the National Council of La Raza. NASCAR has grown quickly into a big business, and in a few years, diversity will certainly thrive in NASCAR because the sport has got the correct perspective. As chairman and CEO of NASCAR Brian France says, "We do not see it as an obsta-cle; we see it as an opportunity."

The Warner-sponsored truck didn't finish all that well in Martins-ville, but that didn't matter to the voters of rural Virginia. Of much more importance was the fact that Virginia race fans instantly embraced the partnership of Warner and the Wood Brothers.

In NASCAR marketing, one of the most important ingredients of a solid program is "support marketing," or exposure created in addition to the actual racing. We used shots of the truck in TV ads and bought billboards—some featuring the truck—at nearly every short track in rural Virginia. Our deals with the short tracks always stipulated that they would play a "Warner" song in between races. Of course, Warner always men-tioned the truck and his teaming up with the Woods everywhere he traveled in rural Virginia. The greatest voter impact of the NASCAR pro-gram was probably generated by one radio ad. We made a large race-day buy on the "Motor Racing Network" (plus other country venues) and saturated the market with young Jon Wood's testimony to Mark Warner. Jon's testimony connected NASCAR fans with Mark's message of hope for rural Virginia.

> (MUSIC: "Warner" down-home instrumental . . .) JON WOOD: Hi. I'm Jon Wood of Stuart, Virginia's Wood Brothers and driver of Roush Racing's No. 50 truck in NASCAR's Craftsman Truck Series. Like lots of young folks, I don't know squat about politics, and I could care less if somebody is a Democrat or a Republican. The important thing is what they stand for, and whether they're genuine. And that's why I'm voting Mark Warner for governor. I know Mark personally, and let me tell you, he's been there for folks all over Virginia. When Tultex closed down last year in Martinsville, Mark Warner *was there*. When Lane Furniture announced the closing of its factory in Rocky Mount, Mark Warner *was there,* trying to help. And Mark's sponsorship and support helped me move into the Craftsman Truck Series, where I'm hoping to make Virginia proud. This is NASCAR driver Jon Wood. Vote for my friend Mark Warner for governor this November 6th. He'll be there *for* all of us.
>
> Music fades up, lyric: Warner, for public education . . . Warner, what a reputation . . . Warner, vote in this election . . . to keep our children home.

There are many in the Democratic Party, including some in the Democratic National Committee, who still scoff at Warner's NASCAR strategy. But there was empirical evidence as to the power of NASCAR political marketing in that campaign. The Warner campaign conducted a phone and door-to-door canvass program to help determine Mark's political support or opposition, as well as to test issues that were influencing likely voters. Young interviewers fanned out all over Virginia and sent in their results every night to the statewide coordinated headquarters in Alexandria.

The survey was short, seven questions, but it revealed a wealth of information, from party identification to candidate support, while gauging voters' positions on several key issues. The final question of the survey, however, was telling. It asked simply, "Is there anything we have not talked about, but that you have seen in this campaign, that is influencing your vote?" As we looked at the results every evening, something began to stand out. Traditional responses to that last question, such as crime, education, and jobs, were not rising to the surface as dominant or salient issues influencing voters. Instead, night after night, the response to that open-ended question that was beating out the traditional responses was that Warner's affiliation with NASCAR was positively influencing voters to vote for him. Responses such as, "If NASCAR is good enough for Warner, Warner is good enough for me," were stacking up. In short, our imprinting NASCAR onto Warner was turning into political gold. In fact, when our canvass was completed, *Warner's affiliation with NASCAR was the number one response* to the open-ended question. For those Democrats who still scoff at the power of NASCAR, put that in your cherry pipes and smoke it.

After the Warner campaign, we jumped onto John Edwards's campaign and his leadership PAC, the New American Optimists (NAO). As Iowa is a Mecca of dirt track racing, we decided the NAO would hit the dirt tracks. We slapped decals onto the Late Model car of Dave Schrader, former Democratic leader in the Iowa house and one helluva dirt track driver. Dave not only raced it but also parked it at everything from campaign events to the entrance of the Iowa State Fair, the "Woodstock" of state fairs. Unfortunately our plan of taking Edwards into the world of NASCAR in 2003 came to an end when "chemistry" and strategy differences with other Edwards staffers culminated in our exit in early 2003.

By March, we had gotten the call from U.S. Senator Bob Graham of Florida, who in a late decision (postponed by open-heart surgery) jumped into the race. Although neither of us wanted to get back in the nominating battle, we both strongly believed then and still do today that Graham, a two-term Florida governor and three-term U.S. senator, would have made a great American president. His credentials for the job were by far the most impressive of any of the candidates. We were compelled to jump in with him.

We had been talking with Roush Racing president Geoff Smith and their marketing vice-president John Miller for some time about the possibility of Edwards sponsoring Jon's No. 50 Roush Ford F-150. And when we joined Graham, we were able to close that deal for him. We guess the

"NASCAR Dad" was born shortly after the Roush-built "Graham truck" made its debut July 5, 2003, at Kansas Speedway in the O'Reilly Auto Parts 250 in front of nearly 70,000 spectators and a live national television audience. It didn't take long for Jon to go to the front. As the race progressed, our cell phones lit up as we were in different parts of the country. There is no drug or drink that can match the buzz of winning a race (political or NASCAR), and we all caught that incredible high as we watched Jon pull away at the end and take the checkered flag.

And about the time *The Washington Post* placed Liz Clarke's story on the Democrats' inroads into NASCAR with a picture of the winning Graham truck above the fold on the front page, the seed had begun to germinate. NASCAR fans all across America began asking each other, "Who is Bob Graham?" Unfortunately, Graham was plagued by his late start, which killed fund-raising (as well as unfair media portrayal of him as "quirky" because he kept a detailed notebook the way his dairy farmer dad, Cap Graham, had taught him to). We never got the opportunity to roll out much in the way of "support marketing," which anybody in the NASCAR business will tell you is critical to the success of a program.

Within a month of that cup race, Graham was out of the presidential race. In what we believe was an unfortunate occurrence for the 2004 presidential campaign, no other Democratic candidate executed a NASCAR strategy. We will go to our graves wondering what would have happened in Iowa if the John Edwards campaign had put it into action. Edwards and his rural North Carolina roots would have fit the bill perfectly. So as the 2008 election approaches, the question still lingers. Can a national Democratic candidate drive voters with a NASCAR program? Although many Democrats will quickly say "No," the campaign of George W. Bush apparently thought so, because it shifted gears big-time in 2004 and came up with its own NASCAR program. It was a joke. Bush brought every cup driver (who would come) to the White House for a photo op, which ended up a one-day story. They expended valuable campaign resources and started an ill-conceived NASCAR voter registration drive. Their clueless race-day registration strategy may have registered as many as 500 NASCAR fans. Bush's campaign didn't understand that when a fan plops down a hundred bucks or so for a ticket, the last thing he wants to do at the track is go sit down and fill out a form. That said, we did think it was a smart move for the Bush campaign to fly Air Force One, even though it was on the taxpayer's dime, into Daytona for the 2004 Daytona 500.

As far as the question of a national Democratic candidate "driving votes" with NASCAR, we still ardently believe what we learned in the Mark Warner race. A Democrat can't win in the rural South or Heartland unless that Democrat can navigate the culture and get to the Democratic message of hope. And if you want to get through the culture, there is no better vehicle than NASCAR.

The Music Campaign

If you want to get a message down into the soul of a God-fearing, native-to-the-earth, rural-thinking person, one of the surest ways is through traditional country music. For the best example of this powerful phenomenon, go to Knoxville, Tennessee, one fall afternoon and watch as the University of Tennessee's band strikes up the Osborne Brothers' Tennessee anthem "Rocky Top." Along the Tennessee River, 100,000-plus Bubbas stand up in Neyland Stadium and nearly go into convulsions. We believe most Americans love at least some genre of music. We find no fault with opera or classical music lovers, but without question opera and classical guitar, for example, don't touch the soul of rural America. And it must be said that rural America saw right through the John Kerry sixties rock charade the Electras. Mr. Kerry, you might have provided the best rock-and-roll on Cape Cod, but rural America wouldn't walk across the road to see your act. While a few rural Americans may enjoy a symphony every now and then, they really enjoy, and respond to, bluegrass and country musicians like Tim McGraw, the Del McCoury Band, Alison Krauss, Dr. Ralph Stanley of the Stanley Brothers and the Clinch Mountain Boys, his son, Ralph II, Patty Loveless, and, of course, the independent-minded tunes of John Prine, just to name a few. We understood this from the beginning and were determined to use music to break through the culture and get to the heart of the rural areas of Virginia during the Warner campaign.

We were five days away from the campaign kickoff, which Mark had agreed should start in Southwest Virginia. The advance team had come to Roanoke's City Market Building, and the only song for the kickoff that was mentioned was Paul Simon's "The Boy in the Bubble." That song is no doubt a classic, but its foreboding lyrics about the complications of modern life obviously didn't reinforce our branding of the campaign as "hope for rural Virginia." We had gone through what seemed like every traditional song imaginable, and we still hadn't found the right song with a perky and rollicking message of hope. We are fans of the music of rural America, including Flatt & Scruggs, Bill Monroe, Reno & Smiley, the Stanley Brothers, and the Dillards, who gained national notoriety as the "Darlin boys" of *The Andy Griffith Show*. And we found the perfect tune when we recalled a song of theirs entitled "Dooley." It's a Dillards standard about moonshining that goes, "Doo-ley, slippin' up the holler, Doo-ley, tryin' to make a dollar / Doo-ley, gimme a swaller / and I'll pay you back someday." It was one of the catchiest of the Dillards' tunes. We replaced "Dooley" with "Warner" and came up with lines like, "War-ner for public education . . ." After a ton of help from Lansdowne-Winston Music Publishers' Lynne Robin Green, the great Rodney Dillard and Mitch Jayne, and others, our campaign song done in the Dillard classic melody was ready:

WARNER

Mark Warner is a good ole boy from up in Novaville,
He understands our people, the folks up in the hills;
He first came to the mountains many years ago,
His interest in our future then began to grow.

Chorus

War-ner, for public education,
War-ner, what a reputation,
War-ner, vote in this election,
To keep our children home.

Mark Warner is ready to lead our Commonwealth,
He'll work for mountain people and economic health;
Get ready to shout it from the coal mines to the stills,
Here comes Mark Warner, the hero of the hills.

FOXES IN THE HENHOUSE

Chorus

Mark Warner, he needs us as much as we need him,
No more tricks in politics that leave our future dim;
So you folks in the mountains at the end of your rope,
Get on out and shout it out, Mark is our hope.

Chorus

Picking the rural campaign band was one of our easiest tasks. In order to establish any legitimacy where we were heading, we had to have a real hillbilly band. There could be no imitations, and very important, they had to be perky and rollicking musicians. With roots and mannerisms sprouted from deep in the coalfields of Russell County, the Bluegrass Brothers were made for this gig. Victor, Robert, and Steve Dowdy are as hillbilly as they are incredibly talented. Victor, next to Dr. Ralph Stanley, has the weariest voice in the mountains and can innately sing songs that capture the sad problems of the region. Robert, who at the time was a regional legend, is now recognized as one of the best banjo pickers in America, and Steve, Victor's son, is a bluegrass version of Eric Clapton on the guitar. They are rollicking. They rollicked on the way to the events, rollicked during the events, and rollicked after the events. The only time they didn't rollick was early in the morning after an event. They had everything we needed to pull in and fire up a rural crowd. Ralph Stanley II, the son of bluegrass legend Dr. Ralph Stanley, said it best: "Them boys can heat it up." And heat it up they did. It took one verse for the crowd to get into the spirit of the tune. It was the first time that Mark had heard the song. He turned to reporters and said, "They're singing about me." Cameras moved to the risers where Warner's daughters were flatfootin' and dancin'. Since Virginia and New Jersey were the only two states that had elections going on in 2001, the national press was well represented. They were all over the Bluegrass Brothers, and after the show they requested an encore presentation of the song so they could get a good recording of it. Later that afternoon, Judy Woodruff ran the song on CNN's *Inside Politics,* and by nightfall it was playing continuously on Warner's and other political websites. The song became a hit in rural Virginia after it was played in ads produced by Frank Greer (Clinton's media guy), in between innings at minor-league baseball games across the state, in between races at most of the short tracks in Virginia, at early-fall football tailgating parties at Virginia Tech and the University of Virginia, at every bluegrass festival, at every fair, and, of course, at every main Warner event (it played nonstop the night Mark was elected). Even rural radio stations got copies and ran the song.

We knew Warner wouldn't object to using the song to help introduce the message to the strategy. He liked it and more important to him, his girls loved it. Maddy, Gillian, and Eliza Warner's spontaneous dancing throughout rural Virginia had to have gotten us a couple thousand votes. The only question Warner ever had concerning the song originated with some northern Virginia "smart Democrat" who had suggested changing the lyric "from the coal mines to the stills" to "from the coal mines to the mills." Apparently, this particular Democrat was afraid of Republican attacks on Warner for supporting untaxed, illegal liquor. We told Warner, "Mark, if we could only be so lucky. The still is nearly as sacred as the cross in the hills." Mark laughed and responded, "OK," and that was that. The Republican foxes sidestepped that trap and we never heard a word about it.

We stuck to the bluegrass brand throughout the election. It served us wonderfully, as it became one of the major efforts in advocating progress in rural America. Matt Bai, a feature writer for *The New York Times Magazine,* was covering the Virginia rural campaign for *Newsweek* when we arrived at the Galax Old Fiddler's Convention in August. By this time, Warner was the political king of "traditional country music." The Fiddler's Convention is huge in the southern Appalachians and draws crowds in the 50,000 range. This is what Matt observed on Warner's arrival at Galax:

> *The entrance to the Fiddler's Convention in Galax was at the top of this steep embankment, and when Mark Warner hopped out of his SUV and started to make his way down the slope, dressed in a polo shirt and pressed jeans like he'd just left the country club, I think I actually cringed for him. Thousands of families from Southwest and Southside Virginia and neighboring Appalachian states were camped out in the mud, sending their kids for fried dough and cotton candy while they listened to the bluegrass all around them. This was not a place for politics, and Warner's opponent, the state's attorney general (Mark Earley), seemed to get that; he shook some hands here and there—uneasily, it*

seemed to me—and gave interviews to local reporters. But here came Warner, the Harvard-educated millionaire Democrat, striding confidently into the throng, shouting to be heard over the banjos.

To my surprise, the families did more than tolerate him—they actually seemed to like him. Hands shot out from all directions, and Warner shook as many as he could, asking where they had come from and how long they were staying. He smiled broadly when he saw the Bluegrass Brothers huddled together, playing for scores of fans. It took me a minute to realize why: they were playing the one they put out about Warner and how he would keep your children home, the one that stuck to your brain like pine tar, until one day you found yourself singing bluegrass out loud at a table full of co-workers. Warner clapped along for a few beats, but he didn't pretend to be a fiddle buff. The point was that he knew the music mattered to them, and to those voters, that seemed to say a lot about the man.

I remember that before we left I stopped and talked for a while with a guy who worked for coal companies in the seams near West Virginia. His face was hard and gray from a life spent in the mines. He was active in local politics, and he told me he thought Warner actually was going to win. By the time I left Galax, I thought so, too.

Without question, the fruits of Warner's bluegrass push ripened and peaked at the right time. The Blue Ridge Institute and Museum at Ferrum College, Virginia, has their annual Folklife Festival the fourth Saturday in October. The one-day festival drew between 20,000 and 25,000 visitors that year, and the statewide candidates were there in force. In the spirit of authenticity, the director of the institute, Roddy Moore, had cut down a tree at an appropriate spot on the campus so that the candidates would have an actual stump to use as a podium for speech making. Roddy is known as a "Big Byrd Democrat," a reference to the esteemed champion of the Appalachians, Senator Robert Byrd of West Virginia. Roddy has mainlined the history of the southern Appalachians all his life and believes that the Republican foxes have always fed on the little people in the hills. In a nutshell, Roddy was no stranger to our foxhole. The entertainment at Ferrum that year included some of the truest of mountain legends, including Dr. Ralph Stanley, his boy, Ralph II, and the Clinch Mountain Boys. Anywhere you go in the southern Appalachians and say the name of Dr.

Ralph, you will see heads bow much as they did in Munchkin Land at the mention of the Wizard of Oz.

Much to the sorrow of Virginia Republicans that day, Dr. Ralph was in the Warner foxhole too, and it was no accident that Roddy and Dr. Ralph were prepared for Mark Warner's arrival. Dr. Ralph got a cue when Warner arrived, and he stopped playing. "Laaa-dddies and gennn-lllll-men," Dr. Ralph twanged in his unblemished Appalachian accent, "th' next guv-nah of th' Common-wellll-th of Vaginnia is heah. Mark, where are ya? Come on up heah, boy, and let these fine folks see you . . ." Dr. Ralph Stanley, in a blink of his sincere eye, had made up the minds of most of the remaining undecideds in attendance. If Warner was Dr. Ralph's guy, then he was Bubba's too.

Music is, of course, just one piece of the strategy. But if you are a Democrat in a high-performing rural Republican area, consider incorporating *good* music into your message delivery. The importance of *good* music cannot be stressed enough. With any kind of imagination at all, it is easy even for a Democratic campaign to figure out how to pay for *good* music. That's what happened in the Warner campaign—you can't buy free media, and that's what you get when you draw a big crowd. Plus, music is versatile and can be utilized in any cultural strategy. While we were using music in the ridges and the hollers, Mark had convinced Williamsburg resident Bruce Hornsby to do a number on the yuppie-filled high-growth areas of the "Golden Triangle" of Virginia. A great way to get Bubba, or anybody for that matter, to listen to your message is to gather a big crowd with some high-powered musicians. And if you give people the right message to the beat of the music, they'll listen and respond.

Game Day

In most of the Heartland and the entire South, no single phenomenon spurs more pure passion than college football. There are many in academia who will tell you the megaprograms of college football compromise academic integrity. We think they supplement it. The truth is that these megaprograms generate millions of dollars a year in donations for their schools, based on their number of wins. And that money is given not just to the athletic departments but across the entire campuses. People give large sums of money to their passions, and as Coach Paul "Bear" Bryant said, "You can't rally around a physics class."

In the Warner campaign, we took Coach Bryant's wisdom to heart. Everybody, especially Warner (a huge college sports fan), felt it was a no-brainer for the campaign to embrace both the cultured fans of Mr. Jefferson's University of Virginia and the raucous fans of Virginia Tech. Not only did we buy time on the two schools' radio networks, we ordered a pile of mascot-based "Wahoos for Warner" and "Hokies for Warner" lapel stickers to give out at the games. On game days at both schools, the campaign had staffers and college-age volunteers working the tailgaters and entry gates, sticking lapel stickers on anybody who would let them. And most did—they did not want to turn down a sticker with their team mascot's name on it. At Tech's home opener, we had the Bluegrass Brothers band moving from tailgate party to tailgate party in the parking lots, taking requests for famous bluegrass songs. Of course, they always played the "Warner" election song we had written before they moved on. And when they were gone, all the tailgater radios set to Bill Roth and Mike Burnop's pregame Tech show gave Tech fans a dose of Tech's Outland Trophy winner and all-time NFL sack leader, Bruce Smith, letting them know what a good guy Warner was. Our staffers and volunteers did such an overpowering job of getting lapel stickers on Tech fans that we ran out.

There is an ironic sidebar to the Warner campaign's college football push. Mark is a splendid retail politician, and after his working many "tailgates" at Tech, a tremendous number of Hokies fell in line behind Warner. The wonderful irony is that after he was elected, Mark put his ass on the line and fell in behind them. In the late spring of 2003, we were out in Iowa working for John Edwards when we got the word that Virginia Tech's fellow members of the Big East Conference—Miami, Boston College, and Syracuse—had been secretly meeting with representatives of the Atlantic Coast Conference. The plan was for the three schools to join the ACC, turn the nine-team conference into a twelve-team conference, and with the additional media markets and a conference championship game, everybody could get a little richer. Of supreme concern to us, Virginia Tech would be left in a denuded Big East Conference, and the University of Virginia would benefit immensely from its position of being Virginia's only team in the expanded megaconference. While the extra exposure would give UVA a huge advantage in recruiting, new fan support, and of course, money, the Wahoos' gain would be at the Hokies' expense. UVA, with a smile on their face, claimed they wanted the expansion to include Virginia Tech, but their vote proved otherwise. Seven of the nine ACC schools had to agree to a three-team expansion. The University of North Carolina and Duke University were against the expansion. Virginia's vote, in the smoke-filled rooms of a private ACC meeting, gave the expansion the seven needed votes. In a cute political move, the University of Virginia's leadership announced it had "highly recommended Tech for membership." We did not believe them.

Virginia Tech is located in the Southwest Virginia town of Blacksburg, with the university being the largest employer in the western half of the state. It is an outstanding academic institution whose graduates include Chris Kraft, the NASA scientist who led America to the moon. Southwest Virginia native and Tech football coach Frank Beamer had done a great job of getting Virginia Tech into the national limelight. From 1993 to 1998, Beamer led Tech to a couple of Big East championships and had taken the team to bowl games every year, including the Sugar (beat Texas) and the Orange (lost to Nebraska) bowls.

Like every highly rural area in America, Southwest Virginia has been disproportionately hit with loss of jobs from federal trade policy and subsequent imports, but the high-profile football program brought massive exposure and investment dollars for Virginia Tech, the region's economic development engine. Admission applications soared. Tech's national success on the gridiron has resulted in six or seven weekends a year when you can't find a hotel room in the region and provides a huge shot into the arm of "Mom and Pop" businesses.

When we got the news while in Iowa of the proposed expansion, we were at first in disbelief that such a devastating blow to Tech's future could actually be unfolding. As we ate breakfast that morning at the Hotel Fort Des Moines, we discussed the ramifications of such an expansion for Tech and Southwest Virginia, if Tech were not included. We got on the phone to Mark Warner to find out what the hell was going on.

Warner, who had been under massive lobbying from UVA, had been told to stay out of the process because the UVA Athletic Association was a "private" association. After telling the sixty-ninth governor of the Commonwealth of Virginia that if the UVA Athletic Association was "private," they should get the hell off public land, Warner readily agreed to take an unobstructed look at the situation. After assessing the big picture and the potential damage to rural Southwest Virginia, Warner told us to call Virginia Tech president Dr. Charles Steger and tell him to stay close by the phone: Warner would be calling Steger in a few minutes to say he was entering the fray as Virginia Tech's advocate.

Once he made the decision to get involved and had a little instructive chat with UVA president John Casteen and the board of Mr. Jefferson's university, our confidence soared. We had enough experience with Warner to know that Tech was somehow going to get an invitation to join the ACC. When Warner instructs, he's clear, and when he knows he's right, he instructs like a pit bull.

Just to give the governor backup cover, we went about the task of developing Tech and Warner a secondary plan of attack. The politics were easy. There are four times more Tech graduates in Virginia than UVA graduates, and Tech's fan support is much more rabid. The backup plan would involve legislation introduced in the Virginia House of Delegates by Democrat Jim Shuler and Republican Dave Nutter, whose districts cover the town of Blacksburg and Montgomery County. The bill was simple. The University of Virginia and Virginia Tech, the state's two flagship programs, *would have to be members of the same athletic conference* unless both agreed to a different scenario. If any athletic conference was going to have a presence in one of the top ten media markets in America, neither of our Division I programs could be hurt. To put it clearly, the University of Virginia would have to either tell Tech "Welcome to the ACC" or say goodbye to the ACC, if the ACC expanded without inviting Virginia Tech to the dance. We made calls to other members of the legislature and, with the help of some very powerful political numbers, found that getting support for the legislation was as easy as dynamiting fish. To ensure the bill's credibility, Warner agreed to sign the legislation if passed. The deal was sealed. The ACC blinked. It could not afford to lose UVA. It now got Virginia Tech. Dr. Steger called to tell us to call off the June 25, 2003, press conference announcing the legislation because Casteen had called and told him Tech was getting an invitation to the ACC.

Mark Warner is now a revered name in the history of both Virginia Tech and Southwest Virginia. In his four years as governor, Mark Warner repaid rural Virginians in a lot of ways for their support in his election, but all the other things he did collectively paled in comparison to his leading Tech's charge into the Atlantic Coast Conference. Frank Beamer and the Virginia Tech Hokies got to return the favor of the governor's leadership. In their first year in the ACC while Warner was still governor, Mark got to lead the pregame "Hokie Walk," and when the 2004 football season ended, the Hokies had won their first ACC Football Championship.

This is just one example, but we believe Warner's commitment to Virginia Tech, rural Southwest Virginia, and, ultimately, college football really helped him gain even more respect in the rural parts of the state. Democrats should follow his lead. Anybody who lives in the South or the Heartland knows that college football is more like a religion than a sport. By showing some respect and passion for a sport that is close to the rural voter's heart, Democrats can increase their profile in Bubba country and get some votes.

The Sportsman

It seems these days that most major campaigns have a "Sportsmen for Their Guy" strategy. When big campaigns head into rural battle, both parties get all fired up to go after the sportsmen vote, because in many cases, sportsmen tend to vote "single issue." Their passion for the outdoors, not underemphasizing that you need a gun to hunt, dictates which lever they pull.

Political campaigns are notorious for putting together sportsmen committees of Mark Trail types who dress like the guys who grace the cover of L.L. Bean catalogs. (For those who don't know Mark Trail, he was the ultimate pipe-smoking naturalist and a cartoon character.) Other than bagging a few bucks from their big wallets, these sportsmen have little else to offer. These "Mark Trail" committees invariably come up with some vanilla conservation plank that makes them feel good and produces a few blaze orange bumper strips and signs for them and their buddies. And of course, such committees never forget to do a handout flyer with a picture of the candidate, looking as if he knows what he's doing—holding a gold-triggered Browning or working an Orvis fly rod. Frankly, these committees seldom, if ever, generate any real buzz and drive few votes.

As we ourselves do not indulge in the fine products L.L. Bean has to offer, we were determined that the sportsmen committee for Mark Warner would not be comprised of only rich, politically influential outdoorsmen. The committee would include all geographic, demographic, and economic profiles. It would also include *all* outdoor sportsmen—deer hunters to turkey hunters, coon hunters to bear hunters, frog giggers to fur trappers, freshwater fishermen to saltwater fishermen, and even the fastest-growing segment of outdoor sports—watchable wildlife.

As sinfully avid sportsmen ourselves, our egos made us determined to put together the most energetic and active sportsmen committee in the history of Virginia politics. The first job was to come up with a chairman for the committee. The chosen one would have to be willing to do much, much more than just brandish a title. This person had to have a complete understanding of how to drive the targeted constituency, be willing to go all hours of the day and night, and most important, be a person that the sporting Bubbas of the commonwealth would trust.

Our chosen one would not be called chairman. The chosen one was an uncommonly beautiful former Tennessee woman named Sherry Crumley. Why choose a woman as chair for any committee targeting white Bubba males? Sherry was our first and only choice as chair simply because she was the only person in Virginia who met all the criteria. Sherry, who at first glance seems more apt to be seen on Rodeo Drive than a deer stand, has lived outdoor sports her entire life. Her dad, Carl Smith, was chairman of the Tennessee Game and Fish Commission. Sherry's husband, Jimmy Crumley, was her brother Tom's best hunting buddy. In the early eighties, Jimmy came up with an invention that would revolutionize the sport of hunting. After years of pondering what to wear to keep game from seeing him, Crumley came up with the first nonmilitary hunting concealment material and named it "Trebark." His new camouflage turned the American market for hunting clothes and accessories upside down, and within a couple of years, Jimmy and Sherry Crumley, who now reside near Springwood in Botetourt County, Virginia, became national household names among hunters.

Over the next twenty years, Sherry took time from helping Jimmy sell camouflage to also serve on the boards of the National Wild Turkey Federation and of "Hunters for the Hungry," and as chairman of the Virginia Wildlife Foundation. In 2000, Virginians voted in a referendum on a constitutional amendment that guaranteed them "the right to hunt, fish, and harvest game." Sherry was chairwoman for the effort that won statewide, 60 percent to 40 percent. Since the Hunting and Fishing Amendment campaign had just been completed, Sherry still had her team pretty much in place and, with her honest word, could move her troops over to Warner and not skip a beat. The only problem was that she wasn't a partisan voter. She could care less about Democrats or Republicans. She's an advocate of the outdoors, not a party. The only possible chance we had to get Sherry was to get Mark to go to the hills, turkey hunt for a day, and sell him to her. She agreed to invite Warner out to Botetourt County for a spring gobbler hunt.

Upon our arrival, Sherry, Jimmy, and former Chicago Cub All-Star catcher Jody Davis greeted us at the backdoor. We sat down for a somewhat heated conversation and Mark Warner was at his best. Sherry, who would never support anybody who proposed so much as a micro-threat to our sporting culture, had prepared her own questionnaire. Warner hit every question into the seats and Sherry accepted the position. The only thing that went wrong was the Warner campaign didn't kill any turkeys the next morning. We righted that campaign wrong two weeks later when we were back at the Crumleys to work out the final details of the sportsmen strategy.

We rapidly put together a cover-all strategy and began the drive for the 223,931 licensed hunters and the 403,227 licensed fishermen in Virginia. Once the massive push began and word got out in *The Washington Post* that we had talked to the NRA, the "smart people" once again had no problem letting us know of their serious skepticism of the entire rural strategy and our "running off the liberal base." We fired back with numbers from the year before on the Hunting and Fishing Amendment referendum. The referendum had only lost in the Northern Virginia suburbs, by 51 to 49 percent. In addition, we asked the "smart people" where were these supposed defectors going to go? To the Republicans? We have talked about it a lot since then. One, or as many as two, of our party's wackos (it's not just the Republicans who have them) may have stayed home, but we honestly don't think we lost a vote to the Republicans with the targeted sportsmen strategy. At the same time, we know the group expanded our base.

Our message was simple: (1) Mark Warner isn't taking anybody's guns, (2) Mark Warner is going to improve wildlife habitat, and he's going to fight for the quality of our air and water. (Please note that in part two of the message, the word "environment" is omitted and rightly so. Because of the right-wing's stereotyping of *all* environmentalists as left-wing extremists over the last twenty-five or so years, most rural Americans would rather be labeled as a lying, cheating, no-count son of a bitch than an "environmentalist." We don't use that word.)

As far as Warner and his sporting pedigree was concerned, we never, ever, ever, ever suggested to anybody that Mark was a big outdoorsman. Presenting a Harvard-trained, Connecticut-raised, high-tech millionaire and businessman to the sportsmen as anything other than eager in his support of them would have been like presenting a sow's ear as a silk purse. In fact, we drove hard in the other direction. Associated Press writer Bob Lewis was obviously cynical about Warner's "sportsmen" movement and asked us how Warner's first turkey hunt went. We told Lewis that Warner "didn't know shit" about what he was doing but "had a big time" tromping around the woods and asking questions.

Ethical members of the fourth estate love the truth, especially when the truth comes out of such an unlikely source as a political campaign. Lewis and the rest of the Virginia media accepted the truth, printed it, and moved on. The truth was we weren't selling Mark Warner as a sportsman. Instead, we were selling Warner as a friend of the sportsmen, who respected the culture of hunting and its importance to tens of thousands of Virginians he hoped to represent. With all the antigun, antihunting stereotypes that have been pasted to Democrats, most Democratic candidates have to be careful to not come off as being disingenuous when chasing sportsmen votes. John Kerry tried to lay the notion on American sportsmen that he was an avid hunter. In his defense, John Kerry *is* an avid hunter, but that reality was doomed before it had the chance to sink in with sportsmen. The first good look Bubba had at Kerry was of him windsurfing off the coast of Martha's Vineyard in "spandex shorts." No staged goose hunt can remove that scene from Bubba's memory banks. For that matter, Kerry could have bagged the new world records for whitetail, grizzly, and elk using only rocks, while catching the new world record largemouth bass with a safety pin as a hook, and Bubba would only remember those "spandex shorts." If that wasn't bad enough, the Sportsmen for Kerry website had "full funding of our national parks" at the top of their agenda. The problem is, hunters can't hunt on "park" land and that pisses them off. In our opinion, W didn't do much better with his "sportsmen" campaign. Other than answering Kerry's full funding of national parks by opening up a "few" parks to hunting, Bush's "sportsmen" relied on the wedge issue of guns and simply touted his endorsement by the NRA. If Sportsmen for Kerry had taken to the offense and portrayed W as an enthusiastic hunter of pen-raised quail—planted in just the right spot under the supervision of the Secret Service—real Bubbas would have quickly learned that Bush is no sportsman. Ask any real Bubba about hunting pen-raised quail, and he'll quickly tell you that's the way "wusses" hunt and it's akin to shooting chickens. And why didn't Sportsmen for Kerry use the somewhat abandoned tactic of truth, spend just a little money, and show sportsmen how the air and water policies of W were ruining wildlife habitat? They could have at least made Bush's campaign squirm enough to make him respond and spend valuable resources where he hadn't planned.

By contrast, during the Warner campaign, Sherry quickly brought on several key volunteers from the Hunting and Fishing Amendment referendum, and we were out of the blocks quickly. Before she was finished, the Sportsmen for Warner group enlisted 1,250 eager volunteers from traditional Democratic ranks, independents, and even crossover Republicans. The main crux of the strategy, obviously, was to get the word to Virginia sportsmen that Warner was behind them and serious about gaining their support. You can have dimes for sale for five cents, and if nobody knows about it, you won't sell any. That meant the group's presence in their support of Warner had to be more than just visible. For a Democrat to win sportsmen, it had to be dominantly visible. If visibility was a commodity, Sherry and Warner's army of sportsmen could have opened a store called Visibility Is Us. They slaughtered the Republican version of Warner opponent Mark Earley's sportsmen campaign. Sportsmen for Warner signs started showing up from the hills of the Blue Ridge to the Eastern Shore. By the time the campaign was over, 10,000 four-by-eight-foot Sportsmen for Warner signs were plastered across rural Virginia, and while we are using 10,000 as a number, 10,000 Sportsmen for Warner hats (in native Virginia "Trebark" camouflage) were resting solidly on the heads of Virginia outdoorsmen. The "Sportsmen" were not just present on signs and hats. Staff and volunteers were seen behind Sportsmen for Warner booths—loaded with information and giveaways—at every big gun show, hunting show, fair, and major NASCAR race. We produced ads for outdoor magazines. We did direct mail touting Mark's commitment to the sportsmen. In Southwest Virginia, we even teamed up with Brian and Jason Reger at Buck Mountain Outfitters in Roanoke and sponsored our own outdoor show. Together, we brought in hunting supply vendors, all types of sporting demonstrations, the Bluegrass Brothers, three live monster white-tailed bucks from Ohio, and plenty of good food. We drew 7,000 sportsmen over the two-day event.

You've got to have a good horse to win, and Warner always did a great job of pointing out at sportsmen events that he himself wasn't an experienced outdoorsman, but he never failed to articulate clearly that if he were elected, he would champion the sporting culture. By the end of the campaign, Warner was honestly into it. He hunted geese. He hunted doves. All of us, especially Warner, were having fun with it. It is always fun in politics to kick ass, and Warner's "sportsmen" were doing just that in rural Virginia. During the campaign, Mark's enjoyment of the rural strategy evolved to the point that he seemed more at ease with a group of Bubba-type hunters than he did with the stuffed-shirt business crowd of Northern Virginia. And as his enjoyment grew, so did his confidence—even with a gun. One day late in the campaign, Mark and Sherry arrived at a huge hunt-club gathering in Eastern Virginia where one of the activities was an old-fashioned southern "turkey shoot." You don't actually shoot turkeys at a turkey shoot. It is in reality a shotgun shooting match, with the winner being the shooter who places a shotgun pellet closest to the center. It is called a "turkey shoot" because in the old days that's what you won—a live turkey. Somebody asked Warner if he wanted to take a shot, and he responded that he didn't have a shotgun with him, but if somebody would lend him one he would love to "take a crack at it."

Warner loves basketball, played it every day as a kid, and possesses good hand-to-eye coordination. However, as Sherry watched somebody hand Mark a shotgun to the delight of several hundred interested onlookers, her thoughts concentrated only on the worst. But Warner not only hit the target solidly, he finished second out of approximately fifteen very experienced shotgunners.

As election day approached, Warner would gleefully and honestly tell rural sportsmen he wished he had more time to hunt, fish, and get outdoors. Bubba believed Warner, and sportsmen's cynicism for this Democratic candidate all but disappeared. Bubba understood time restraints because common sense told him that Mark couldn't have much time and all them millions, too. Mark genuinely liked Bubba and his sporting culture, and more important for him on Election Day, Bubba had grown to like Mark, too.

The point of all of this is that culture matters to people, and in rural and southern America, culture often means NASCAR, hunting and fishing, college and high school athletics, and country and bluegrass music. If Democrats wish to be successful, they must tap into and connect with this culture and with the people who practice it. We believe culture is a more powerful verifier of the credibility of a political candidate than any policy issue ever could be. And once candidates connect with rural and southern voters through their culture, they will have built up a trust and connection that will open the door for connecting on issues as well.

Chapter 5

FIVE SIMPLE LESSONS

From the 1930s through the 1970s, several generations of Americans witnessed firsthand the power and compassion of a government dedicated to equality, justice, fairness, and opportunity. During this time, workers were increasingly seen as valued assets rather than disposable commodities. Our nation and its people began to understand the fragility of our land, air, and water, and took bold new steps to protect and preserve our planet. Overcoming the ills of poverty, homelessness, joblessness, and sickness became the great causes of our nation. Government was viewed for the good that it could do, not publicly derided while privately looted. Our political leaders worked from the premise that a nation is only as good and strong as the weakest in it. In short, for nearly forty years, Americans were able to believe that our federal government's visionary and compassionate ideals could conquer all frontiers.

The world saw it too. The fuel of America's opportunity, liberty, and justice ignited an unparalleled beacon of hope for hundreds of millions of people throughout the world. America and the world witnessed the dawn of the American century.

Yet, beneath the surface, cynicism still resided. Greed, ignorance, hypocrisy, and bigotry still courted suitors. And increasingly, in the 1970s and 1980s, they found them. By the 1980s, cynicism captured the attention of a host of willing and seemingly mindless political opportunists, and greed fueled their causes. Smoke and mirrors became the refurbishers' building materials for political renovation. By the 1990s, cynicism had taken root, and by November 2, 2004, greed, ignorance, hypocrisy, and bigotry had firmly repelled the forces of hope, opportunity, liberty, and justice.

The results have been numbing. From redistribution of wealth and unprecedented debt and deficits to misguided and malevolent social and economic policy, from scorched-earth preservation and conservation practices to unmitigated assaults on free speech and due process guarantees, the vehicle of America's government is out of control. And Republican leaders and their misanthropic cheerleaders happen to be driving the bus.

Now we'd like to begin providing Democrats with a blueprint for running the Republicans out of power. It starts by urging Democrats and their candidates to learn five simple lessons. We believe this is the first step on the road to political recovery.

Lesson 1:   Learn How to Count

People in politics often attempt to put themselves on pedestals, thinking they're brain surgeons or rocket scientists. "Well, what really happened in the 2004 election was that Karl Rove's a friggin' genius. He figured out that Christians vote." We're sorry, Karl Rove may be a genius, probably in mathematics or astrology, but even a middle school civics class could have seen the rise of the Christian right.

Or you hear, "Well, the Republicans just had better candidates than the Democrats." Please. Tom Coburn, Jim Bunning, Jim DeMint, much less W? Democrats could have picked better candidates out of a police lineup.

Or you hear, "Well, the Republicans had computer chips installed in every voting machine and just stole the damned election." Okay, that one might be true.

The point is, people in politics are not geniuses. It doesn't take geniuses to win elections. Otherwise the *Chicago Daily Tribune* headline of November 3, 1948, would have read "Dewey Defeats Einstein." If only geniuses won in politics, Stephen Hawking would have been studying astronomy in the White House in the eighties instead of Nancy Reagan consulting her astrologist there. In fact, if brains were the criteria for success in politics, Democrats in 2000 could have picked up any phone book in America, opened it, randomly put their fingers on any name, run that person for president, and the odds are pretty good that there would be a smarter man or woman occupying the Oval Office at this very moment.

So, if it's not brains that guarantee electoral success, what is it? It starts with people who can count.

That's right, people who can count. Geniuses can count. Democrats can't.

How do we know Democrats can't count? We watched them.

Case in point:

In the United States, presidents are not actually elected by popular vote. Instead, presidents are elected by electors allocated to each state. Every state has an elector for each of its members of the U.S. House of Representatives and one elector each for its two U.S. senators. (The District of Columbia—the nation's capital—doesn't get senators or even real members of Congress, but it gets three electoral votes; that's America's way of saying that people who live there count, but apparently only every four years.)

When a candidate for president wins a state, he (or she) wins all the electoral votes of that state. (There are a couple of states that allocate electors by congressional district, but you get the picture.) All of the electoral votes for each candidate are added up, and, regardless of the popular vote, whoever gets the most electoral votes wins. Representative democracy at work!

In the fifty states, there are 535 electoral college votes; add in 3 for D.C. and there are 538 total electoral college votes. Divide 538 by 2 and you get 269 votes. Thus, to win the White House, a candidate has to get 269 plus 1 to have a majority of electoral college votes.

Pretty simple math here. But Democrats don't seem to get this math. They should have asked for a tutor because they really needed to understand this stuff.

Early in the 2004 campaign—in fact, even before the election really began—John Kerry either believed or was convinced that he should write off twenty primarily southern and rural states and their total 164 electoral votes. Simply write them off. Don't spend any time there. Don't spend any money there. Don't have a message there. Give them to W.

Give them to W! Twenty states with a total of 164 electoral college votes!

In effect, the Kerry camp said to W: George Bush, here's an early Christmas present—twenty states! A hundred and sixty-four electoral college votes! Were you surprised! Does it fit! Do you like the color red!

Here are the twenty states and their electoral votes: Alaska (3), Utah (5), Idaho (4), Montana (3), Wyoming (3), Texas (34), Oklahoma (7), Kansas (6), Nebraska (5), North Dakota (3), South Dakota (3), Mississippi (6), Alabama (9), Georgia (15), South Carolina (8), North Carolina (15), Tennessee (11), Kentucky (8), Indiana (11), and West Virginia (5).

Now some Democrats claim that W and the Republicans wrote off regions of the country as well. They did not. Name the region. The Northeast? Where is New Hampshire if not in the Northeast? Bush campaigned hard there and almost won it. The 2004 Republican National Convention was in New York City for God's sake, and Bush was even competing in New Jersey until late in the campaign. Did the president write off the Northwest or the Southwest? Don't think so. He campaigned hard in Washington State, Arizona, and New Mexico. No, the president and the Republicans did not write off any regions.

They did not do so because they wanted to maximize their votes in *all* states. They wanted a Republican message nationwide, not regionally. They wanted to hedge their bets. Sure, they didn't campaign hard in Massachusetts, but they were never so arrogant as to announce they were "abandoning" the Northeast. Bush never stood up and asked why a Republican would go to the Northeast or the Northwest! He went there. He went *everywhere*. Thus, the Republicans had a message *everywhere*. They spent money *everywhere*. They gave cover to all of their down-ballot candidates *everywhere*. The Republicans knew how to count, and they were never so elitist or shortsighted as to think they couldn't make the case for the president and their candidates in every corner of the country. Democrats would be wise to study from this section of the Republican playbook if they want success in the future.

If Democrats could count, they would stop and think, Hey, wait a minute. If we give George W. Bush 164 electoral votes and he needs 270 votes to win, he now needs only 106 additional electoral votes to win the presidency! That's only 106 of the remaining 374 electoral votes out there!

Let's make sure we get this right. For Bush to win now, he needs only 106 of 374 votes—or 28 percent of the remaining votes. By contrast, Kerry needs 270 of 374—or a whopping 72 percent.

Okay, we're starting to get this stuff now.

But the Democrats weren't. Instead, they huddled together and announced: "Since we're in a giving mood, why not concede even more states and more electoral votes!"

So they did. Shortly after John Kerry became the official nominee of the Democratic Party, inexplicably at a national Democratic Party convention held in liberal Boston (strange for a party struggling to attract moderate voters), and after an inexplicable love fest with nary a word informing voters why George W. Bush's reelection would be a disaster for the nation, the Kerry camp announced that they were "suspending operations" in an additional seven states! Seven more states!

Suspending operations. Out. Gone. No money. No appearances. No staff. No message. All you voters in these states, vote for the other guy. We don't care about you. We don't need you.

What were these seven states? Virginia. Louisiana. Arkansas. Missouri. Nevada. Arizona and Colorado.

What are the electoral votes of these seven states? Virginia: 13. Louisiana: 9. Arkansas: 6. Missouri: 11. Nevada: 5. Arizona: 10. Colorado: 9. Sixty-three additional electoral votes. Two hundred twenty-seven electoral votes now conceded.

And it wasn't even Labor Day.

In this election the Democrats conceded 227 electoral votes in twenty-seven states to Bush before any votes were actually cast. So of the 270 electoral votes needed to win the election, Bush already had 227, or 84 percent. In other words, in the remaining twenty-three states, the Republicans would have to get 43 electoral votes, or 14 percent of the total votes left out there to win reelection. Just 14 percent!

Let's repeat the moral of the story here: Politics is the art of addition, not subtraction. So when did Democrats begin to think that elections are the art of subtraction?

The truth is that not all of the Democrats' demise in 2004 was John Kerry's fault. Nor was it the fault of Kerry's campaign. For all the hope, the hype, the hoopla, and the hysteria surrounding Democratic expectations of victory in 2004, many of the seeds for the party's crushing defeat on November 2, 2004, had been sown long before.

The Republican Party's grasp around the necks of rural and southern America has been tightening for the better part of the past quarter century and transformed itself into its current manifestation in the eighties with the rise of the Religious Right and in the nineties with a new breed of Republican legislators led by the politics-first, win-at-all-costs tactics of progressive and democratic Cro-Magnons such as Newt Gingrich and Dick Armey.

But let's be clear: Democrats have no one to blame but themselves. For a generation, the national Democratic Party has ignored the South and much of rural America. They have belittled people who live there as rednecks, racists, trailer trash, and gun-toting simpletons. They refused to campaign in many of these areas. They simply wrote them off, conceded them to Republicans, and seemed all the happier for the decision. That is the root of the problem. And too many Democrats do not get it.

But look at what happens when Democrats do understand it.

In 1986, in his first race for the U.S. Senate, Tom Daschle got it. He was running in a red state against a very popular incumbent Republican, Jim Abdnor. Abdnor had a job approval rating above 70 percent, and according to voter registration figures, Republicans outnumbered Democrats in South Dakota by 13 percent. To win, Daschle needed every vote he could get. So his staff, headed by a calm yet meticulous vote counter named Pete Stavrianos, orchestrated one of the first "coordinated campaign" operations in modern American history. This campaign contacted every voter they could find in every corner of the state. They wrote off nothing. They telephoned the voters whom they could call, and for those they could not reach by phone, they sent staff to knock on doors. They did all of this to ask voters whether they were supporting Daschle or Abdnor or were undecided. They also asked voters what issues were most likely to influence their votes.

The names of those indicating support for Daschle went into a computer so they could be turned out on election day. To undecided voters, Stavrianos sent persuasion mail and targeted them with specific advertising reflecting the issues the voters said were most salient to them. And when it appeared that there might not be enough existing voters who supported Daschle, his staff mounted an aggressive registration drive to identify and register new Daschle voters. Ten thousand Daschle supporters were added to the voting rolls this way. It was the most aggressive voter contact effort in South Dakota history.

Stavrianos was brutal in his quest to get every vote in every corner of the state. Night after night as his campaign canvassers returned to the headquarters, he would tally their numbers of people interviewed and voters registered, and invariably would admonish a staffer to return the next day and register more new Democrats there because his numbers showed that there were still one hundred unregistered voters in a certain precinct that had a Democratic performance of 40 percent, thus, there were forty unregistered Democrats in the precinct, and it was the campaign staffer's job to root them out.

The registration effort was so intense that staffers were stopping people on the street and registering them to vote. One day, two campaign staffers walking through a park in Sioux Falls came upon a man and a woman sitting at a picnic area. The staffers screened them, found out they supported Daschle but were not registered to vote. They registered them. Back at campaign headquarters, the two staffers were watching the 6:00 P.M. news when they recognized the two people they had registered in the park. Their faces were on the news because, apparently shortly after the staffers had registered them, the man and woman got into a fight and the woman killed the man. She was now in police custody. One of the staffers turned to the other and said, "We registered those two people, but now one of them can't vote because he is dead and the other won't be able to vote because she will be a convicted felon." To which the other staffer replied, "Yeah, we should have voted them absentee."

Pete Stavrianos knew how to count. Daschle won by 7,000 votes.

In Virginia in 2001, everybody knew that businessman Mark Warner could not win the governor's race. Nothing against Warner, but the state was trending Republican faster than almost any state in the union. Republicans controlled everything at the state level—both houses of the legislature and every statewide elected official. The previous November, the Republican George Allen had unseated the Democratic incumbent U.S. senator Chuck Robb by 100,000 votes. Pundits figured Warner would be merely the latest Democrat to go down in this red state.

There was just one problem with that theory. It presumed Warner did not know how to count. Turns out, he did.

Warner's campaign saw that the Virginia Democratic Party had identified only 360,000 voters out of nearly 4 million registered voters as Democrats (Virginians do not register by political party). If Warner knew so little about so few of Virginia's voters, he knew he could not win. Moreover, Warner's staff estimated that unless he broadened the base from traditional Democratic constituencies, he would not have enough votes to win. So his campaign mounted the most aggressive voter canvass in Virginia history—no region was ignored or left out. Warner knew that he needed huge votes from traditional Democratic areas in Northern Virginia and from the traditional Democratic constituencies of women and African Americans. But he also knew that if he did not cut into traditional Republican strongholds in rural Virginia, he would lose. So from April through October 2001, his campaign telephoned into the 2.7 million Virginia households and reached 1.3 million voters, finding out for whom they were voting and, if they were undecided, what issues might influence their vote. In addition, his organization hired 135 staffers statewide to knock on doors of voters who had not been reached by telephone. An additional 800,000 voters throughout the state were contacted in this fashion.

Warner specifically targeted rural voters. He did so by aggressively campaigning in rural Virginia, by offering concrete policy proposals to help the people there, and by tapping into the culture of rural Virginia, including sponsoring a NASCAR truck, adopting a bluegrass theme song, and establishing the largest sportsmen's group of supporters in Virginia history. On election day Warner's efforts paid off. He won by 101,000 votes—and the bulk of his margin came from rural Virginia. He shocked pundits and analysts by actually winning rural Virginia, with 51.4 percent of the vote. Mark Warner knew how to count.

Unfortunately, more and more it seems guys like Tom Daschle and Mark Warner are the exception, not the rule, for Democratic politicians.

Let's face it, if Kerry had won the presidential election on November 2, 2004, Democrats would have been high-fiving each other all over Washington, D.C. They would have been singing their own praises, telling each other and anyone who would listen how smart they were. They would have missed the point.

If Kerry had threaded the needle, and won that race while Democrats had completely written off the South and much of the rural Midwest to the Republicans, the cancer of neglect would still have been growing inside the body Democrat. More than likely, Democrats would have done nothing to address the neglect, and this ticking time bomb would have gotten much more threatening, not less. Eventually—whether in 2008 or in 2012—it would have killed the host.

Threading the needle was the only way Kerry or any Democrat who had written off the South and much of rural America could ever have won the 2004 election and is the only way a Democrat will win in the future unless Democrats wise up and quit conceding such important and, in the case of the South, *growing* parts of the country. Let's be real clear. The South is not getting *less* politically important, it is getting *more* so. Today 102 million Americans live in the South—defined by the Census Bureau as the states of Georgia, Florida, Texas, North and South Carolina, Alabama, Mississippi, Louisiana, Kentucky, Oklahoma, Arkansas, Tennessee, Virginia, West Virginia, Maryland, and Delaware, and the District of Columbia. In election 2004, 32 percent of all voters came from the South. But census projections indicate that by 2030 fully 143 million people, or 40 percent of the American population, will live in the South, compared with 92 million people living in the West, 70 million in the Midwest, and 58 million in the Northeast. Democrats, do you think we ought to keep ignoring the South?

We don't.

We are already seeing the shift of power through the addition of congressional seats in the South and Midwest and, with them, electoral college votes. The 2004 presidential race was the first to be affected by the shifts in congressional seats that followed the 2000 census. And the South and Midwest were the biggest regional winners in congressional seats. This is how the landscape changed from 2000 to 2004: Arizona went from 8 electoral college votes to 10; Florida from 25 to 27, Georgia from 13 to 15, Texas from 32 to 34, Colorado from 8 to 9, North Carolina from 14 to 15, and Nevada from 4 to 5. Bush won all of these states.

Are you thinking what we're thinking? How many more electoral college votes will the South get as its population balloons by 40 million people in the next twenty-five years! If you do the simple math and see that the South will go from 32 to 40 percent of the population, an 8 percent increase, it stands to reason that the region will gain 8 percent more electoral college votes. Eight percent of 538 is 43. Democrats, are you still thinking it wise to concede the South to the GOP?

Meanwhile, to help drive the point home that Democrats have to learn to play in the South, here are the more traditional Democratic-leaning states that lost congressional seats and with them important electoral college votes: New York and Pennsylvania each lost two seats, while Connecticut, Wisconsin, Illinois, and Michigan each lost one seat.

Democrats cannot afford to keep writing off the South. If you don't start getting a message there, if you don't start listening to people there, if you don't start spending time, energy, and money there, and if you don't stop belittling the culture of those who live there, you can say good-bye to any notion of regaining political power and instead say hello to the numbing reality that you are relegating yourselves to the status of a permanent minority party.

The truth is, the cultural elitism that national Democrats have been showing toward people in the South and in rural areas was and is not only politically shortsighted but morally repugnant.

If Democrats are so concerned that Republicans are using moral issues as a wedge, how morally right is it for the Democrats to tell 100 million people that they don't matter?

How do you think the voters—much less the Democrats—in Kentucky and Mississippi felt in November 2003, when Democratic National Committee Chairman Terry McAuliffe told a national television audience that the losses in gubernatorial races in those two states were not that important to Democrats because the Democrats were focusing on "the number 270"—as in 270 electoral votes needed to win the White House?

Well, let's let the DNC leadership in on a little something: If Democrats continue to ignore and belittle people who live in southern and rural America, Democrats will not only never get to 270 but will never have any realistic shot at recapturing the Senate or the House, and their chances at winning gubernatorial and state legislative races in these areas will diminish exponentially.

And it wasn't just McAuliffe. How morally correct is it to have a presidential candidate ask, as John Kerry did an audience at Dartmouth College in January 2004, "Why would a Democrat go south?"

Perhaps because 100 million voters live there today and in the next twenty-five years 40 million more people will be born there or have moved there? Perhaps because when one runs for president in a representative democracy there is an implied assumption that he (or she) is running to represent *all* Americans?

Would Democrats not be repulsed if a candidate for president, much less any office, stood up and asked, "Why would a Democrat go into black neighborhoods?"

Would Democrats not be repulsed if a candidate asked, "Why would a Democrat go into areas with old people?"

What's the difference?

"Why would a Democrat go south?" Senator Kerry? Perhaps so he can at the end of a campaign be referred to as President-Elect Kerry?

From a political perspective, why would you begin any race by writing off huge segments of the population? Isn't it intuitive that, to win, you have to try to make the case to all voters? And, why would you *ever* concede any votes to these Republicans? What the hell have *they* done for rural and southern America?

The truth is, voters in southern and rural regions of the country have been devastated by Republican policies. These voters are yours, Democrats. Go get them.

Aren't the Democrats the ones who have always carried water for rural and southern America? From rural electrification to the Tennessee Valley Authority, from Pell Grants to student loans, from Head Start to hospice, from Social Security to Medicare, from unemployment insurance to health insurance, from job training to workers' rights, from land-grant colleges to the G.I. Bill, from clean air to groundwater protection, from preserving our parks to conservation and preservation programs that allow hunters, fishermen, and other outdoor enthusiasts to enjoy a rural way of life, the Democratic Party is the party that has provided for people in the South and rural America.

By contrast, Republicans have sold out the environment to corporate polluters and campaign contributors, have gutted educational and child-care programs, have waged war against workers' benefits and rights, have treated family farmers as disposable commodities in favor of faceless corporations who ravage the land and turn waterways into open sewage lagoons, have jumped in bed with big oil, have conferred death sentences on families through misguided and self-serving moral and political agendas, have sold out to drug manufacturers at the cost of dignity and quality of life for senior citizens, and have threatened the future growth and productivity of millions of Americans by adopting narrow-minded and narrow-interested health-care policies.

If Democrats continue to lose to this phony, sanctimonious, hypocritical, moneygrubbing band of blowhard brothers, they deserve to lose.

So, after learning how to count, what else do Democrats have to do so that they *won't* continue to lose these voters?

Democrats have to learn how to reconnect with voters by reaching out, by listening to them, by embracing their culture, and by defining the issues of the campaign before their opponents do.

Lesson 2: Define Yourself and Define Your Opponent (Not the Other Way Around)

There is a simple device used by media and polling advisers known as the message grid or the message quad. It is so widely used and respected that we have seen at least six media and polling consultants—in both political parties—take credit for it. It is a simple device. It merely says that, at the beginning of any campaign, candidates and their advisers should take some time to answer four simple questions:

1. In this campaign, what will I tell voters about myself? (You on you.)
2. In this campaign, what will I tell voters about my opponent? (You on them.)
3. In this campaign, what will my opponent tell voters about him- or herself? (Them on them.)
4. In this campaign, what will my opponent tell voters about me? (Them on me.)

Some Democrats clearly understand this grid. In Montana's 2004 gubernatorial race, the Democrat Brian Schweitzer did a terrific job of telling voters who he was—a blue-jean-, bolo-tie-, cowboy-boot-wearing farmer who was far more Montanan than he was Democrat. Schweitzer connected with red-state Montana voters—particularly the "difficult for Democrats" white male voters—by shooting his television ads while sitting on a horse's back or brandishing a gun. Last fall he told *The Washington Post,* "I spoke to men visually and showed them I am like them. Hell, I can be on a horse and talk about health care. Ninety percent of them don't ride horses, and many of them don't shoot a gun, but my ads said visually that I understand Montana. My gender gap disappeared. I think I have just summed up why Democrats lose elections."

We agree.

Schweitzer won by 4 percentage points in one of the nation's biggest upset victories of 2004.

Yet, in the most high-profile race from 2004, the presidential race, most observers have noted that Kerry did not do a very good job defining himself or defining Bush. By contrast, most observers contend that Bush did an excellent job of defining Kerry and a good job defining himself. Bush succeeded in painting Kerry as out of touch with average voters—using footage of his opponent windsurfing and snowboarding; noting that Kerry spoke French, and even contending that Kerry *looked* French at a time when Americans were upset at France's lack of support for the Iraq War. Bush was able to paint Kerry as a flip-flopper on defense issues who had a litany of antimilitary and antiveteran votes. He even convinced many voters that Kerry would ask the United Nations's permission before committing Americans to war. Most of the charges, as it turned out, were false, but that did not matter. Bush's team was able to convince voters they should be wary of Kerry as a potential commander in chief.

Meanwhile, Bush was able to paint himself as tough and unwavering in his support of our troops. He was able to gloss over his failure to bring Osama bin Laden to justice by convincing Americans that Iraq and bin Laden were essentially one and the same, so by fighting a war in Iraq, America was really fighting to root out terrorists. Bush was also successful in convincing Americans that the economic downturn was a result of wartime pressures and additional spending needed to deal with additional terrorist threats on American soil.

Bush's success in defining himself was important, but the way in which he defined Kerry was textbook perfect. And W's defining Kerry is probably best illustrated by the way the Bush campaign questioned Kerry's military service, his medals, and even his war wounds, while the draft-dodging W smirked all the way to the ballot box. What was inexplicable to many observers was why Kerry let Bush do it.

When we first heard that Bush was hammering Kerry over Kerry's Vietnam service with a Swift Boat television ad, we were eating ribs at Brother Jimmy's barbecue in Harvard Square in Cambridge, Massachusetts, where every Wednesday a southern ID gets you 25 percent off your tab. We couldn't believe the ad. We jumped up and down, saying, "The stupid son of a bitch Bush. He just gave Kerry an opening to take his draft-dodging, whiskey-drinking, Tricia-Nixon-attempt-at-dating, Alabama-loafing, Yale-cheerleading, goofy-looking head off."

But it never happened.

Opportunity missed.

We were very disappointed.

Why would you *not* do that? It was pretty clear that all Bush was doing was trying to define Kerry before Kerry defined himself—which reflects another political rule: *View every campaign as a blank chalkboard.* Whichever candidate writes on that chalkboard first, describing who he is and who his opponent is, will have the best chance of winning.

Bush spent $40 million in the spring of 2004 defining Kerry—in, shall we say, less than flattering terms. Kerry did virtually nothing to respond. Bush was the first to define Kerry on the political chalkboard. His definition to the American voting audience was so thorough, compelling, and crude that Kerry never recovered.

Bush was also performing another obvious political gimmick that is an outgrowth of the message grid: *When you find a strength in your opponent, where possible turn that strength into a weakness.*

Taking Kerry's decorated military record and turning it into a weakness was nothing short of political brilliance. It ranks up there with Pat Robertson and Jerry Falwell taking checks from the poor and preaching of biblical doctrine to help the poor as they retire to their castles and shrines, and with the four-times-divorced, drug-laced Rush Limbaugh claiming he represents the values of America.

This was a draft-dodging, AWOL, deer-in-the-headlights-on-hearing-of-the-attacks-on-the-World-Trade-Center, wimpy shrub, tearing the medals from the chest of an honest-to-God war hero and stomping them beyond recognition.

John Kerry should have called him out on it immediately. Bush crossed a line, and Senator Kerry needed to be indignant as hell and rip his militarily impudent, Alfred E. Neuman–look-alike head off. This was a Ronald Reagan (who wasn't a veteran either but thought he was because he played one on TV) "I paid for this microphone" moment.

And God knows, it is not just with the issue of war that Democrats get beat.

Democrats, if you ever again allow this blabbering bunch of deceitful, insincere, hypocritical, knavish, sanctimonious phonies call you tax-and-spend liberals, you deserve to lose.

Democrats, if you ever again allow this band of pompous, pious, petulant, pharisaic, heretical, blasphemous blowhards, with their disastrous record of protecting families, brand you as amoral and antifamily, you deserve to lose.

Democrats, if you ever again allow these wimpish, ingenuous, guileless, slovenly, shameful, despicable, discreditable G.I. Joe wannabes, with their disastrous personal, political, and policy credentials in carrying out military policy and caring for our military personnel, label you as antidefense, you deserve to lose.

Democrats, if you ever again allow these habitat-destroying, water-polluting, air-fouling, corporate-coddling demolishers of all that is sacred about the outdoors tag you as antisportsmen, you deserve to lose.

This rule is perhaps the simplest of all. Do not let these guys get away with defining the terms of the debate. And every time they try to do so, expose them for what they really are.

There are scores of instances where they do this and you let them get away with it, and in doing so you are, in many instances, literally letting them get away with murder. When they do this, you should get angry, you should get indignant, you should get even.

Which brings us to Lesson 3.

Lesson 3:   Show Some Passion!

Democrats need to show passion in a couple of ways. First, you have to show passion in a positive way. Show people you understand that politics is about those who would be served, not about those who serve. Show them that you enjoy serving them, that you relish fighting for them against the special interests. Show people you understand that lives are at stake in the actions or inactions of elected officials. People want heroes. They want underdogs who are willing to take on the big, faceless special interests who take far too big a piece of the American dream. Be a Bob Kerrey, who as governor of Nebraska stood on the tracks and stopped a trainload of high-level nuclear waste from entering his state. Or the same Bob Kerrey, who told a group of college students—who it turns out were hired by the Republican National Committee to stand in front of Kerrey's 1988 Senate campaign office carrying signs that read "Draft Dodgers for Kerrey"—to "go to hell." Or be a Brian Schweitzer, who as a candidate jumped on a bus to Canada with a group of senior citizens to buy prescription drugs at cheaper prices than they could get them in Montana. Or be a Paul Hackett, the marine who served in Iraq before coming back to Ohio and who narrowly lost a special election for a congressional seat in a very Republican district but, in doing so, showed Democrats that passionate honesty, candor, and fearlessness transcend ideology or party affiliation for huge percentages of the American voting public.

Democrats, be optimistic and offer solutions. For millions of Americans, hope is a vision lost. Life intervenes. And life can be cold and uncaring. Find the needs and insecurities of your constituents, and show them you have the passion to fight to give them greater opportunity to live the American dream. And once elected, don't forget the promises you made or the fears and insecurities you witnessed. Act on them, and deliver hope once again. Do so whether the picture is local, as was the case with Kerrey, Schweitzer, and Hackett, or large—Franklin Roosevelt telling America it was wrong that a third of the nation was ill-fed, ill-housed, and ill-clothed; or John Kennedy vowing to make America the educational leader in the world, capped with landing a man on the moon in a decade; or Lyndon Johnson vowing to end poverty in our lifetime.

Second, Democrats, you need to be able to show passion when you are attacked. Sometimes, you need to get pissed. It's okay. People actually like a little indignation. This is what happens when you don't get indignant or show some anger or enough passion.

Max Cleland, the former U.S. senator from Georgia, is one of the most decent, respectable human beings God ever breathed life into. Max Cleland lost both legs and an arm in Vietnam thanks to an ugly grenade explosion. He is the former head of the Veterans Administration and is without question one of the greatest advocates for veterans' causes in America. Max Cleland ran for reelection in 2002 and was defeated in no small part because his opponent, Saxby Chambliss, who never served in the military, ran television ads questioning Cleland's patriotism.

Chambliss ran an ad featuring images of Osama bin Laden and Saddam Hussein and suggested that Cleland was essentially voting to help them when he voted against the Homeland Security Bill (which essentially gutted the U.S. Constitution in the name of granting W authority to search for "evildoers" in America—including you, by the way—without any cause).

Before we go any further, let us state clearly that we know there *are* a lot of reasons people lose elections. The bin Laden–Hussein ad was not the only reason Cleland lost. Cleland was also running under the weight of an unpopular Democratic governor who had gotten into a horrible hornets' nest involving the Georgia state flag and the Confederate flag.

But wouldn't it have been great, and might it not have turned things around, if Max Cleland had run an immediate television ad—just Cleland to camera—wherein he said something like this:

Saxby Chambliss, don't you ever, ever challenge my patriotism or my commitment to this country or to our military personnel serving it. You have not earned that right. You have made a mockery out of legitimate support of our country and our military. To suggest that I would do anything that would support the murdering gangsters Osama bin Laden and Saddam Hussein is inexcusable. I left a lot in Vietnam. But I did not leave everything. I did not leave my heart and my soul, and I did not leave my patriotism. If you are man enough to meet me one-on-one, I will kick the hell out of you with the one arm I have left. And if that costs me reelection, so be it. My character and pa-

triotism are far more important to me than any personal political gain ever will be.

Cleland did not have to go negative on Chambliss; he did not have to attack his opponent. He just needed to show the passion that said Chambliss's actions were unacceptable. If ever anyone could have delivered such a message to a person like Saxby Chambliss, it was a legitimate American hero, Max Cleland.

Another case in point:

Tom Daschle. Without question the most powerful political figure with whom South Dakotans have ever been blessed. Daschle was not only the Senate leader for the Democrats but the number one advocate for his home state. After he steered hundreds of millions of dollars to South Dakota over his twenty-six-year legislative career, one could not argue that Tom Daschle didn't deliver. Tens of thousands of South Dakotans were stronger, were better educated, and were healthier; they had better jobs, got better prices for their agricultural crops, and had more opportunity as a consequence of Daschle's unselfish service to the Sunshine State.

But then came the 2004 Senate campaign between Daschle and the upstart pretty boy John Thune, a former congressman who ran as a "family values" candidate. In this race, Thune did a lot of despicable things, including paying two people to create an anti-Daschle website filled with lies and distortions about Daschle, his family, and his record.

But of all his lies and distortions, none touches the allegation Thune made that Daschle, who served as an intelligence officer in Vietnam, uttered words that "emboldened the enemy" when he questioned the U.S. government's policies in the Iraq War. Thune, who never served in the military, made the allegation to Daschle's face on NBC's *Meet the Press* several weeks before the election. Daschle's reply was that he was "disappointed," that those were words that would have gotten one taken to the woodshed when Daschle was growing up.

Daschle should have called Thune on this immediately and with passion. Thune had just accused Daschle of a treasonous act. Daschle shouldn't have merely been disappointed, he should have been mad as hell! He should have demanded an apology and told Thune he was tired of this crap and so were the people of South Dakota. Had Daschle gotten in Thune's face, we believe Thune would have looked very weak and small.

And we know it's not just Kerry or Cleland or Daschle. We know it's not an easy thing to do. We know that many public officials have a natural inclination to be reserved. But Democrats are getting killed out there. They need to put aside their reserve and stand up for themselves. In fact, Democrats should do what one guy did when asked about the Swift Boat attacks on John Kerry. The one guy who did the right thing was the same Kerrey we mentioned earlier, Joseph Robert Kerrey, the former senator from Nebraska.

Bob Kerrey had left the Senate in 2001 and was serving as president of the New School in New York City—he was also a Medal of Honor recipient who had left a leg in Vietnam and didn't take kindly to a draft dodger whose congressman daddy had pulled strings to get him off the front lines and into a limousine ride to Alabama so he could go AWOL.

Asked by the New York *Daily News*'s James Gordon Meek what he thought of the Swifties accusing John Kerry of volunteering for Vietnam combat duty to "pad his political résumé," Kerrey said, "Oh, fuck them. Quote me on that. The idea that you'd volunteer for [Swift Boat duty] be-cause you're thinking about a political career. . . . That's what you think about doing if you want a posthumous political career."

You think Bob Kerrey would have let Bush question his character or integrity?

It would appear not.

Bob Kerrey got angrier at George W. Bush assassinating John Kerry's character than John Kerry did.

Which brings us to Lesson 4.

Lesson 4:   When Someone Assassinates Your Character, Retaliate!

This one is an easy one.

It's very simple. Every American will understand it. When people impugn your character or integrity, when people suggest that you are a loathsome human being, when people question your patriotism, your commitment to humanity, your morals and values, you have license to fire back with a bigger gun than they fired at you.

In fact, not only do people think it's acceptable for you to fire back, they expect it! And worse, if you don't fire back with anger and indignation to attacks on your character, to attacks on your essence as a human being, people may think the original attack must have had some merit. Politics is a contact sport. The odds are very good today that in almost any race for public office there will be attacks. You need to expect them and respond to them. Don't ignore them; don't be uncomfortable with them. Retaliate against them. Look at these moments as opportunities to show the real you.

There are two ways to retaliate. First, if the attack on you is true, you may want to address the charge, but then you should get off the issue and onto turf that better suits your chances of winning.

Case in point:

In a state legislative race in Virginia in 2005, a first-time Democratic candidate, Eric Ferguson, was running against the twelve-year incumbent Allen Dudley. A week before Labor Day, Dudley found himself in a closer race with Ferguson than he wanted. Dudley's response was to begin calling through his district with a push poll, a device disguised as a telephone poll of constituents whose real purpose is to provide negative information about one's opponent. Dudley's callers were informing voters that Ferguson as a young lawyer had been sued for malpractice.

Ferguson's initial response was anger, and he wanted to debate Dudley on the issue, but there was one problem—Ferguson *had* been sued for malpractice twenty years earlier. He decided he had to make sure the campaign would not spend any time arguing this malpractice suit. So he changed turf. He immediately began running radio ads defining Dudley as out of touch with the district. His ads pointed out that Dudley, who served with the state's Republican majority on the Appropriations Committee, had done a poor job of bringing state funds back home to the district—in fact, in the past legislative session there had been 194 appropriations projects, 0 of which came to Dudley's district. Ferguson's ads also pointed out that Dudley received most of his campaign funds from lobbyists with no connection to his district, and they showed that he had taken

$150,000 from the state in twelve years to run an office out of his home—a legal but sordid practice. Finally, Ferguson was able to get local news organizations to expose Dudley's ownership of a mobile home park that tenants claimed was ill kept and that happened to house illegal aliens.

The point is, Ferguson knew he could not win if the race centered on whether he had been sued for malpractice, so he fired back with damning research on his opponent's political and business record.

By contrast, if the attack on you is untrue, you should immediately respond to it with indignation and disgust. This is an opportunity to paint your opponent as a politician who will say or do anything—even lie—to win. Turn the false attack into a question of your opponent's own lack of character. People who cheat and lie to get elected would seem to be putting their own interests before those of the constituents they supposedly wish to serve.

When people question whether you were actually wounded in a war, whether you truly deserved your medals, whether you really were patriotic—when you *were* wounded in war, *did* deserve your medals, and fought, bled, and killed for your country—annihilate them. Particularly do so when the attacker's record is one of dodged service, questionable excuses, and a powerful daddy pulling strings to keep the attacker out of combat.

The Swift Boat attacks on John Kerry were particularly galling because Kerry had the opportunity to use them not just to expose flaws in Bush's character but also to rally veterans to his side. An indignant Kerry calling Bush out on these charges would have shown toughness, pride, and an instinct for fairness and honesty. Kerry could have relatively easily used this attack to contrast Bush's own questionable military service record as well as his suspect record on terrorism and on the Iraq War. Moreover, an indignant Kerry pointing out that, when Bush questioned whether Kerry deserved his medals, he was suggesting it would be acceptable to question any soldier who ever received a medal would have been a powerful rallying tool for veterans everywhere. Not just John Kerry but the band of brothers were being attacked on this one. Decorated war heroes coming forward asking whether Bush would question their medals next would have been a powerful visual and would have shifted the attacks from ones on Kerry to ones on Bush's character, military competence, and patriotism.

Kerry should have gone head to head with Bush on this. He should have done it for himself and for those of us who are livid at these Republican phonies who routinely question the military records of Democrats. But Kerry should also have done it because he had the opportunity to suggest that Bush would question *anybody* who had received a medal if he thought he could gain politically from doing so.

Can you imagine if John Kerry had been the draft dodger and George W. Bush the highly decorated veteran? The Republicans would have had a field day. How unpatriotic the Democrats and Kerry would have been to question "the war hero George W. Bush"!

Can you imagine if it had been John Edwards who had headed Halliburton when it made a plethora of illegal payments and bribed government officials to win multibillion-dollar deals; who had invited oil executives to his vice presidential office so they could write our nation's energy policy; or who was still receiving monetary benefit from Halliburton *after* he left the company to become vice president and *while* Halliburton was getting billions of dollars in no-bid contracts in the Iraq War?

And, just to add a bit of icing to the cake, what if it had been the former CBS News anchor Dan Rather who was accused of sexually harassing a young woman in his employ and had to pay her a reported multimillion-dollar settlement to go away? Where is the outrage from the moralists in the Republican Party at Fox News's Bill O'Reilly, who actually was accused of sexually harassing a young woman in his employ and *did* pay her millions of dollars to go away?

Come on, Democrats. Politics is not what it used to be. It's a contact sport. You are going to have to play by Republican rules on this stuff. If their rules allow character assassination, you had better be ready for it and know how to strike back. If character is fair game, blow the hell out of theirs.

Get mad! It takes time for a message to get through, so don't give up. Fight back and fight hard. If you don't fight back, if you don't play by their rules, there will be no one left standing in the Democratic Party.

You want some help with passion? See if the exploits of the following list of Republican leaders and cheerleaders doesn't get your blood boiling and your passion for change exploding.

Republican Confederacy of Dunces

Ann Coulter: Where does one begin with this mendaciously painted lady who looks more like Bullwinkle J. Moose in a tight skirt and cheap wig than the blond bombshell to which she aspires? This shrill, loudmouthed puppet for Republican causes is the darling of the GOP leadership. But the truth is, Ann Coulter cannot hold a job.

She was fired by MSNBC. She was fired by *USA Today*. She was fired by National Review Online.

Ask GOP leaders whether they support Coulter on these points: During an interview with the Vietnam Veterans of America Foundation president, Bobby Muller, on MSNBC, Coulter did not agree with one of Muller's responses, so she declared, "No wonder you guys lost." MSNBC rewarded her quick wit by firing her.

Coulter aligned herself with the Reverend Jerry Falwell when he said the September 11, 2001, terrorist attacks on America were punishment for the activities of gays and abortionists.

Coulter described Democratic women as "corn-fed, no-makeup, natural-fiber, no-bra-needing, sandal-wearing, hirsute, somewhat fragrant hippie-chick pie wagons."

Finally, this modern-day Clara Barton slurred the Vietnam War triple amputee Max Cleland.

That would be Army Captain Max Cleland, who volunteered for service in Vietnam. On a mission in 1967, Cleland was exiting a helicopter after setting up a radio relay station for his unit. But upon jumping to join his fellow soldiers for a break, he noticed a grenade under the helicopter. He feared that if he did not remove the grenade, it would explode when another helicopter landed at the site. Unfortunately for Cleland, the young enlisted man who had dropped the grenade had not secured the pin. When Cleland picked it up to dispose of it, the grenade exploded, shredding both his legs and an arm, and mangling his body.

This is how Cleland remembered the moment in his gripping autobiography, *Strong at the Broken Places:*

> *Shifting the M-16 to my left hand and holding it behind me, I bent down to pick up the grenade. A blinding explosion threw me backwards. The blast*

jammed my eyeballs back into my skull, temporarily blinding me, pinning my cheeks and jaw muscles to the bones of my face. My ears rang with a deafening reverberation as if I were standing in an echo chamber. Memory of the firecracker exploding in my hand as a child flashed before me. When my eyes cleared I looked at my right hand. It was gone. Nothing but a splintered white bone protruded from my shredded elbow. It was speckled with fragments of bloody flesh. Nausea flooded me. I lay where the blast had flung me for a moment, fighting for breath. I found myself slumped on the ground.

Then I tried to stand but couldn't. I looked down. My right leg and knee were gone. My left leg was a soggy mass of bloody flesh mixed with green fatigue cloth. The combat boot dangled awkwardly, like the smashed legs on the dead soldier after the rocket attack.

What was left of me? I reached with my left hand to feel my head. My steel helmet—now gone—had apparently protected it. My flak jacket had shielded my chest and groin from shrapnel. Intense pain throbbed my body with each heartbeat. I seemed to be falling backwards into a dark tunnel.

I raised up on my left elbow to call for help. Apparently, surrounding troops had mistaken the blast for incoming rocket fire and frantically scattered. I tried to cry out to them but could only hiss. My hand touched my throat and came back covered with blood. Shrapnel had sliced open my windpipe.

I sank back on the ground knowing that I was dying fast. A soft blackness was trying to claim me. No! I don't want to die.

Coulter was angry at Cleland for campaigning for John Kerry and against George W. Bush's Iraqi policies, so in February 2004 she wrote in a column, "Max Cleland should stop allowing Democrats to portray him as a war hero who lost his limbs taking enemy fire on the battlefields of Vietnam. Cleland lost three limbs in an accident during a routine noncombat mission . . . he saw a grenade on the ground and picked it up. He could have done that at Fort Dix. . . . Luckily for Cleland's political career and current pomposity about Bush, he happened to do it while in Vietnam."

So, according to Coulter, Cleland was lucky to have lost three limbs.

Oh, one other thing. A week before he picked up that grenade, Cleland had *volunteered* to be a communications officer for the Second Infantry Battalion on a mission to assist American troops trapped behind enemy lines at Khe Sanh. During that mission, and while under heavy enemy fire, he came to the aid of and saved wounded American soldiers. He was awarded a Silver Star for battlefield heroism.

Shame on Ann Coulter. Republicans do not renounce her slanderous, scurrilous statements. They encourage her. They buy her books, they listen to her on the radio, they read her columns. She would not exist without their support. The Republicans who enable her are not patriots. Democrats, hold accountable those supporting and encouraging her.

Dick Cheney: Let's look at his record.

Dick Cheney represented Wyoming in the U.S. House of Representatives from 1978 through 1988. These are some of his votes.

- He voted to cut food stamps to poor people.
- He voted to cut funding for the Occupational Safety and Health Administration, the agency responsible for workplace safety rules.
- He voted to cut food stamps again.
- He voted to cut food stamps again.
- He voted to cut Pell Grants for college students.
- He voted against a bill designed to help homeowners facing foreclosure.
- He voted against unemployment compensation for laid-off workers.
- He voted against reauthorizing the Federal Water Pollution Act.
- He opposed Environmental Protection Agency research and development programs.
- He voted against reauthorization of the Clean Water Act (one of only eight congressmen who opposed reauthorization).
- He voted against extending aid to low-income home buyers.
- He voted against a resolution calling for South Africa to release Nelson Mandela from prison.
- He voted not once but twice to block sanctions against the apartheid regime in South Africa.
- He opposed reauthorization of the Superfund program, designed to clean up America's major hazardous waste sites.
- He disliked cleaning up toxic waste so much he voted against this one again.
- He was one of only twelve members of Congress to oppose the Older

Americans Act amendments designed to provide nutrition and support services to the elderly.

- He was one of only sixteen House members who opposed reauthorization of the Endangered Species Act (even Newt Gingrich voted for this one).
- He was one of only thirty-nine members who backed capping cost-of-living allowances for Social Security recipients.
- He voted against the Older Americans Act again.
- He voted (twice) against creating the Department of Education.
- He voted against reauthorization of the College Student Loan Program.
- He opposed funding the Safe Drinking Water Act.
- He voted against the Head Start program, which provides nutrition, and education to preschoolers.
- He voted against the Head Start program (this is not a typo; he did it again).
- He voted to cut college student aid, which provided funds for colleges and for needy students.
- He voted against the Federal Immunization Program.
- He opposed a bill that would have helped states combat crime.
- He opposed the Family Violence Protection Program.
- He opposed a police-backed bill to ban armor-piercing bullets.
- He voted against guaranteeing death benefits for firefighters' and cops' widows.
- He was one of only nine members to vote against allowing federal employees to take time off to care for sick family members.
- He voted against a program to collect hate crime data by race, religion, sexual orientation, or ethnicity.
- He voted against federal nutrition programs.
- He voted against the Hunger Relief Plan, which would have expanded eligibility into the Food Stamp Program for families who could not afford to feed themselves.

So, what did Cheney vote for?

- He voted for the testing of U.S. antisatellite weapons against a target in space.
- He voted for the Binary Chemical Weapons Program, which authorized

the appropriation of $124 million for the production of these sophisticated and dangerous weapons.

- He voted for Ronald Reagan's Strategic Defense Initiative—the so-called Star Wars defense system the Gipper just had to have.
- He voted to allow testing of nuclear explosives greater than one kiloton.

So let's get this right. Cheney voted against children, women, education programs, old people, poor people, black people, sick people, working people, against cops and firefighters, against families, against clean air, clean water, clean land, against birds and animals, but he voted for virtually every weapons system on which he could lay his hands.

And this is the same Dick Cheney who got out of Vietnam on a 3-A deferment (that means he had dependents—Cheney had four other deferments before this one). Years later (in 1989 to be exact), Cheney was quoted as saying, "I had other priorities in the sixties than military service."

Then there were the years (1995 to 2000) Cheney spent as CEO of the oil services and defense contracting giant Halliburton.

Halliburton wanted Cheney because they wanted someone who could use government *contacts* to get government *contracts*—from the U.S. government and from governments around the world. Even terrorist-coddling governments. Halliburton did not care. And as it turns out, neither did Cheney. But there were problems with how Cheney and Halliburton made their money.

- Cheney and Halliburton soon acquired Dresser Industries, making Halliburton the revenue leader in the oil services industry. But after the merger, Dresser executives found that Halliburton projects were less valuable than they appeared on the books.
- In 1996 Cheney and Halliburton entered into a joint venture to build undersea pipelines and received one of its biggest contracts that year in Myanmar, formally known as Burma. However, the United States had withdrawn its embassy in Myanmar in 1990 and banned new U.S. investments there in 1997 because the Southeast Asian country's military junta had one of the worst human rights records in the world. Not only was the junta accused of killing tens of thousands of pro-democracy protesters over the years, but they also were notorious for

using forced labor. Cheney didn't care. He had a contract signed in 1996, one year before U.S. sanctions kicked in. Halliburton was grandfathered in.

• Under Cheney's watch, Halliburton was accused of bribing the Nigerian government in order to win oil contracts.

• During Cheney's tenure, Halliburton sold millions of dollars' worth of equipment to Iraq.

• Also under Cheney's leadership, Halliburton was accused of fabricating billings in a base-closing case. They were sued for fraud and had to pay the federal government $2 million.

• Even though America had sanctions against Libya and Iran for being sponsors of terrorism, Cheney and Halliburton did business with both nations. So Cheney was doing business with two of President Bush's "axis of evil" countries.

• The U.S. Securities and Exchange Commission, our nation's watchdog against corporate fraud, investigated Halliburton for inflating its revenue by over $234 million. That's important because it artificially kept Halliburton's stock prices high. It's also illegal.

• Cheney put Halliburton on very dangerous financial footing by exposing it to potential asbestos claims against businesses bought while he was CEO.

• The conservative group Judicial Watch even sued Halliburton, claiming the company's fraudulent accounting practices hurt its shareholders—on Cheney's watch.

Perhaps all these problems help explain why Cheney wanted out of Halliburton. And he got out all right. Upon nominating himself to be W's running mate, Cheney cashed out to the tune of $36 million.

But his soul was long ago sold to big oil, and that wasn't about to change just because he was back in Washington. When he became vice president, his regard for Halliburton and for oil companies in general skyrocketed. Halliburton is the major contractor for the rebuilding of Iraq with billions of dollars in no-bid contracts. When critics cried foul, Cheney feigned ignorance. But after the Defense Department selected Halliburton to help rebuild Iraq's oil production facilities on March 8, 2003, a Pentagon memo surfaced that indicated the plans for the contract had been "coordinated" with Cheney's office. Cheney claimed that he received only a heads-up about the contract decision but had no involvement in the contract process.

And come to find out, Halliburton was still the same questionable company Cheney had built. No sooner did Halliburton start receiving contracts than the Defense Department found out the megacorporation was overbilling the government for services. In just one example, the Pentagon found that Halliburton had overbilled $175 million in its contract to provide meals to our servicemen stationed in Iraq. What happened to Halliburton for defrauding U.S. taxpayers out of millions of dollars? Not much. The Pentagon settled and agreed to pay virtually all that had been billed—even though Halliburton could not provide "adequate documentation to justify its expenses." In fact, the Pentagon gave Halliburton a "no-fault grace period" for several months of the contract. These just happened to be the months during which the greatest overcharging occurred.

• But the vice president's shilling for Halliburton was only the tip of the iceberg. Just to make sure the spoils were shared industrywide, Cheney invited a who's who of the oil, electricity, coal, nuclear, chemical, and natural gas industries to his office to hammer out America's national energy policy. And on May 16, 2001, Cheney submitted to President Bush more than one hundred proposals for our new energy policy—all preapproved by big energy companies, with little attention to environmental or consumer concerns.

Finally, we remind you of the many personal moments with Cheney, like the time he and George W were caught on tape calling the *New York Times* reporter Adam Clymer "a major league asshole." Or the time Cheney told Senator Patrick Leahy on the floor of the U.S. Senate to "go fuck yourself."

Democrats, make Cheney the poster boy for greed; for ethical lapses; for destruction of our habitat; for voting against children, women, working men and women; for voting against education programs, senior citizens, our air, land, and water; for voting against better health care and better housing; and for obliterating the hopes and dreams of millions of working families. We think Dick Cheney is a coward. He has shown nothing but contempt for our laws and indifference for our citizens. His arrogance is exceeded only by his callousness. This modern-day Grinch deserves nothing short of our disdain and disrespect.

Bill O'Reilly: As the Fox News Channel anchor-host of *The O'Reilly Factor* and talk radio commentator, Bill O'Reilly claims to be a moralist, a pro–family values guy, and a no-spin commentator. The truth is, Bill O'Reilly is none of these things. To watch his program is painful. He often blubbers and bumbles, and never lets the facts get in the way of a good story. His insecurities are so massive he routinely resorts to shouting down guests, and if that doesn't work, he has his producers shut off the microphone of the offending guest.

Bill O'Reilly is also a liar. He claimed that a television show he hosted, *Inside Edition,* won a Peabody Award.

It did not. Indeed, the only award it won was a far less prestigious Polk Award—oh, and that award was won long *after* O'Reilly left the show.

O'Reilly even claimed to have been a football champion. In the end piece for a guide for the 2005 Super Bowl, he said he had "won a national punting title for his division" in college. There is a slight problem with this.

It didn't happen.

O'Reilly attended little Marist College in Poughkeepsie, New York, graduating in 1971. But Marist College did not have a varsity football program until 1978. At best O'Reilly would have played for some intramural or club program. Hard to win a "national" much less "division" punting title when you don't have a national program, you don't have a division, and you don't even have a varsity football program.

But even all of this would not compel us to mention O'Reilly here.

Yes, Bill O'Reilly is biased. But he works for Fox News. Fox News is by definition the rendering plant of broadcasting.

No, what particularly galls us about O'Reilly is that he wrote a book, published on November 1, 2004, which pretends to give moral advice to children ages nine to sixteen. In its rambling, disjointed pages, O'Reilly talks about the evils of bullying and cheating—clearly he did not read his own copy, or perhaps he is a very slow learner. O'Reilly also warns of the evils of sex and sexual harassment (he actually lectures boys about treating girls abusively).

Two weeks before the unveiling of O'Reilly's ode to growing up moral and valued, a lawsuit was filed in New York by Andrea Mackris, a producer for O'Reilly's Fox TV show. The suit contended that he had repeatedly sexually harassed her from 2000 to 2004 and then threatened her if she went public with the harassment.

The suit was very specific. At a dinner in May 2002, it claimed, O'Reilly told Mackris to "just use your vibrator to blow off steam." At which point Mackris, understandably, became embarrassed. Sensing her embarrassment, O'Reilly said, "What, you've got a vibrator, don't you? Every girl does."

In August 2004, the suit said, O'Reilly called Mackris at her home, excited because he had just interviewed two porn stars (Good work, Fox), and he wanted to talk about sex and vibrators. According to the suit, "It became apparent that [O'Reilly] was masturbating as he spoke."

In another instance, the suit alleges that O'Reilly told Mackris and her college friend, "Boy, I would've had fun with you two." It also says he told Mackris he had had many trysts, including a rendezvous with a pair of Scandinavian airline flight attendants. And keeping with his Caribbean fetish, according to the suit, O'Reilly told Mackris on another occasion that he wanted to take her on a Caribbean vacation and fantasized about foreplay with her using a loofah sponge.

It gets worse.

On the many occasions Mackris complained to O'Reilly to stop the harassment, Mackris alleged that O'Reilly routinely became threatening. In one particularly intimidating response, she alleged that O'Reilly invoked the name of Roger Ailes, who heads Fox TV's News division and who used to work for Richard Nixon, Ronald Reagan, and George H. W. Bush: "If any woman ever breathed a word, I'll make her pay so dearly that she'll wish she'd never been born. Ailes knows very powerful people and this goes all the way to the top," O'Reilly said, according to the suit.

Wonder what O'Reilly might have meant by that? "Pay so dearly that she'll wish she'd never been born."

Sounds serious to us.

"Powerful people" and "this goes all the way to the top."

O'Reilly, of course, was furious about the lawsuit. He denied breaking the law but not that he used the language quoted in the lawsuit, and actually countersued Mackris, claiming in a statement, "I will not give in to extortion."

Oh, yeah, and then Mackris, we suspect, told him about the audiotapes she had made of their conversations.

Bill O'Reilly, the family values venerator and potentate of adolescent maturation, dropped his countersuit and settled out of court. O'Reilly sent Mackris a check for several million dollars—with one estimate as high as $10 million.

And the Republicans were outraged and embarrassed, right? They called on Fox to fumigate *The Factor,* right? They denounced O'Reilly, right?

Wrong.

Nary a word was uttered by those paragons of piety.

But at least Fox News owned up to the scandal, right?

Let's see. MSNBC covered the story with a total airtime on its news programs of one hour, twenty-two minutes. CNN gave the scandal thirty-one minutes on its news shows. Fox ran a total of thirty-six *seconds* of coverage on the scandal.

Next time Republican phonies scream about Democratic family values, next time they wail about morals in the media, ask them what they think of Bill O'Reilly and his morals and values. Ask them what they think of Fox burying their coverage of the scandal.

Oh, yeah, one more thing. O'Reilly is married with two children.

Rudy Giuliani and Bernie Kerik: Enter Rudy Giuliani. He's America's mayor, remember? Well, really, he was first New York City's mayor. Before September 11, 2001, Giuliani was probably best known as the mayor who had a very public mistress. But then September 11 happened.

Rudy got reinvented. In fact, Rudy was everywhere. He stood at Ground Zero. He attended over two hundred funerals. He showed up at Yankees games—it seemed like all of them—always in the front row and always wearing New York City firefighter 'or New York City police baseball caps. It was so overdone it was tacky.

Rudy turned himself into the face of 9/11. It was a pretty good gig. He got a reported $3 million advance to write a book on it. He pompously and presumptuously titled the book *Leadership*—and put his smiling picture on the cover. Then he suggested throughout the book that *he* personified leadership because of what he did after 9/11. We thought he was just doing what anyone would have done—showing compassion when people are hurting, doing the job you are paid to do. But he did more than that. He started giving speeches around the country, apparently making as much as $100,000 per speech. He formed companies and made millions of dollars. He started talking about becoming president of the United States.

Some thought Giuliani was taking advantage of 9/11. The columnist Tina Brown even wrote in *The Washington Post,* "The city [New York] has become just a tad cranky about Rudy's naked branding of 9/11 for his own political and pecuniary ends. Increasingly, his speeches seem to turn New York's saddest day into shtick to dramatize his own heroism."

We think Brown is right.

In fact, even Rudy's handling of affairs before and after September 11, including his preparedness and leadership, came under attack. The 9/11 Commission, formed to determine what really happened on and after September 11 and to help us learn how to avoid or better prepare for future disasters, was very critical of Giuliani. Their 2004 report cited a lot of evidence suggesting that there were huge gaps in command and cooperation between New York agencies in charge of emergency response.

In fact, one of the 9/11 Commission members, the former Navy secretary John F. Lehman, who served under Ronald Reagan, blasted the city for its response. Lehman particularly criticized Bernard Kerik, who was New York police commissioner on September 11, 2001. Lehman said that Kerik played games and had turf battles with the Fire Department, which "hampered the rescue efforts." He called these failings "a scandal" and Kerik's leadership "not worthy of the Boy Scouts."

Perhaps Rudy should put out a second edition of his book and title it *Questionable Leadership.*

It got worse for America's mayor.

During 9/11 Commission hearings in New York in May 2004, Giuliani was heckled by outraged relatives of World Trade Center victims. One woman shouted, "My son was murdered because of your incompetence."

Sounds like a lot of Americans would like to recall this mayor.

We think Rudy Giuliani milked the September 11 tragedy way too much. We agree with Tina Brown. We agree with the 9/11 Commission.

But Rudy doesn't. Rudy apparently thinks he can do no wrong. That's why he pushed hard, really hard, for Bernard Kerik, who happened to be Rudy's former driver and was at the time his business partner, to be America's new Homeland Security secretary in December 2004. George Bush took the word of America's mayor and nominated Kerik.

But Bernie Kerik withdrew from consideration before the Senate could even get a shot at him. It turned out that Bernie Kerik had a lot of warts. It turned out that Rudy Giuliani knew about a lot of them and should have said something.

Here are some of those warts:

- Kerik failed to report lavish gifts he received as a New York City public official (that's illegal).
- Kerik's nanny was an illegal immigrant (that's pretty bad in light of the fact that the secretary of Homeland Security is in charge of immigration).
- Kerik was supposed to pay taxes for this same nanny. He didn't—that's illegal too.
- Kerik had declared bankruptcy.
- Kerik, who was married, apparently had not one, but two, mistresses.
- Kerik apparently frequently had trysts with his mistresses in an apartment overlooking Ground Zero that was supposed to be reserved for exhausted firefighters and other workers at the site.
- A New Jersey judge had once issued an arrest warrant for Kerik because he owed $5,000 in condo fees.
- Kerik made $6.2 million in profits from a stun gun company. He was appointed director of the company *after* he had the New York Police Department purchase guns from them.
- Kerik was fined for using city cops on city time to help him research a book he wrote.
- *Newsweek* magazine even reported that Kerik was named in a lawsuit for creating a scheme that forced prison guards to work for Republicans in their off hours.

Using the murders of September 11, 2001, for personal gain leaves a pretty bad taste in our mouths. Attempting to pawn off a scoundrel to direct our Homeland Security efforts is offensive.

Democrats did not do this. Republicans did. Hold them account-able. While you are talking to people about these hypocrites, talk to them about something else as well—like why their lives matter to you.

Lesson 5: Talk to People Where They Live—About Their Lives, Their Fears, and Their Interests

The Democrats must get off this cultural high ground they have been liv-ing on for the past twenty-five years.

When you want to represent people, you have to talk to them where they live. Talk to them about what they like to do for fun, what makes life enjoyable for them, what their fears are. And when you find out that they like NASCAR races, that they like country or bluegrass music, that they like to hunt or fish, don't pass judgment on them. Embrace them.

Quit segmenting your constituents. Embrace all of them and all of their culture—even if you personally don't do some of the things they do. So what? Understand that they may be different from you but that you have a responsibility to represent all of them.

This stuff isn't about you. It's about the people you wish to represent. You only work for them; you do not sit above them.

You need to let people know that you will care for them. Sometimes you may even have to redefine for them what their needs are. You under-stand that Constituent X just got laid off, has no health insurance, has a sick kid and a spouse working two jobs—who has no health insurance ei-ther—and can no longer afford the rent.

To show them you really understand this, go to where they live. Talk *to* them, not *down at* them. Don't tell them they are voting against their own self-interests. Show them that you hear their fears and insecurities. Get to know them. Then go out and fight for them, and you will win a lot more races through rural and southern America than the Republicans who sold these poor bastards down the river to corporate greed and cor-porate campaign contributions.

In his 2001 campaign for governor of Virginia, Mark Warner trav-eled to every corner of the commonwealth. And he learned a lot that he did not know before about the people he wanted to represent. He found out that tens of thousands of them in rural areas did not have indoor plumbing in their homes; he found out that vocational education really mattered to them; he found out that thousands of people hunted and fished not so much for the sport of it but because they needed the food. He found out there were a lot of have-nots in a fairly wealthy state who were just trying to get by. All of this shaped his policy agenda and his message. It also connected Warner to these voters in meaningful ways often missed by politicians.

This also raises a point about the Democrats' message. Why are Democrats afraid to talk about class warfare? They had better get over their fear of this battle, because it's not some hypothetical possibility. It is happening right now. *And Republicans are waging it!*

Warren Buffett, America's second wealthiest man, with a personal wealth estimated at near $50 billion, has no problem calling corporate greed what it is. In his annual letter on March 8, 2004, to shareholders of his Berkshire Hathaway company, Buffett said, among other things, "Tax breaks for corporations (and their investors, particularly large ones) were a major part of the Administration's 2002 and 2003 initiatives. If class warfare is being waged in America, my class is clearly winning." Buffett called the lavish pay packages of corporate America an "epidemic of greed."

Amen, brother.

Class warfare is not a way-off notion. It is real, and the classes that are getting screwed—middle and poor America—are desperately looking for someone who will fight for them in this war.

Look at what is happening to the middle class in America.

The Drum Major Institute for Public Policy studies, among other things, how federal legislation affects the middle class in America. In 2003 alone, the institute found that the average score for supporting the middle class on fourteen votes of interest to those earning between $25,000 and $100,000 dropped from 61 percent to 43 percent in the House and from 76 to 52 percent in the Senate. The institute reports that the biggest drop in middle-class scores came from Republican lawmakers. Republicans are screwing the middle class in order to pay back their greedy corporate donors.

Look at what the haves, who control the reins of corporate America, are doing to the have-nots, the workers who build the products that produce the profits. The haves' commitment to American workers is to cut their pay, break their unions, get rid of overtime wages, take away health care and retirement benefits (if workers ever had them), threaten layoffs, and, if this isn't enough to keep corporate profits up, simply close the factories and move the jobs overseas—you know, outsource them to nations where corporations can get away with paying workers less than a dollar an hour with little or no regard for their benefits or safety.

This only helps the bottom line of some company that tops it all off by locating their corporate offices in the Cayman Islands so they can avoid paying taxes in the good old U.S. of A.

And who carries the water for these greedy corporate haves? *The Republicans!* Do you think it's an accident that 90 percent of corporate political action committees today give more money to the GOP than to Democratic candidates?

George Bush has created a quid pro quo atmosphere with his political hacks and donors. Literally hundreds of his "Pioneer" fund-raisers have been "paid back," not just with favorable legislation but with overnight stays at the White House and Camp David, as well as with trips abroad as part of U.S. delegations. And during Bush's first term, fully one-third of his Pioneer fund-raisers received ambassadorships or agency appointments or were given positions on advisory committees. We need to look no further than the horrible job the underqualified Federal Emergency Management Agency director Michael D. Brown did surrounding Hurricane Katrina in 2005 to see that these political appointments have real and often dire consequences. Brown's main qualification for the job was that he was a college friend of Bush's former campaign manager, Joe M. Allbaugh. It surely wasn't the experience he gained from his previous job, as commissioner of the International Arabian Horse Association.

The point is, not only are the Republicans practicing class warfare but they are cashing in on it. And the quid pro quo that companies and greedy donors receive in the form of favorable legislation and White House perks makes the practice one that is going to stay around as long as they do.

It's simple really. Corporate America gets these guys elected, and these guys then pass laws that redistribute wealth from the middle class to the upper and corporate class; they pass laws that cut workers' rights and benefits; and they pass laws that allow corporate America to turn our air and waterways into their personal sewage lagoons. Then, to pay for tax cuts to these wealthy elites, Republicans have to dismantle health-care programs, educational programs, retirement programs, in short, any program that was designed to give middle Americans and their children opportunities to grow, succeed, and compete in society. Republicans need the money to pay for their giveaways to the greedy, so they are taking it out of your pocket, middle America. How in God's name is that not class warfare?

But Republicans say that challenging corporations to be good corporate citizens makes you antijobs and anti–corporate America.

That's bullshit.

We ask our individual citizens to respect one another, to respect our land, to take personal responsibility. We don't allow our neighbors to come into our yards and defecate. Why do we let corporations shit all over our land, air, and water? Why don't we demand that they be good corporate neighbors and citizens just like we expect our individual citizens to be? What ever happened to the concept of fairness? Most middle-class Americans do not ask that corporations be made to pay more than their fair share in taxes. Most middle-class Americans do not ask that corporations eliminate profit margins or put themselves at a competitive disadvantage. They just ask that when profits are up, when things are going well, the corporations share a bit of that wealth.

When a Republican attempts to label you a practitioner of class warfare, ask him or her since when is it class warfare to stand up for men and women who go to work every day, pay their taxes, and literally give their lives for this country? Ask them since when is it class warfare to expect corporations to quit destroying our air and land, to quit sending our jobs overseas, to quit avoiding paying their fair share in taxes. In fact, before they have the chance to accuse you of practicing class warfare, ask them why *they* are.

We believe most corporations want to do what is right—and a large share of them, in fact, *do* what is right. As a party, Democrats need to push for fairness, for ethical practices, for common sense. And you need to work with companies that are playing by the rules while you work for laws that force bad companies simply to do what is right. Democrats need to show corporations alternatives to their current practices, and guide and lead them. But Democrats need to make them know that they have a responsibility to take responsibility.

Democrats, become the voice for all working people across America. If you keep ignoring people in the South and in rural areas, if you don't offer perspective and fight hard for all of the middle and working classes, particularly those in the South and in the Heartland, who have been ignored for too long by the Democratic Party, if you write them off, if you don't go talk with them, if you mock their culture, if they don't hear a message from you and instead hear only the poisonous lies the other side is spewing at them, you will never convince them that you are the embodiment of their voice and the representatives who will truly look after their needs. Go talk to all of your constituents, and make sure they hear your side. They deserve to hear the truth.

Democrats need to embrace the five simple lessons. They need to get comfortable with them and practice them. Doing so is the first step on the road back to majority status.

Part III

REPUBLICAN LIES AND HOW TO COUNTER THEM

If Democrats learn the five lessons outlined in Chapter 5, they will be better prepared to address a small but volatile group of issues on which they have been losing elections for the better part of a generation. These include family values, fiscal conservatism, national defense and patriotism, and gun issues. These are key issues throughout the country, but nowhere more so than in the South and in rural America. Much of the reason that these issues seem more salient in these parts of the country is the culture of these regions. In much of the South and rural America, a family is not just parents and children but a collection of integral parts, each dependent on the others and all with key roles to play. In the farming culture, children operate machinery, milk cows, feed livestock, and maintain specific roles in the day-to-day work of the farm. In rural small towns, children work alongside parents to run Main Street businesses and help care for younger siblings.

These strong family units are very often religious as well. When financial ruin is but one hailstorm or drought or disease away, faith may be the only value that sustains you. One of the most compelling arguments for helping to maintain America's rural culture is that the family farm and small-town America produce much more than the food we eat. They also produce a strong work ethic, a great appreciation of the family unit, and a value system based on the Golden Rule of "do unto others." It is just as likely that families in the South and in rural America understand fiscal conservatism, because they have no choice. Credit is often hard to come by, and millions of our parents and grandparents would not have dreamed of purchasing anything with a credit card. Patriotism tends to run deep in the South and in rural America, in no small part because for generations these regions have tended disproportionately to send their children into battle. Finally, guns are a way of life. Hunting and fishing are not just ways to spend idle time; they are often vital activities to help put food on the family table and "fill the freezer" for the winter.

Yet, in each of these issue areas, Democrats have increasingly tended to lose out to Republicans, particularly in the South and in rural America.

The truth is, if voters in these regions had all the facts, and if Democrats spoke with a loud and confident voice on these issues, Democrats would once again start winning elections in the South and in rural America. When the facts are known, Republicans' arguments that they better represent the beliefs of a majority of Americans on these issues would be exposed for the lies that they are.

It is time to start exposing the lies.

Chapter 6

LIE 1: REPUBLICANS ARE THE PARTY OF FAMILY VALUES AND GOD

*It is a truism that almost any sect, cult,
or religion will legislate its creed into law if it acquires
the political power to do so.*
ROBERT HEINLEIN

When it comes to God, we are biased. We consider ourselves spiritual people, and we are both believers in God. We believe God is truth, and the truth is we don't have all the answers. But we don't like the way God, Jesus Christ, and religious figures of the day are being used in a political sense. It makes us angry when Republicans and their religious cheerleaders tell us they are merely espousing the wishes of God while they misuse the words of God. We believe that too often those in politics—generally Republicans, who most frequently mention God and Jesus, and who too often pretend to know how God or Jesus thinks or what God or Jesus wants— have ulterior motives and personal and often financial or political stakes in their interpretations. We don't like it that Pat Robertson said God told him George Bush would be reelected, or that Tom DeLay told a group of conservatives that God sanctified Terri Schiavo and her vegetative state so as to strengthen the conservative cause, or that Republicans suggested that if Democrats did not support certain Supreme Court nominees it meant Democrats were antifamily and anti-God.

We believe most Americans do not like it either. We believe most Americans are much more likely to appreciate a politician like John Edwards, the former North Carolina senator and 2004 Democratic nominee for vice president. Edwards is a deeply spiritual person, as is his wife, Elizabeth. But they did not wear their spirituality on their sleeves. Instead, in their words and in their interviews, people saw their faith come from their hearts. They are pretty good examples to follow.

However, we believe that when Republicans throw Bible passages at Democrats in an attempt to justify their narrow spiritual logic, Democrats should not back down. Instead, we argue that Democrats are legitimately doing significant amounts of God's work as mandated in biblical passages, and they should not be afraid to challenge Republicans and cite those passages. This is how we believe Democrats should deal with the God and family values issues.

> *Power always thinks . . . that it is doing God's service*
> *when it is violating all his laws.*
> **JOHN ADAMS**

God in Politics—Let's Be Honest

Let's begin with this notion that God actually pays attention to politics and, worse, gets involved in it.

That is, on its face, ridiculous. There is no way God is a Republican. And there is no way God is a Democrat. The truth is, God does not give squat about politics, and He cares even less about political parties.

And He cares even less than that about those who use Him for political gain and who masquerade as messengers of God, wrapping themselves in Jesus' name—while they make a mockery of Jesus' message and, on top of that, heretically tell people that God *told them* He wants people to vote a certain way.

How can God be the least bit moved by the will of man when the will of man is so often jaded, impure, selfish, and sometimes downright evil? Take, for example, polls showing that more people claim they are praying today than ever before in American history—the odds are pretty good that they're praying for the wrong things. In fact, according to surveys, the number one thing people in America are praying for today is to win the lottery.

And look at how religion seems to be increasingly interjected by American sports personalities. Some well-intentioned person wins a race in NASCAR, scores a winning touchdown, or makes the winning basket and points to heaven and says, "Thanks, God, for helping me win." When these people are interviewed after the race or the game, they often proclaim something to the effect of "The Lord God was with me today. I could not lose."

It is one thing to thank God for one's athletic ability; it is quite another to suggest that a victory was aided by divine intervention. God doesn't help a person win a race or score a basket or hit a ball. He just doesn't. If He did, He would be blowing off all those players and fans on the other team who were praying to Him that they and their teams would win. It wouldn't really be fair for God to be in the business of determining the outcomes of sporting events, would it? Let's see, one team has Michael Jordan, Larry Bird, Magic Johnson, Karl Malone, and Oscar Robertson, and the other has . . . God. Okay, we'll bet on God's team.

In a story attributed to the legend of college basketball Coach Bobby Knight, a sportswriter supposedly once asked Knight, who was coaching at the University of Indiana at the time, why he didn't believe in his team praying before the game. Knight, so the story goes, said it was because "God doesn't give a damn about college basketball." To which the shocked writer responded, "How can you be so sure?" Knight is said to have replied, "Because if he did, them lying, cheatin' sons of bitches down there at Kentucky would never win a game."

The Knight example can be applied to God and politics. If the All Powerful gave a damn about politics, the best, most righteous guy (or gal) would always get elected and all of God's children would be fairly and equally taken care of. One has to look no further than our current crop of public policy makers to know that ain't happening.

Quite simply, God is not into the lawmaking business, much less the business of politics.

Pointing out the ludicrous nature of such an argument should in and of itself be sufficient for any honest, sensible person. Yet, unfortunately,

Democrats' offering this little bit of common sense is often not enough to combat Republicans' arguments that God is on their side because they claim to be "the party of faith and family values." Democrats have to engage the argument a bit further.

What if you indulge the Republicans and agree with them that God indeed pays attention and intervenes to assist candidates He believes help His children the most?

Now look at what George W. Bush and his Republican mimes have done to the least of God's children in just the past five years:

- Thirty-six million Americans, one-third of them children, live in poverty. Two million people have fallen below the poverty line on the watch of George W. Bush and the Republicans.
- Forty-five million Americans lack health insurance—5 million more since Bush came to power.
- Over 3 million Americans lost jobs with Bush and the Republicans in power—the first net job loss for any American president since the government started keeping records on employment figures.
- America's debt, which hits the poorest Americans the hardest, has skyrocketed. Bush and his Republican-controlled Congress have racked up more debt than all previous administrations combined.
- The number of homeless Americans has mushroomed under Bush and the Republicans. Nearly 4 million Americans are homeless, and one-third of them are children.
- Under Bush and the Republicans, the number of Americans going to bed hungry has blown through the ceiling, with fully 12 percent of households lacking enough food. A shocking 20 percent of all children live in homes where there is not enough food to feed them.

The list goes on and on. If Republicans keep contending that God supports their candidates, make some of the preceding arguments. History shows that Democrats have been the ones fighting for the homeless, the hungry, the sick, and the unemployed. Presidents like FDR, Lyndon Johnson, Jimmy Carter, and Bill Clinton have fought to keep families together by supporting programs that provided jobs, food, shelter, health care, and opportunity for them. Democrats have risked political capital to serve the least among us.

By contrast, George W. Bush and the Republicans have been brutal to these people. How are tax policies and programs that have screwed these families consistent with any definition of providing for the least among us? While George W. and his Republican parrots in Congress passed tax legislation that provided the greatest redistribution of wealth from the middle and working classes to the richest Americans, the least among God's children have suffered unmercifully.

But if Republicans and so many of their Sunday morning cheerleaders still want to have a battle over whether God is a Republican, Democrats should say, in the words of a somewhat suspect religious convert of convenience, George W. Bush, "Bring it on."

The question is, How do God-fearing Democrats retrieve God's stolen endorsement from the religious right wing of the Republican Party?

The first thing they must do is attack the ridiculous but still very real perception the Republicans have created in many areas of America that the Democratic Party is a godless party. Democrats are routinely tagged by the Republican right as heathens or, on their kind days, as some sort of *half-assed Christians*. When the former Virginia House majority leader C. Richard Cranwell, who was no slouch when it came to blowtorching hypocrisy, was confronted with this piece of GOP sanctimony right in his state, he snapped back, "A half a loaf is better than no loaf at all." What Cranwell had figured out was that there are a lot more people who attend church for their own spirituality and who pray to God for things like health and opportunity for their children and families than there are fanatical fundamentalist Christians who are being hypnotized every Sunday and being told God wants them to vote a certain way. Cranwell was right, and his words still ring true. Who are these Republicans to label anybody's spirituality "half-assed"?

The truth is, Democrats need to reach out to these Christians who do not wear their Christianity on their sleeves. Yes, these people have Christian values, but more likely than not they are the broader Christian values of feeding the hungry, healing the sick, and tending to the poor, which Democrats espouse, than they are the narrow, polarizing issues Republicans have championed.

In fact, Democrats shouldn't even assume that Christians who attend even the most fundamentalist churches will always buy the stereotype that Democrats' values are not values they want or need. The former congressman and secretary of agriculture Dan Glickman recalls that one day when he was running for reelection in Kansas a woman approached him and said, "You're a Jew. You killed Christ, and you're going to hell." A somewhat stunned Glickman told the woman that he did not know what to say, to which she replied, "You don't have to say anything. I'm going to vote for you anyway. That was then. I need help now."

If you touch their culture and reach out to all people with a legitimate message of hope, opportunity, and real family values, they begin to see through the heavy-handedness if not the hypocrisy of the seersucker sermonizers who regularly preach to them.

Perhaps the best evidence of this is that in 2001, in winning Virginia's governor's race, the Democrat Mark Warner carried Lynchburg. The nation's most prominent fundamentalist megachurch, Thomas Road Baptist Church, and its far-right polarizing pastor, Jerry Falwell, are headquartered in Lynchburg, as is Falwell's Liberty University. In Lynchburg, Warner's pro-family, pro-growth agenda, coupled with his attachment to other tenets of the culture of the region, trumped Falwell's dichotomizing dogma.

Exit polls following the 2004 election suggested that "values" issues were the most important to over 20 percent of the voters—the largest single type of issue affecting the vote. We should note that these numbers are suspect, and the surveys came under fire for the way they were worded and implemented. But let's assume for a moment that those numbers were accurate. If these people had had an alternative definition of what it means to practice the teachings of God—like feeding the hungry, tending the sick, providing shelter for the homeless—might they have voted differently? We think so. Indeed, a poll conducted by the Center for American Progress showed 33 percent of voters believe that greed and materialism are the nation's most pressing moral problem and another 31 percent said the most demanding moral issue in America is poverty and economic justice. That's encouraging.

But Democrats do a poor job of defining issues like greed and materialism in moral terms. In fact, they routinely say nothing, while Republicans are all too happy to define moral issues as gay marriage and abortion. Were Democrats to offer a competing definition, we believe most voters would see failing to feed the hungry, provide shelter to the homeless, and take care of the sick as a greater threat to our nation's moral fiber. It's all about how the debate is shaped and who shapes it.

We need to unite the Christians within the Democratic Party and get after the self-righteous, the greedy, and the blasphemous. We are not the only Democrats who are tired of being looked down upon by the spiritually self-righteous Republican right. Democrats need to make this "God is no Republican" strategy a reality. Perhaps they should start a PAC or a 527 called the Half-Assed Christian Coalition.

We believe Democrats can unite Christians within our party, particularly in the South and in rural America, precisely because of the strong values and family base of people who live there. Families in rural and southern America understand the tremendous pressures on families because they live them. They know that families are torn apart more often by poverty, by a lack of job opportunities, by lack of health care for sick loved ones, by lack of food, and a general lack of opportunities than by any of the single polarizing issues Republicans tout. They also know biblical teachings mandate that they "do unto others" and that they take care of the sick, the homeless, the hungry, and the feeble. Democrats fight for these values. They just need to remind people of that fact.

When Republicans Use the Bible to Justify Their Positions, They Are Playing with Fire

We hear it all the time, "The Bible says this" or "The Bible says that." Republicans are particularly vocal in contending "The Bible says God supports all life (just not the life of the mother, or the life of the young woman whose doctor tells her she will die if she delivers)" or "God opposes homosexuality." Republicans often state that if a Democrat supports equal rights for homosexuals or if Democrats believe the abortion issue is between a woman, her doctor, and her God, they are defying the Bible, must be anti-God, and thus should be defeated for public office.

But the Bible says many, many things, and literal interpretations are tricky at best. Should we take Leviticus 25:44 literally when it states that we may possess slaves? Exodus 35:2 tells us that people who work on the Sabbath should be put to death—do we want to apply a literal interpretation to that? Should we begin selling our daughters into slavery, as sanctioned in Exodus 21:7? Or should we gather all townspeople together to stone to death those who curse, as commanded by Leviticus 24:10–16?

We think people would be far better off if they studied the teachings of God and attempted to live through the laws of God that say love God with all your heart, mind, and soul, and love your neighbor as yourself. In fact, we long for the day when preachers feel their role is to tell us the word of God and let us interpret it for our own lives rather than tell us what God meant as well.

When preachers and panderers pull from it passages to justify some selfish personal and political position, they really are doing the Bible a disservice. That is why we would just as soon politicians and phony preachers would quit using it to divide God's people while they pad their own political or pious pockets.

Sadly, we don't think these politicians and preachers will quit using the Bible this way unless challenged on their own turf. One way to challenge them is to fight biblical fire with biblical fire.

So, when Republicans tell you they are merely reciting biblical teachings to justify their brand of "family values," ask them how they are living up to the following passages on the real values of loving thy neighbor.

These are the biblical passages we grew up on and were taught to memorize. Back before politicians jumped in bed with ministers and vice versa, it was simple. We were taught that the Bible said, Believe in God and take care of the least among you and you will be fine. But the blasphemers of today tell us nothing of the sort. What they often tell us seems to benefit them more than it benefits biblical orthodoxy. They might begin by reading the first book of the New Testament.★

★ We realize that, when we are talking about the Bible, we are talking primarily to politicians and people of the cloth who identify themselves as Christians. We do so because it seems as if those who misrepresent and misuse God the most for their own personal or political gain are those who masquerade as Christians.

Matthew 25:41-46

Then I will say, . . . "For I was hungry and you wouldn't feed me; thirsty,
and you wouldn't give me anything to drink; a stranger, and you refused me
hospitality; naked, and you wouldn't clothe me; sick and in prison, and you
didn't visit me."
Then they will reply, "Lord, when did we ever see you hungry or thirsty or a
stranger or naked or sick or in prison, and not help you?"
And I will answer, "When you refused to help the least of these my brothers,
you were refusing help to me."
And they shall go away into eternal punishment; but the righteous into ever-
lasting life.

If Republicans who wrap themselves in the Bible really had read Matthew, they sure seem to be ignoring Jesus' words, mocking Jesus' teachings, and defying Him by often doing the exact opposite of what His words prescribe. Frankly, we're very tired of friends and even family members who inform us that they are voting Republican because some preacher told them Democrats are baby killers or because Democrats support two men getting married—in direct violation of biblical teachings. Where is the sanctimony of these people when these preachers and their Republican robots pad their own personal and political pockets and defy the Gospel of Matthew and many other Bible teachings, allowing millions of the least among us to suffer? Republican callousness has sentenced tens of millions of Americans to go to bed hungry, homeless, or sick with no way of getting well. And we hear nothing out of these lemmings who are spoon-fed lies in the name of Jesus and who jump off political cliffs at the first call from these masquerading ministers.

Republicans do not have the right to question other people's Christianity or spirituality. They have plenty to worry about with their own. Their ignorance of the Bible is alarming, and the way they cling to a couple of narrow biblical passages does not excuse them from defiling so many other passages. In fact, one could argue that in voting for Republicans whose policies are hurting millions of God's people, one is complicit in their actions. Republicans make that claim about Democrats all the time. But now the shoe is on the proverbial other foot. So, to our friends who conveniently question our spirituality, know that we won't question yours, but we sure as hell pray for it.

We believe the Bible is a spiritual guidebook for how we should act in our own lives and for how we should treat our fellow human beings. So, when Republicans reduce the Bible to self-serving sound bites, Democrats should throw a few more passages back in their faces.

Deuteronomy 10:18–19 gives guidance for how we should treat immigrants and strangers: "He loves foreigners and gives them food and clothing. You too must love foreigners, for you yourselves were foreigners in the land of Egypt."

Galatians 3:26–28 suggests that Jesus viewed *all* people as God's children and taught that all should be held in equal standing before God: "For now we are all children of God through faith in Jesus Christ, and we who have been baptized into union with Christ are enveloped by him. We are no longer Jews or Greeks or slaves or free men or even merely men or women, but we are all the same—we are Christians; we are one in Christ Jesus."

Proverbs 29:7 tell us, as did Matthew, that "the good man knows the poor man's rights; the godless don't care."

Leviticus 19:32 cautions mankind: "You shall give due honor and respect to the elderly."

Matthew 19:13–14 admonishes us to protect, care for, and give opportunity to children: "Little children were brought for Jesus to lay his hands on them and pray. But the disciples scolded those who brought them. 'Don't bother him,' they said. But Jesus said, 'Let the little children come to me, and don't prevent them. For of such is the Kingdom of Heaven.' "

Matthew 5:7 further tells us that if we do care for the sick, feed the hungry, shelter the homeless, and address all of the fears and troubles of our fellow men and women, there is a greater reward: "Happy are the kind and merciful, for they shall be shown mercy."

In fact, for those who use the word of God to pad their thousand-dollar suit pockets with collection plate collateral, who build castles and shrines to their almighty selves, who ignore the teachings of scripture and let themselves be used by politicians, Matthew 6:19–21, 24 has a word of warning: "Don't store up treasures here on earth where they can erode away or may be stolen. Store them in heaven where they will never lose their value, and are safe from thieves. If your profits are in heaven your heart will be there too . . . You cannot serve two masters: God and money. For you will hate one and love the other, or else the other way around."

Finally, Matthew 6:5–6 has a rather stern if not ominous admonition to those who would politicize the word of God: "And now about prayer. When you pray, don't be like the hypocrites who pretend piety by praying publicly on street corners and in the synagogues where everyone can see them. Truly, that is all the reward they will ever get. But when you pray, go away by yourself, all alone, and shut the door behind you and pray to your Father secretly, and your Father, who knows your secrets, will reward you."

The Bible is a beautiful book. Republicans don't own it, and they often misuse it. When they synthesize, redefine, and distort His teachings, they are actually working against the will of God.

Democrats, when Republicans reduce all scripture to the damnation of abortion or homosexuality, do not shrink from the debate, take control of it. No one likes abortions, and everyone knows the debate over homosexuality is often painful, but the Bible has thousands of lessons to guide our actions. Democrats need to stop allowing the Republicans to gut the body of the work by intentionally ignoring the bulk of its teachings.

Finally, a word for those who are not God but attempt to play Him on Sundays and on cable TV: You keep messing with God and His message, and keep falsely claiming that He told you to tell people how to vote, while millions of His children are suffering in seemingly direct proportion to the increases in your bank account, and your trip to the pearly gates may have a lengthy stopover in a slightly balmier climate.

Republicans Versus Democrats on Family Values: The Winner Might Surprise You

Although they may constantly claim they are, Republicans are clearly not the party of family values. Their actions speak much louder than their words. And their actions in recent years have been nothing short of alarming. The consequences have been a relentless blitzkrieg on the American family.

The truth is that family values land fairly and squarely on the turf of the Democrats. To illustrate this fact, we should start by defining "family values," since the Republicans have distorted its meaning way out of proportion.

An obvious definition would go something like this: "Family values are those principles that keep family units together, that make families stronger, healthier, more secure, happier, more productive, more content, and more aware of the importance of the family unit." It all seems simple enough.

Democrats must remind rural and southern voters of the true definition of "family values." A good way to see what keeps families together is to look at what tears them apart.

Without a good education, good jobs become scarce. Without good jobs at fair wages with fair benefits, parents lack the confidence that they can feed their children, give them a safe and loving home, provide them with a good education, and secure a better future for their children and a comfortable retirement for themselves. Unemployment breeds despair, hopelessness, and feelings of inadequacy, while overemployment— that is having to work multiple jobs just to make ends meet—keeps families apart. Without good and affordable health care and health insurance, the fabric of a family is shredded. There is no more helpless feeling than being unable to afford to care for a loved one who is sick.

Republicans don't want to define "family values" this way. They know these are the real family values, but they don't want voters to know it. Republican leaders have sold out so completely to corporate and moneyed interests that *real* family values are the first thing sacrificed. The Republicans had to sell out because they need the big corporate dollars to win elections and can't get them if they don't cut family values programs and give that money in huge tax breaks and government spending to their greedy cronies.

Knowing the importance of family values to rural and southern voters, Republicans had to redefine the term to fit their agenda. They had to convince voters that things like jobs, health care, decent and affordable housing, family and retirement security, and even the ability to provide food and clothing for your family, are secondary to *their* definition of "family values," which focuses on two hot-button issues: abortion and gay marriage.

They defined "family values" as narrowly as they could. Abortion and gay marriage are issues that most people face seldom if ever. Yet these are issues that can evoke strong and polarizing reactions.

If most families did have to confront the abortion issue, they would see up close how personal and painful that decision is. Republicans wanted this issue to be the boogeyman in the closet, something people have heard about but have never seen. It is easier to be sanctimonious and self-righteous about an issue if it has never affected you personally.

Republicans knew that most families will never be personally confronted with homosexuality either (the rate of homosexual desire is estimated to be about 7.7 percent in men and 7.5 percent in women). All the better. Make it scary. The truth is, if every family were confronted with a loved one's homosexuality, greater instincts of love, understanding, and the need to come together would very likely take over.

The Republican politicians then made their "family values" seem all the more real by getting religious groups who were torn about or uneasy with these issues to join them in opposing abortion and gay marriage. They convinced religious groups to condemn politicians who understand that abortion is a private matter between a woman, her doctor, her God, and sometimes her family. (Because of incest or abuse by family members, it is sometimes difficult if not impossible to include family members in this decision.) Republicans persuaded religious groups that homosexuality is rampant. So much the better if they could use scripture to condemn gay lifestyles and marriages.

With opposition to abortion and gay marriage as the newfound indicator of moral zeal, Republicans could obfuscate the generations of work done by Democrats for families. They even got religious groups to ignore all the work Democrats had done to make sure the hungry were fed, the sick were healed, the homeless had shelter, and the naked had clothing. This was no easy feat. The Democrats had a compelling record, and Republicans knew it. They knew that in just the past two generations, under Democratic leadership, poverty had been cut by two-thirds; infant mortality rates had dropped by one-third, 200 million poor people had been served by Medicaid in a thirty-five-year period, and another 85 million senior citizens had been served by Medicare in the same period; the number of people living in substandard housing was cut in half; 16 million preschool children had benefited from Head Start, and 29 million students had gotten 86 million college loans.

The Republicans had cracked the electoral code, but they know that this bait-and-switch act sits on tenuous ground. The alliance between self-serving politicians and legitimate men and women of the cloth can never be a strong one. This alliance with falsely pious politicians ultimately makes the church look bad. It is only a matter of time before churches take their Bible back from the GOP.

In 2000 and 2004, however, Republicans got religious voters at the lower end of the economic spectrum to ignore their own best interests and vote on these two hot-button issues. And if the voters wavered, these Republicans knew the churches would threaten them with eternal damnation. But, just to be sure, the GOP held out things like vouchers, and new Housing and Urban Development regulations that allow federal grants for construction of "social service" facilities at religious institutions.

It was a brilliant strategy, and if they want to succeed at the polls, Democrats have to let people know that they understand this shotgun marriage between church and state, and they don't like it. Legitimate churches are being used by this arrangement. The churches must listen to their members. Churches survive only with the participation and support of their parishioners. A mandate to get churches to go back to teaching God's word and stay out of politics is not too much to ask. And if churches wish to stay involved in politics, the Democrats must show them how Republican policies are affecting rural and southern America.

The Democrats must highlight the real definition of "family values," compare it with the Republican definition, and see which one passes the smell test.

Try this: A family is sitting around the kitchen table. There are literally millions of them doing this very thing this very evening. The parents are fighting. Dad just lost his job. Mom is holding down two jobs, but neither of them offers health insurance. They have three children, one of whom is chronically ill. They can no longer afford day care for the two youngest ones and the doctor bills for the sick child. They are very worried about next month's rent, and, on top of that, the car's engine is smoking. They live paycheck to paycheck. They shop at Goodwill for the kids' clothes, and they buy the cheapest food they can find to stretch their food budget regardless of nutritional value.

What if Dad doesn't get a job soon? What if his new job—as is likely—pays less than his old one? What about health insurance? And this family doesn't even bother worrying about retirement.

This family is in trouble. Maybe the parents will turn to drugs or alcohol to ease the pain. Maybe their anger and frustration will boil over and one of the kids will become a victim. Almost assuredly the parents will lash out at each other. This family may not even manage to stay together.

Do the Republicans really believe that this family, and the millions of others just like it, are sitting around that kitchen table and actually deciding that, all things considered, the greatest threat to their family unit is whether two consenting men are getting married? Or whether some poor, mixed-up kid got in trouble and, with her family, her doctor, and her God, is making a decision about an abortion? Of course not.

It would be laughable if it were not so devastating. Republican family values are doing nothing to hold this family—or millions of others—together.

Indeed, because Republicans pontificate on these issues while ignoring real family values and, in fact, while voting against real programs that keep families together, they have actually become antifamily. The truth is, these Republicans in the White House and Congress today are the most antifamily group of politicians in modern American history. You saw the empirical evidence of their neglect and disdain for families in Part I. It is a shameful record.

To reach rural voters on the family values issue, Democrats should remember that "Feed 'em, clothe 'em, house 'em, and heal 'em" trumps "Greed 'em, loathe 'em, douse 'em, and steal from 'em" every time.

Try adding in the following arguments when it comes to abortion and gay rights.

Abortion: Putting a Face on a Human Tragedy

Don't let Republicans get away with defining themselves as pro-life. Most of these Republicans are antichoice rather than pro-life. They are antichoice because they clearly do not want a woman to have the right to make a decision regarding abortion.

But they are not pro-life. Pro-life suggests they support all life, not just the life of a fetus. Their record suggests just the opposite.

Second, don't let Republicans define your position on abortion. *You* define it. Let people know that, even if you fall on the side of giving a woman the right to choose, you think abortion is wrong. There is sanctity in life, and we should do everything in our power to find an alternative to abortion, including greater incentives for adoption. People need to know that you respect human life. But you also realize that, in some instances, a difficult decision will be made to have an abortion. We should all do everything we can to make needed abortions safe, legal, and rare. The truth is, if voters were given other ways to look at the abortion issue, they might not be so quick to embrace the Republicans on it.

That is why we would not concede the pro-life mantle to people merely because they claim it. Expose their hypocrisy. There are a lot of things about the way people wrap themselves in the moral pro-life robe that bother us.

First, it is so convenient. If I call myself pro-life, I need no additional evidence of moral consistency. I don't care about the homeless, the hungry, the sick, the children. So what? I'm pro-life. You take a different position than I do, *you* are evil.

What they are saying in reality is, I am pro-life so long as the fetus is in the womb. Once it is born, God forbid that their tax dollars might have to help feed it, house it, heal it, and care for it. When these moralists vote on the abortion issue alone, they are too often supporting politicians who are imposing a death sentence on children every day through macho "pull yourself up by your bootstraps" bullshit, feel-good rhetoric. Their moral obligation ended when the doctor slapped the kid on the behind and the baby wailed.

What if the baby—once born—doesn't have health care and gets deathly sick?

Not their problem. The parents should have thought of that before they bred like rabbits. People have to take personal responsibility. They should get jobs.

And what if both parents have jobs? But the jobs are part-time at Wal-Mart, so they lack income security, and health insurance.

They should have thought of that before they had kids.

What about birth control?

What if it is against their religion?

They should get help from their parents.

Grandparents cannot provide health insurance for their grandkids, and besides, what if the grandparents lack the resources to help? Or what if there are no grandparents?

The point is, of course, that every situation is different. Rarely are things as black and white as people make them out to be.

Now here's a fact that should shock the pious pretenders: Abortion rates have risen 25 percent since George W. Bush took office. Analysts will tell you that the rise in abortions is in direct correlation to Bush and the Republicans' cuts in sex education programs and to increased poverty rates.

But so many of the antichoice people don't seem to care. Indeed, if people call themselves pro-life, they can be immoral in so many other ways. They can even be for the death penalty. So much for the sanctity of human life. The hypocrisy and sanctimony of these people begs to be challenged.

Throw a moral argument back at them: WWJD? What *would* Jesus do? Abandon the child after birth? Condone the votes of politicians that cause His children harm and even death? Whisper in the ear of some money changer in the Temple that he wants these politicians to be elected under the guise of being "pro-life" when their actions taken in whole actually abuse and destroy life? Don't think so.

Make these politicians, preachers, and people who selectively use biblical passages be moral in *all* life, not just selective lives. If they are not, scorn them for conveniently taking some of God's words while violating so many others.

Another thing that bothers us about the sanctimony surrounding so many of the pro-life crowd is that they attempt to justify their abortion position by suggesting that women who have to make the decision to terminate a pregnancy somehow *want* to have an abortion. As if it's a manicure. Most people who have to have an abortion go through emotional and physical hell. And that hell often involves more than the decision to have the abortion.

- What if the pregnancy came because of a rape?
- What if the pregnancy came to a girl who was a child herself?
- What if the pregnancy would cost a young woman her life if she delivered?
- What if the pregnancy resulted from a case of incest?
- And what about when a girl or young woman knows that there would be abuse and neglect were the baby carried to term?

We do not believe people would be nearly so judgmental and sanctimonious if the abortion decision fell to one of their loved ones.

When the face confronting an abortion decision belongs to a loved one, the holes in the Republican argument become glaringly personal. Look at some cases in point.

Case Study 1: A true story: The thirteen-year-old daughter of pro-life parents becomes pregnant by her fourteen-year-old boyfriend. Her parents are devastated. Their daughter believes her life is ruined. She talks about killing herself. Her parents turn to their church. Their pastor tells them that their daughter needs to carry the baby to term. Their pro-life congressman gives them the same advice.

To make matters worse, the girl's gynecologist tells the parents that if their daughter carries the child to term, she will die.

It's not so easy now, is it? Does God value the life of an unborn baby—who may not survive to term anyway—more than He does the life of the thirteen-year-old girl? And who should make the decision about the abortion? A congressman? A pastor? The government? Seems like a pretty personal decision to us.

Case Study 2: A true story although the names have been changed: Sally and Dan were both twenty-four. They were madly in love and had been married since they were twenty. They did not make a lot of money, but both worked. They had two children, a one-year-old and a two-and-a-half-year-old. They were devout Catholics. They listened when the church bulletin told them to vote Republican because of the abortion issue.

Then Sally became pregnant again. They were elated. Both sets of parents rejoiced at the news. Both sets of parents were decidedly pro-life. All was going well as Sally entered her third trimester. Then something went terribly wrong. After eating at a restaurant, Sally became violently ill. She was rushed to the hospital. Tests confirmed that she had been poisoned by undercooked, contaminated meat. If the doctors did not perform an immediate so-called partial birth abortion, Sally would die. Her two children would lose their mother. Her young husband would be left alone to care for his children on an insufficient income. Whether or not she had the abortion, Sally would almost assuredly lose the baby. Without an immediate partial birth abortion, Sally would die. There was not a lot of time. Dan called his parents and his in-laws. Everyone was stunned. They knew that if they stuck to their pro-life convictions, Sally would die.

Put yourself in their shoes, and all of a sudden the decision becomes personal. You do not want someone else—clergy, politician, government—to tell you what you must do.

Case Study 3: A true story, although the name has been changed: Jane was a nineteen-year-old sophomore at a small southern university. She was a good student, studying to become a doctor. Her parents had not been able to afford her tuition, but Jane was on scholarship. She studied hard and partied little. But one night she did party—at a fraternity house. Late in the evening, Jane began to feel disoriented. She did not think she could drive and asked one of the frat brothers if she could lie down. Four guys followed her into the bedroom. She screamed and fought, but no one heard her over the music. She was repeatedly raped. When she woke up, she was ill, naked, and still in the strange bed. There was blood. Hospital tests showed that she had been drugged and gang-raped. She was also pregnant.

Jane had recurring nightmares about the rape. She could see faces, hear the guys talking and even laughing, and she could feel pain. Jane and her parents were pro-life. But they now knew how personal and difficult this decision is. They also felt ashamed for having acted like there was an obvious answer to a situation like this. Now the obvious answer was not the one they ever thought they would have picked.

The point is, Democrats, you need to be able to show people that you support the sanctity of life. But you also need to show people that these are not the easy, black-and-white decisions that so many politicians, preachers, and armchair parents attempt to make for others every day.

Democrats, you have done so much to save lives, to make all life healthier, smarter, and more fruitful. Don't ever again let Republicans define for the voter what constitutes "pro-life." Show voters that you respect all life, including the life of the unborn. Show them as well that you know when it comes to abortion, there is more than one life involved. Then define the debate about what constitutes "life" as one which is much broader than just the abortion issue. All human life is sacred. Saying you are pro-life is not a license or justification to ignore the needs of a life once it leaves the womb. That is an insult to humanity, and Republicans and their followers on the abortion issue need to be reminded of that fact.

Gay Rights and Gay Marriage

Of all the issues politicians have to deal with, gay rights and gay marriage tend to be the ones with the most land mines. We believe this is in no small part because of the ignorance surrounding homosexuality, the recent elevation of these issues to the public fore, and the long-standing stigma attached to homosexuals and their lifestyles. We also believe this is in no small part because Democrats have allowed Republicans to define the issue for much of America. Democrats have been much more supportive of granting rights for homosexuals, but they have done so rather tepidly, under the radar. On its face, that approach may be understandable in light of how polarizing these issues are. But such a strategy left the door open for Republicans to define "gay rights" for the American people. And define they did.

Republicans have tended to pander to their base by warning of grave consequences of homosexual lifestyles. This far-right turn, of course, ignored any personal implications for homosexuals and their families. Republicans know that the rate of homosexual desire is estimated to be only about 7.7 percent in men and 7.5 percent in women. And only 2.8 percent of men and 1.4 percent of women identify themselves as gay or lesbian. According to the 2000 census, only 1.2 million adults live with a gay partner, and this is spread out over 99.2 percent of all U.S. counties. Thus, most Americans are not personally confronted with the issue of homosexuality or with attacks on homosexual loved ones. If they were, personal instincts of acceptance, understanding, and support would likely take over.

As a consequence of the stereotypes surrounding homosexuality and the somewhat tepid voices supporting gay rights, the Republicans have been able to define "gay rights" as acceptance or rejection of gay marriage. This narrow and divisive definition has ignored greater issues of civil and human rights for the gay community while it has helped Republican electoral chances.

Surveys show that by margins as great as two to one, a significant majority of Americans oppose legalizing gay marriage. Indeed, most Americans still oppose allowing gays and lesbians to form civil unions, giving same-sex couples the same rights and benefits as married couples. But surveys also show that Americans are less enthusiastic about changing the Constitution to ban gay marriage. And when people are given the choice of whether to leave the issue of gay marriage to the states, fully 60 percent favor letting states make their own laws. Yet in the elections of 2004, eleven states had same-sex marriage amendments on the ballot, and all eleven rather overwhelmingly voted against same-sex marriage. (The states were Mississippi, Montana, Oregon, Arkansas, Georgia, Kentucky, Michigan, North Dakota, Ohio, Oklahoma, and Utah.)

All of this would suggest that Republicans have defined the issue of gay rights clearly to their electoral advantage. The bottom-line question on this issue in the minds of the American public is, should we condone gay marriage? And when that issue is the lens through which America views gay and lesbian issues, gays and lesbians lose.

To attack this position, we suggest Democrats define gay and lesbian issues from a different perspective.

John Kerry and John Edwards in the 2004 election had the right idea when they took the position that gay marriage issues should be left up to the states. And while that angered some in the gay and lesbian community (the Human Rights Campaign, the largest gay rights organization in the country, for instance, said they were "disappointed" by it), the community was generally very favorable to the Kerry-Edwards ticket regardless. This was not all that surprising. Much of the gay and lesbian community is weary of gay marriage initiatives because they believe the question polarizes Americans and diverts energy from more important matters, such as civil rights and private benefits such as health insurance.

We would argue that Democrats could get a whole lot more mileage out of defining gay and lesbian issues as ones involving civil rights for all Americans. We believe Americans have far less tolerance for discriminating practices than they do hatred for any category of people. Perhaps it is our history dating back to our being relegated to second-class status by Great Britain, which led to the Revolutionary War, or our fights for workers' rights or women's rights or civil rights for African Americans, or our tremendous pride in our constitutional freedoms. Whatever the reasons, Americans tend to change their perspective when issues of discrimination are raised. This is far better turf for the Democrats.

Former Nebraska senator Bob Kerrey had a powerful retort to cynical questions about his support for the rights of gays and lesbians. When he was asked about his support of gay and lesbian issues, his response was an unequivocal "I do not accept discrimination in any form." Kerrey, who had lost a leg in a firefight in the jungles of Vietnam, followed with "I am a cripple. I have been discriminated against. I don't like it, and I don't accept that someone can discriminate against another human being for any reason." Pretty powerful stuff. Who the hell could argue with it?

And for those without Kerrey's compelling personal history, national statistics on hate crimes against homosexuals are compelling. According to the FBI, in 2003 there were 1,479 reported hate crimes based on sexual orientation. Of those, 6 were murders (all gay men), 3 were rapes, 162 were aggravated assaults, 426 were simple assaults, 433 were intimidation, 42 were robbery, and 337 were destruction of property or vandalism. Students who describe themselves as lesbian, gay, bisexual, or transgendered are five times more likely to miss school because of feeling unsafe, and fully 28 percent are forced to drop out. The vast majority of victims of antilesbian or antigay violence, possibly as many as 80 percent, never report the incidents because of fear of being "outed."

According to a study at the University of Maryland, lesbians earn 14 percent less than their heterosexual female peers with similar jobs, education, age, and residence. Yet, according to a *Newsweek* survey, 84 percent of Americans say they oppose employment discrimination on the basis of sexual orientation. Forty-two percent of homeless youth identify themselves as lesbian, gay, or bisexual, and lesbian, gay, and bisexual youth are at a four times higher risk for suicide than their straight peers. We believe most Americans would abhor such discrimination were "gay rights" defined for them as applying to people who merely wanted to get through life, work at a job, go to school, and live without fear of being beaten or killed.

Personalizing the issue also helps make the case that violating someone's civil rights should not be acceptable in the United States of America. That is, asking people if they had a son or daughter or a brother or sister who was gay, would they find it acceptable for these family members to be discriminated against as a consequence of their sexual orientation? Ask people if they had a family member who was gay, would they tolerate someone openly and hatefully mocking them? Beating them? Withholding employment from them? Refusing benefits to them? The question is simple. Would you want your child or sibling to be vilified and singled out solely based on sexual orientation?

We wouldn't. Our instincts as parents or siblings would kick in, and we would not tolerate such words or actions. We would do everything in our power to stop them. When these issues become personal, the values of love, understanding, acceptance, and compassion will generally trump hatred, ignorance, and selfishness.

So when someone says to you, "What do you think about gay rights?" change the scope of the debate. Ask them why they believe some of God's children have less value than others. Ask them, after homosexuals, what group of God's children would they discriminate against and hate? Ask them if they believe God would be pleased with their hateful and discriminatory practices upon a certain group. Gay rights are really basic human rights. That's the argument we would use. It undermines the Republicans' entire premise. And we believe it should be the trump card played every time these bigots play the gay card. We are not trying to oversimplify a difficult issue. We just believe the arguments for tolerance, understanding, and equality are much more powerful than the arguments for hatred and discrimination.

We cannot reconcile biblical references that condemn homosexuality any more than we can reconcile biblical references that would allow us to sell our children into slavery, kill someone who works on the Sabbath, or stone to death someone for wearing garments made of two different fabrics. All of these things are in the Bible. What we can reconcile is that *all* human beings are God's children. We do not have the luxury or arrogance to suggest that we know some of God's children are better than others. We would rather offer people Jesus' laws, which say to love God and to love our neighbors as ourselves. Period.

Chapter 7

LIE 2: REPUBLICANS ARE THE PARTY OF FISCAL CONSERVATISM

Let's begin this chapter with a quiz.

Name the last three Republican presidents of the United States who all campaigned on a platform of fiscal conservatism.

That's easy.

Ronald Reagan, George H. W. Bush, and George W. Bush.

Now name the three greatest liberal spenders in American presidential history.

Same answer.

George W. Bush, Ronald Reagan, and George H. W. Bush—in that order.

According to U.S. Budget Office numbers, in Ronald Reagan's eight years as president, he quadrupled the national debt to a whopping $4 trillion. When George H. W. Bush left office, four years later, he had added another $1 trillion to the debt.

The *Democrat* Bill Clinton then drove the deficit *down* for eight years, leaving office with a $557 billion surplus. Indeed, the $230 billion surplus Clinton built in his last year in office was the largest in U.S. history. His economic policies, had they been continued by the Bush administration, would have increased the surplus by nearly $1 trillion over ten years.

But back came the fiscally conservative Republicans.

George W. Bush, who had lived a good share of his adult life on Daddy's credit card, went wild on America's. It must have reminded W of his old Yale cheerleading, Delta Kappa Epsilon fraternity partying days, because in his first four years in office, George Walker Bush and his Republican majorities in both houses of Congress went on a spending binge and giveaway orgy that added nearly $1.3 trillion to the deficit. Projections are that W will add another $2 trillion of debt before he leaves office in January 2009. And when you add in the money he transferred from the Social Security Trust Fund, his total deficit spending mushrooms somewhere between $3.5 and $4 trillion. On top of that, the prognosis is that W's enormous giveaway of your money to the greedy, disguised as tax cuts for all, coupled with his mismanagement of government, will add $5.6 trillion to the national debt for the ten-year period 2004–2014.

This makes the compassionate conservative George W. Bush the absolute greatest liberal spender in U.S. government history. We have all seen that Bush's fiscal policies are far from compassionate, but he is at the far *left* edge of the fiscal spectrum. W is America's poster boy for irresponsible, misguided, and reckless liberal deficit spending.

That must have made Poppy proud. Because in the trophy case of all-time liberal spenders in American history, Poppy comes in third, joining his son to offer cozy, irresponsible "Bush bookends" to the second greatest liberal spender of all time, that fraud of a conservative Ronald Reagan. No, George W. Bush, Ronald Reagan, and George H. W. Bush were not fiscal conservatives. They were fiscal phonies.

Democrats and Fiscal Responsibility: The Truth Will Set You Free

History shows that Democrats have a much better record on the economy than do Republicans. A *Forbes* magazine study in 2004 demonstrated that over the past fifty years, Democratic presidents have had far more success with the economy than have Republican presidents. In fact, the three presidents who ranked one, two, and three on the *Forbes* list of the greatest presidents of the past fifty years with regard to creating economic prosperity were all Democrats: Bill Clinton, Lyndon Johnson, and John F. Kennedy—in that order. While the worst three presidents during this time were all Republicans, with Poppy Bush coming in last among the eleven presidents who served during this period. Although, with W's numbing deficit projections, he will likely give his old man a run for his (actually your) money before he leaves office. On a scale of 1 to 11 (with 1 being Bill Clinton and 11 being Poppy Bush), Democrats who served during this period had a strong 3.8 fiscal conservative average, while Republicans had a dismal 7.8 fiscal conservative (liberal?) ranking. And remember, this study was conducted by *Forbes* magazine—not exactly a bastion of Democratic thought. It appears then that W, Ronnie, and Poppy merely perfected the charade of fiscal conservatism—they did not invent it.

Another way economists look at deficit spending is to gauge the national debt as a percentage of gross domestic product. The U.S. national debt peaked at 120.0 percent of GDP in 1946—a result of World War II spending. But from 1946 until Reagan began his term in 1981, presidential belt tightening brought the national debt down to 32.5 percent of GDP. Then, over the next twelve years, the Gipper and his taxpayer giveaways to the ultragreedy, followed by Bush the Elder's bumbling disdain for anything economic, devastated our advances on economic malfeasance. The national debt had skyrocketed to 66.3 percent of GDP at the end of Poppy's term in January 1993.

Clinton, a Democrat, restored fiscal sanity to the budget process and cut the deficit to 57 percent of GDP.

Then came W.

It is projected that by the time George W. Bush leaves office, we will have the highest national debt as a percent of GDP in fifty years—virtually unraveling the progress made by Franklin Roosevelt, Harry Truman, Dwight Eisenhower, John F. Kennedy, Lyndon Johnson, Richard Nixon, and Jimmy Carter—*combined*.

Under George W. Bush, the federal government blew through the back wall of the bank and robbed America of *all* its net savings. In fact, in 2000 our government's net savings rate was a surplus of 2.4 percent. By July 2004 that rate was a *deficit* of 3.1 percent. That was the largest swing from a net surplus to a net deficit in American history.

But the numbers get even worse. According to the 2005 Economic Report of the President, the party with the best record on federal spending, smaller government, and deficit reduction over the past forty-five years is the Democrats. And the numbers aren't even close.

Since 1960 Republican presidents have run up average yearly deficits of $131 billion. Since 1960 Democratic presidents have run up average yearly deficits of only $30 billion. That is a $101 billion *a year* difference.

Democrats, are you listening to this?

Democrats have been far better fiscal managers than these counterfeit conservatives. In fact, of the forty-five budgets from fiscal year 1960 to fiscal year 2004, the fifteen worst deficits were submitted by Republican presidents. And none of the big three—Reagan, Poppy Bush, and Baby Bush—ever submitted a budget that did not result in a deficit.

When it comes to numbers that help working Americans most directly, the Democrats blow the Republican snake oil salesmen out of the water. In raising per capita income for working Americans, Democrats are 30 percent higher than Republicans. Unemployment rates during the terms of Democratic presidents went *down,* whereas they went *up* under Republicans. The same can be seen in inflation: Democratic presidents had an average 3.13 percent inflation rate whereas Republican presidents had an average 3.89 percent inflation rate over the past forty-five years.

The 2005 report shows that over this period, federal spending rose almost twice as fast under Republican presidents as it did under Democratic presidents. Let's repeat that one: Over the past forty-five years, *spending rose twice as fast under Republican presidents as it did under Democratic presidents.* Under Republican presidents, federal spending rose an average of $60 billion a year. Under Democrats it rose only $35 billion a year.

Democrats need to know this stuff and talk about it! If you polled Americans today, you would find that nobody, we mean *nobody,* has a clue that this has been going on—yet you Democrats let Republicans beat you over the head, claiming you are tax and spend and they are fiscal conservatives.

Democrats, you kick Republican ass when it comes to fiscal accountability. We cannot stress this enough—you have to let people know this. Break through the lies, the distortions, the charades of the Republicans. Their economic and fiscal policies have been a sham. They have been liberal, they have been deficit-ridden, they have been irresponsible, they have been deceptive. There is no issue to concede here. Democrats win. It's over. Put a knife in the notion that Republicans are fiscal conservatives, because that notion is done.

In fact, George W. Bush's economic policies were so damning that in October 2004, 169 professors of business and economics at a virtual who's who of American business schools took the unprecedented step of writing an open letter to the president urging, indeed almost pleading with him to change his fiscal policies for the good of the nation.

The group included 56 current or emeritus faculty from the Harvard Business School and 113 more professors from America's top business schools, such as Sloan (MIT), Stanford Business School, Darden (University of Virginia), Kellogg (Northwestern University), Stern (NYU), Wharton (University of Pennsylvania), and Fuqua (Duke University). The list also included two Nobel laureates in economics, Professor Robert C. Merton of Harvard University and Professor Emeritus William F. Sharpe of Stanford.

This is part of what they had to say:

Dear Mr. President:

As professors of economics and business, we are concerned that the U.S. economic policy has taken a dangerous turn under your stewardship. Nearly every major economic indicator has deteriorated since you took office in January 2001. Real GDP growth during your term is the lowest of any presidential term in recent memory. Total non-farm employment has contracted and the unemployment rate has increased. Bankruptcies are up sharply, as is our dependence on foreign capital to finance an exploding current account deficit. All three major stock indexes are lower now than at the time of your inauguration. The percentage of Americans in poverty has increased, real median income has declined, and income inequality has grown.

The data make clear that your policy of slashing taxes—primarily for those at the upper reaches of the income distribution—has not worked. The fiscal reversal that has taken place under your leadership is so extreme that it would have been unimaginable just a few years ago. The federal budget surplus of over $200 billion that we enjoyed in the year 2000 has disappeared, and we are now facing a massive annual deficit of over $400 billion. In fact, if transfers from the Social Security trust fund are excluded, the federal deficit is even worse—well in excess of a half a trillion dollars this year alone. Although some members of your administration have suggested that the mountain of new debt accumulated on your watch is mainly the consequence of 9/11 and the war on terror, budget experts know that this is simply false. Your economic policies have played a significant role in driving this fiscal collapse. And the economic proposals you have suggested for a potential second term—from diverting Social Security contributions into private accounts to making the recent tax cuts permanent—only promise to exacerbate the crisis by further narrowing the federal revenue base.

These sorts of deficits crowd out private investment and are politically addictive. They also place a heavy burden on monetary policy—and create additional pressure for higher interest rates—by stoking inflationary expectations. If your economic advisers are telling you that these deficits can be defeated through further reductions in tax rates, then you need new advisers. More robust economic growth could certainly help, but nearly every one of your ad-

ministration's economic forecasts—both before
and after 9/11—has proved overly optimistic.
Expenditure cuts could be part of the answer,
but your record so far has been one of increasing
expenditures, not reducing them.

What is called for, we believe, is a dramatic
reorientation of fiscal policy, including substantial reversals of your tax policy. Running a
budget deficit in response to a short bout of re-
cession is one thing. But running large struc-
tural deficits over a long period is something
else entirely.

We also urge you to consider the distribu-
tional consequences of your policies. Under your
administration, the income gap between the most
affluent Americans and everyone else has
widened. . . . Some degree of inequality is inherent in any free market economy, creating positive incentives for economic and technological
advancement. But when inequality becomes extreme, it can be socially corrosive and economically dysfunctional. . . . With all due respect,
we believe your tax policy has exacerbated the
problem of inequality in the United States,
which has worrisome implications for the economy
as a whole.

Sensible and farsighted economic management
requires true discipline, compassion, and
courage—not just slogans. Given the tenuous
state of the American economy, we believe that
the time for an honest assessment of the problem
and for genuine corrective action is now. Ignoring the fiscal crisis that has taken hold during
your presidency may seem politically appealing
in the short run, but we fear it could ultimately
prove disastrous. From a policy standpoint, the

`clear message is that more of the same won't`
`work. The warning signs are already visible.`

Think about it. A list of most of the great economic minds in the country chastising a self-avowed (albeit misidentified) fiscal conservative for going on an out-of-control economic binge.

Yet Baby Bush clearly did not get it. Just a few weeks before this letter was sent, a *New York Times* headline blared, "President Asserts Shrunken Surplus May Curb Congress." The lead in that story read, "President Bush said today that there was a benefit to the government's fast-dwindling surplus, declaring that it will create 'a fiscal straitjacket for Congress.' He said that was 'incredibly positive news' because it would halt the growth of the federal government."

We're sorry, but the only straitjacket we see here is the one wrapped tightly around Bush's brain. Let's find out whether shrinking surpluses indeed halted the growth of the federal government under Bush.

According to the Congressional Budget Office and budget historical tables, from the time George W. Bush took office in 2001 through his proposed 2005 budget, U.S. federal spending had increased a jaw-dropping 28.8 percent while nondefense discretionary growth alone soared 35.7 percent! This was, by any definition, one of the most unprecedented rates of uncontrolled spending in American history.

Furthermore, according to a Brookings Institution study, Bush reversed the trend of the Clinton years, which saw government growth decline rather dramatically and, instead, presided over a sharp increase in the size of government. According to Paul Light, author of the Brookings report, the federal workforce grew by over 1 million workers from October 1999 to October 2002. "Although some of the post-1999 growth occurred in the final year of the Clinton administration, most of the 1.1 million new on and off budget jobs appear to reflect increased spending since the Bush Administration entered office." Light concluded, "The Bush Administration is overseeing a vast expansion of the largely hidden federal work force of contractors and grantees."

Stephen Moore, president of the conservative think tank Club for Growth, weighed in. "We are seeing the biggest expansion in government since Lyndon Johnson was in the White House. It is pretty much an across-the-board mushrooming of government." And Daniel Mitchell, of the conservative Heritage Foundation, was even more direct, calling the explosion in the size of government under Baby Bush "very troubling for conservatives . . . particularly since we made so much progress under Clinton in reducing the size of government."

Democrats, you *own* this fiscal conservative, fiscal accountability issue. And you are going to own it for a very long time.

George Bush is not a fiscal conservative. Ronald Reagan was not a fiscal conservative. George H. W. Bush was not a fiscal conservative. It is all a charade.

And so much of this fiscal irresponsibility had to do with one simple, hell-bent intention—George W. Bush, like Ronald Reagan before him, was going to redistribute literally trillions of dollars of wealth and income away from hardworking Americans to their greedy corporate Republican campaign contributors, regardless of the fiscal or economic consequences.

The Republicans are good at smoke-and-mirrors deception. But, as the numbers illustrate, they are bad at fiscal conservatism. Because the truth is, George W. Bush's giveaway to the greedy did not stimulate the economy, it stimulated the checking accounts of the ultrarich. The bipartisan Congressional Budget Office even warned at the time of the cuts that they would have "minimal impact on the economy." Economists cried for an end to the fiscal lunacy. Policy makers warned of the scorched-earth results of such gargantuan redistribution.

And don't kid yourselves. Bush knew that throwing the vast share of the money at an elite greedy few wouldn't stimulate the economy. He just didn't care.

This move by Bush and the Republicans blatantly robbed the working class of $1.7 trillion of their and their children's future, all so that Republicans could basically pay back the corporate harlots who wrote campaign checks to W.

When Baby Bush said, with a straight face, that he thought it better for the American people to have the money than for the government to have the money, he knew he was lying. He knew that virtually every American was *not* going to get any real tax cut. He knew that the numbers were blatantly skewed to ensure only the richest of the rich got the lion's share of the giveaway. That was the idea.

And we shouldn't be surprised.

Look at where King George's taxpayer giveaway went. The bottom 40 percent of America's taxpayers received just 4 percent of the tax cuts. The bottom 60 percent of America's taxpayers received just 13 percent of the tax cuts. Just 13 percent! That means that the richest Americans took home a mind-numbing 87 percent of the tax cuts under the Bush plan. But it is even worse. The richest *one percent* of American taxpayers raked in a breathtaking *43 percent* of the tax cuts. The top 5 percent took over *half* of the cuts. That's not a tax cut. That is the fleecing of America.

People with incomes averaging $1.2 million a year took home $78,460 a year in your money. Even as corporate profits skyrocketed 40 percent from 2000 to 2004, tax revenues from corporations decreased. Bush may have campaigned in 2000 on a pledge to simplify the tax code, but simplification made it harder to hide shelters for the rich and the greedy corporations. So he broke his promise and added 10,000 pages to the U.S. Tax Code. It's true. There is an old line that says, "If Patrick Henry thought taxation without representation was bad, he should see how bad it is *with* representation." Patrick Henry, meet George W. Bush and his Republican bobble-heads in Congress.

Greedy corporations had a friend in King George. A 2004 study by the IRS showed that abuse of Bush-approved tax shelters for corporations had skyrocketed and was costing the government tens of billions of dollars. A Citizens for Tax Justice study that same year found that eighty-two of the nation's most profitable companies paid no corporate taxes in at least one of the past three years. George W. Bush had rewritten the tax code. George W. Bush had blown the doors off the Federal Reserve.

And let's be clear here. We are not suggesting that corporate America be *unfairly* singled out to balance our budgets. But when did a sense of overall equity and fairness leave our values?

At the same time that greedy corporate raiders were given the keys to the bank, American workers were losing their jobs—an alarming 3 million under George W. Bush in his first term alone. Bush became the first president to lose jobs during his term since the U.S. Department of Labor began keeping records. Compare him with Lyndon Johnson, who created over 12 million jobs; Jimmy Carter, who created over 10 million jobs; and Bill Clinton, who created nearly 23 million new jobs during their presidencies. In fact, over the past eighty years, the worst Democratic president increased jobs at a better annual rate than did the best Republican. And for those Americans who were working under Bush and the Republicans, it was often at multiple jobs with low pay, no health insurance, and God, don't even think about a retirement plan.

While Bush's buddies were raiding America's piggy bank, American workers saw their wages decline to the point that in 2004 wages actually fell behind the growth of inflation for the first time in fourteen years. Workers also saw their health benefits dry up, with one-half of the workforce now not provided with health insurance. Forty-five million Americans had no health insurance whatsoever, and, according to a report by Families USA, an advocacy organization for quality health care, as many as 82 million Americans under age sixty-five, fully one-third of the American population, went uninsured for a month or more during 2002–3, with nearly 55 million having been uninsured for six months or more. And all of this was occurring as health and drug costs were soaring.

In addition, the tax burden of working Americans was actually increasing at the same time that the wealthiest Americans and American corporations were enjoying record pay increases and profits while paying less and less in taxes. According to a study by *The Wall Street Journal,* while the average American worker in 2004 saw a wage increase of just 2.5 percent (remember, this was below the inflation rate of 2.7 percent, so workers were actually *losing* money even with the pay increase), the chief executive officers who had been in office at least two years saw their pay explode by nearly 15 percent, to an average of $2.5 million. This marked the largest upsurge in CEO wages since the study began, in 1989. Conversely, the wages of nonunion corporate employees rose at their lowest rate since 1989. Democrats, you have to give voters and opinion leaders this information. You have to talk to all Americans, particularly those in the red states who have bought into the Republican charade. These numbers are powerful and are devastating to the Republican dogma that *they* are the fiscal conservatives and the responsible spenders. They are not. Make the case and do not take a back seat to these phonies any longer.

Under any definition, the Republicans have waged nothing less than an assault on the pocketbooks of working Americans and a violation of all standards of equity, fairness, and honesty. And incidentally, the measly 13 percent of tax cuts spread out to the bottom 60 percent of America's tax-payers was more than eaten up in mushrooming health-care and prescription drug costs, stratospheric housing costs, exploding gasoline and home heating prices, and decidedly lower wages.

These tax cuts coupled with Bush's reckless budgetary spending were causing America to drown in a pool of debt. They were dividing our citizenry. They were making Americans more cynical and distrustful. They were a travesty of gargantuan proportions. They were the most fiscally irresponsible transfer of wealth from the working class to the ultra-rich in American history. They were the most liberal spending, liberal giveaway, liberal malfeasance, greedy charade in American history. And they were all generated by a Republican president, a Republican House of Representatives, and a Republican Senate.

Democrats need to show that the contention that Republicans are fiscal conservatives is a dead issue. They must not allow Republicans to tell the voters or anyone else that the Democratic Party is the party of tax and spend. It simply is not true. While Democrats have led the charge for the past fifty years for fiscally responsible and fiscally conservative policies, the Republican Party and its feckless leaders today are the most fiscally irresponsible, least fiscally conservative that their party has seen in its 145-year history. Indeed, the Republican Party of George W. Bush, of Ronald Reagan, and of George H. W. Bush is the most fiscally irresponsible, least fiscally conservative party in the history of this great nation.

Wanna make 'em pay?

A Democratic Agenda to Recapture the Fiscal Conservative Mantra

Why does the issue of fiscal conservatism matter, and why should Democrats work hard to recapture this issue? It's pretty obvious. First, here's a little background on how Republicans captured this issue as their own.

In the late 1970s, Americans were growing skeptical that our government knew how to manage the economy and spend their tax dollars wisely and efficiently. The hangover of the Vietnam War, double-digit inflation, and spiked gas prices all were taking their toll. Voluminous polling data began to suggest that most Americans thought they were overtaxed, their tax dollars were being wasted, and tax dollars were being spent on the wrong people. They had also come to believe that they could have something for nothing, and that tax cuts were good for the economy and good for the country.

Republicans read these tea leaves. So this is what they did.

1. Republicans told the American people that they agreed their taxes were too high.
2. Republicans told the American people that they, not the Democrats, would cut their taxes.
3. Republicans told the American people that government wasted their tax dollars.
4. Republicans told the American people that tax dollars were being spent on the wrong people. (Read: Poor people or people of a different skin color than theirs.)
5. Republicans told the American people that they could indeed have something for nothing.
6. Republicans told the American people that the Democrats believed none of this and instead were tax-loving, wasteful-spending, deficit-loving, liberal pigs.

The American people chewed on that. They liked the taste, but they wanted to see what the Democrats said. So they asked them. This is what the Democrats said.

1. Democrats told the American people that, while they knew taxes took a bite, we needed the revenue to provide services for our people.
2. Democrats told the American people that they were not sure tax cuts were the right solution.
3. Democrats told the American people that sure, there was always going to be some waste in government, but actually government did a lot of good with their tax dollars.
4. Democrats told the American people that while some people may abuse their tax–dollar–funded services, for the most part, everyone was benefiting from a variety of government services.
5. Democrats told the American people that they could *not* get something for nothing.

6. Democrats told the American people—Well, they didn't really deny the last point made by the Republicans.

Republicans lied and Democrats told the truth.

The people went with the Republicans.

We think Democrats need to modify their responses somewhat. Here is what we propose Democrats say when talking about taxes:

1. Democrats should tell the American people that they agree their taxes are too high.
2. Democrats should tell the American people that they, not the Republicans, want to cut their taxes. (Democrats might want to mention that Republicans want to cut or eliminate taxes only for the ultrarich, who don't pay any taxes to speak of anyway.)
3. Democrats should tell the American people that government does waste their tax dollars.
4. Democrats should tell the American people that their tax dollars are being spent on the rich, greedy bastards who don't need it and who don't pay their fair share anyway.
5. Democrats should tell the American people that they indeed can have something for nothing, but that they could get more if we could just make the rich pay a fairer share of the taxes.
6. Democrats should tell the American people that Republicans don't believe any of this.

It is clear that Republicans abandoned any serious notion of fiscal conservatism a long, long time ago. Say so. What is the matter with you? Just tell voters the truth, for God's sake. You have no one to blame for Republicans capturing the fiscal conservative mantle other than yourselves. You let them. Show some smarts if not some guts and hammer these Republican phonies with it. The people of the South and rural America have not been told the truth for too long. That too is your fault. Because you have ignored people in these areas, they hear only the lies from the Republicans. Tell them the truth. Stand up and fight. Democrats, you are better on fiscal conservative issues, and you have been for the past forty-five years. You might just as well take credit for it.

There is no shortage of talking points when it comes to undermining Republicans on this issue. Republicans basically handed that to the Democrats. They got greedy, and greed, as we know, is one of the seven deadly sins—politically as well as spiritually.

In handing this issue to the Democrats, Republicans allow Democrats to solve half of the equation when it comes to being successful politically on fiscal responsibility. Democrats have all the ammunition they need to make the case that the Republicans failed America on this issue and that, over the course of history, Democrats have done a much better job as stewards of the public purse.

But Democrats have to go a bit further and create a realistic and workable argument for how they would lead again on fiscal issues. They should start with talking about taxes and spending.

While we are not economists, we encourage Democratic politicians and strategists to consult with economic experts in crafting an agenda for fairness and for America's economic rebirth.

Agenda for Fairness and for America's Economic Rebirth (or Some Other Pithy Name)

1. Call for and support a balanced budget amendment to the U.S. Constitution. We did not think we needed one when the Democrats were in control—because we didn't. But we do now. In fact, as we know, Republicans came to power in 1994 in no small part on a platform of balancing the federal budget. (We have not forgotten Newt Gingrich and the Contract with America.) So, now, we need a constitutional amendment to mandate what Republicans did not have the self-discipline to do. Let them bitch about how it cannot be done. Let them whine about how it would break the budget. Let them try to convince the American public that it would be a problem to impose severe belt-tightening tactics because, gasp, we would have to shut down the federal government. Democrats, you used all of those arguments too, and look where they got you.

2. Give most Americans a tax cut—but make it fair for all. That means the

ultragreedy need to pay back what they stole to the American working class, from whom they stole it.

3. Burn up most of those 10,000 pages that Gilded George and the reprobate Republicans added to the tax code so as to hide their giveaways to the greedy. Let's do what Republicans said they would do but didn't (because they lied—they never intended to). That is, let's simplify the tax code. We don't care how—reducing the brackets is probably a good idea, and certainly raising the limit for the upper incomes to where it belongs. Included in this should be the shutting down of hundreds of tax loopholes for which only the greedy need apply—start with the one whereby un-American businesses can open storefronts in the Caymans, not pay any taxes, and then bitch about America. But regardless, shut down these legalized robberies by closing the un-American Bushwhack-backed loopholes.

4. Get rid of that damned alternative minimum tax (which might be effectively handled by closing loopholes). This tax is a crock, and, according to projected forecasts, it will mushroom and snag tens of millions of middle-income Americans by the end of the decade. In fact, find a cute name for it, like Bush's Always More Taxes tax, or Bush's All Money to the Greedy Rich tax. Whatever you call it, hang this one on Boondoggle Bush.

5. As part of fairness and equity, quit taxing different kinds of income at different rates. Republicans routinely fight to shelter income for the wealthiest—capital gains, estate taxes—while the earned income of working Americans has no such advocate.

6. Lead the charge against today's outrageously high gas prices. Bush and Cheney are in bed with greasy oil companies. Bush is in bed as well with the Saudis, and the only people getting screwed are the American people! Democrats, hold them accountable and come up with a real energy plan that, among other things, supports alternative energy sources while it puts pressure on oil companies to quit gouging the American public. Do something about this very publicly, very loudly, and very soon.

The point of all of this is that the Democrats have to take the lead on creating a new American agenda when it comes to government revenues and government spending. Republicans have handed the Democrats an unparalleled gift, thanks to their greed and incompetence. Democrats, quit acting like you are in the minority party. Continuing to play and lose on the

Republicans' turf is no way to lead. Get off Republican turf and create your own. Be proactive. Take some risks. Show some fight, for God's sake.

Speaking of fight. There is one other we would like to have Democrats engage in. We have not forgotten the 1994 Republican Contract with America . . . Let's not let the Republicans forget it either.

The Republicans' Contract with America—Revisited

In 1994, Republicans led by Newt Gingrich told Americans that if they elected a Republican Congress for the first time in forty years, the Republicans would enact and honor a platform they called the Contract with America. It was a bold contract. It promised a lot of sweeping reforms. It made very specific commitments. It became the Republicans' rallying cry.

In fact, Gingrich, Republican members of Congress, and Republican candidates for Congress even held a very public ceremony on the steps of the U.S. Capitol to sign the contract before the election. They made a pledge that day: Give them control of Congress, and they would enact every line item of that contract.

America bought it. Republicans took control of Congress for the first time in forty years. They even made Newt Gingrich Speaker of the House of Representatives. This was a watershed moment. A changing of the guard. The dawn of a new era.

In case you haven't read the Contract with America (apparently, most of the people who signed it did not read it either), this is what it promised:

The Contract with America opened with a preamble. (Nice touch. Apparently nothing was sacred to this bunch of bait-and-switch blowhards.) And right there in the first paragraph, the contract stated that it was a commitment "with no fine print." Well, that was good to know, although, perhaps it was a fatal flaw. As it turns out, they really could have used some.

They didn't even get through the preamble before promising "the end of government that is too big, too intrusive, and too easy with the public's money." Well, that right there pretty much eliminated all the signatories.

We know we could stop here, because all Republicans who signed this contract would have had to resign, but we read further: "We intend to act 'with firmness in the right, as God gives us to see the right.' To restore accountability to Congress. To end its cycle of scandal and disgrace."

This was a problem too. We looked. Tom DeLay signed this contract. Could someone call his office and let him know that when he gets back from his grand jury indictment he should quick write his wife and daughter a campaign check and then clean out his desk?

Thank God we were out of the preamble. But it didn't get any better.

The contract then listed a bunch of things that the Republicans said they would pass "within the first hundred days of the 104th Congress." Most of them looked like they had been written by the people who write actuarial guidelines—a lot of words that don't seem to make any sense. And none of them looked like they would really change things.

But some of the words did make sense, and two of the promises in particular stood out like Rush Limbaugh at a Slim-Fast convention. Republicans now probably wish they didn't:

- They promised to pass a balanced budget amendment.
- They promised term limits for themselves and all members of Congress.

Oh, yeah, they ended the contract with the following: "On September 27, 1994, 300 candidates for public office gathered on the steps of the U.S. Capitol and signed their names to this document. Their pledge: 'If we break this contract, throw us out.' "

Works for us. But many of those Republicans are still serving in Congress, nearly twelve years later.

A word of advice to America. If you want your children to grow up with a sense that a man's or woman's word is bond, and if you want your children to grow up understanding that contracts and promises must be honored, Momma, don't let your babies grow up to be Republican.

As the Democrats begin the road to retaking America in 2006, they must start by calling these people out. They must remind southern and rural America of the Republicans' pledges, contracts, and their lies. Someone once said that the first rule of politics is always to forgive but never to forget.

That was half right.

We haven't forgotten and we cannot forgive. Too much has been lost; too many lives destroyed, too many hopes crushed and opportunities squandered. These guys, with their lies, their deceptions, their perversions, weakened America. In the 2006 election, ask them whether a man's or woman's word means anything.

Ask them whether their rubber-stamp votes on policies that saddled our children with record-breaking debt honored the spirit, not to mention the letter, of their precious contract.

Ask them whether their coddling of the drug and insurance companies that padded their campaign pockets but devastated senior citizens and families was what their contract meant when it said that theirs would be a Congress which "respects the values and shares the faith of the American family."

Ask them whether their trade-off of campaign contributions from energy companies and giant corporate polluters, which has turned so many of our waterways into sewage lagoons, our land into toilets, and our air into malodorous sewer gas, was what they meant when they said that theirs would be an era that "restored accountability to Congress."

These forgers with their contrived contract never intended to deliver on their promises. It was all a sham. It was never about America—it was always about them.

They were elected under false pretenses. They have served under false pretenses. They have broken their word. They are liars. If their word really did mean anything, they would have left a long time ago. When they run again for reelection, scream it from the rafters. Let them know that you haven't forgotten. Make them explain how they can so blatantly lie to their constituents. Ask them how they can live with themselves.

In 2006, let's begin to take back America by extracting these self-serving shills from the body politic.

Chapter 8

LIE 3: REPUBLICANS ARE THE PARTY OF PATRIOTISM AND NATIONAL DEFENSE

The third great lie of the Republicans is that they are the party of patriotism and national defense.

On its face, this is a ridiculous claim.

If Deferments Were Medals They'd All Be Generals

Let's start with the claim that Republicans are more patriotic than Democrats. Give us a break.

Patriotism's simplest and most unadulterated definition is "love of one's country." That is all it is. Very simple, but very powerful.

Patriotism doesn't wear a cloak of partisanship.

Patriotism does not reside with one political party.

Patriotism does not require its adherents to blindly follow a political leader or agenda.

Patriotism does not muzzle dissenting voices.

And when Republican leaders and cheerleaders suggest patriotism does any of these things, they are the true enemies of patriotism, and of our country.

True patriots battle attempts to subvert or politicize another's voice.

True patriots counteract those who would stifle free thought or extinguish public deliberations.

Yet Democrats too often seem reluctant to fight back when phony patriots in the Republican Party attack them. Democrats act like the charge is so ridiculous that it doesn't merit a response.

Wrong.

If the Republicans or their talking heads say Democrats are unpatriotic, the Democrats need to tell them them's fightin' words! And we don't mean slap-across-the-face fightin' words. We mean black-eye, broken-nose, knock-teeth-out, kick-the-hell-out-of-somebody fightin' words.

Yet, in part as a consequence of Democrats' near silence on this issue, Republican leaders and cheerleaders today brazenly hammer Democrats who challenge them as unpatriotic, un-American pinkos.

That has to stop. America is better than that, and Democrats should demand better.

First we have to understand that patriotism in a political world is a two-part equation. If your leaders are doing something you believe will harm the country you love, as a patriot you have a duty to speak out against those actions. But, and this is the part upon which Democrats often neglect to follow through, if somebody then attacks your words as unpatriotic, you need to garner the full force of indignation and anger and respond.

Look at how many people—politicians, academicians, citizens—were castigated and silenced by these frauds just before the Iraq War, when they spoke up because they believed that our nation would be best served by securing a legitimate and truly international coalition to put pressure on Iraq; when they spoke up because they believed more time was needed for UN inspectors to verify the supposed "weapons of mass destruction" in Iraq; when they spoke up because they believed Osama bin Laden was America's greatest threat and argued that resources should not be diverted from a search for him to an attempt to exact revenge against Saddam Hussein. Why did Republicans and their parrots attack these true patriots so violently?

The Republican leaders were using patriotism as a cover for a very cynical and greedy political and economic agenda. We should have seen it coming.

Following the 2000 elections, Republican special-interest guard dogs had gained nearly total power, and they intended to keep it. George W. Bush had a personal, economic, and political agenda, and he was staking his political life on it. For over a decade, special-interest groups had poured hundreds of millions of dollars into this group of Republican leaders—more contributions than had been given to any group of political candidates in American history. These special interests expected payback on their investments.

These greedy moneyed interests intended to reap even greater profits by sticking it to the working class with the sham of bankruptcy reform. They mandated higher oil prices and the resulting windfall profits. They demanded a loosening of environmental oversight so that money would roll in as greenhouse gases rolled out. They orchestrated a watered-down Food and Drug Administration so that billions could be made off faulty, undertested drugs. They manipulated the system to undermine public education so tax dollars could be used to fund their too often suspect religious schools. They were determined to break the backs of lawyers who were the last hope of the little guy when big corporations hurt ordinary folks. They obsessively imposed their religious beliefs on all Americans. Competition was a threat to them, so they jerry-rigged the system into granting them no-bid contracts. They were hell-bent to control the judiciary. They gutted congressional ethics committees so that their fraudulent and illegal personal and political activities would not cost them power. They attacked mainstream media as biased while they bought off commentators, columnists, and the entire Fox News network. They fanatically increased control over our nation's media. They raided the Social Security program and then sought to privatize the accounts so that individuals would have to pick up the tab for their pillaging. They siphoned off trillions of dollars in tax cuts for themselves and shifted the tax burden to the working class.

In short, this was their utopia. This was their nirvana. This was their Eden. To the victor were going *all* the spoils. The looting of America had begun. The pillage of the middle and working classes was on. These special interests, their puppets in politics, and their groups of cheerleading shills in the media were drunk on power and greed.

They would be damned if George W. Bush was going to screw it up because of his stupid-ass, ill-prepared he-tried-to-kill-my-daddy vendetta against Saddam Hussein.

Without question, there would be great consequences—political, social, and certainly economic—if Bush lost his 2004 reelection campaign on the issue of the war. So, patriotism be damned. And true patriots be damned with it. The knives came out.

Case in point:

Senate Democratic Leader Tom Daschle. Daschle was a Vietnam veteran. He understood what bad government policy can do to soldiers in wartime. He lived through Richard Nixon and Spiro Agnew's stifling of antiwar voices as unpatriotic traitors. He deplored that the consequences, in part, of those silenced voices were 58,000 names on a cold black wall in Washington, D.C. Tom Daschle understood the meaning of patriotism.

By March 2003, Daschle was extremely uneasy about Bush's seemingly blind fervor concerning taking out Saddam Hussein. He saw no real attempt to garner an international coalition; he saw no real evidence of imminent danger from Saddam; he knew that the UN weapons inspectors needed more time; he was skeptical about diverting funds to an Iraqi operation at the expense of America's search for Osama bin Laden; and he feared the lack of a long-term strategy, much less a postwar strategy, should things go poorly in an Iraq invasion. In short, Daschle felt that Bush's war would hurt the country he had fought for and loved.

So, on March 17, 2003, Daschle did the patriotic thing. He spoke out.

And remember, Tom Daschle was a somewhat understated leader. He did not flail his arms; he was not prone to vitriolic rhetoric. God knows, he did not accuse Bush of being unpatriotic for plowing amauroticly into war. Tom Daschle respected that different people could have different views on the war.

He simply said he was "saddened that this president failed so miserably at diplomacy that we're now forced to war."

A voice of dissent. A fulfillment of a patriotic responsibility. As we discussed, true patriotism demands that in America. Right?

Wrong.

Republicans did not embrace patriotic dissenting voices. They went bat shit.

The Republican House Speaker, Dennis Hastert, went apoplectic. This man without military pedigree accused Daschle of approaching treason by saying Daschle's remarks "may not give comfort to our adversaries, but they come mighty close."

In a rich twist on bait-and-switch tactics, the White House lapdog spokesman Ari Fleischer, who was in diapers during the early years of the Vietnam War and barely into puberty when it ended, accused Daschle of "politicizing" the debate over the war.

House Majority Leader Tom DeLay said that Daschle's words were treasonous in that they were "emboldening Saddam Hussein." DeLay also told Daschle *in French* to "shut your mouth."

But Daschle wasn't the lone object of these attacks. Republicans were crying treason all over the country. Any elected official, party official, or even patriotic citizen who voiced reservations about the war came under attack. Mothers, fathers, wives, husbands, students, educators, senior citizens, military veterans, you name them—if they uttered a word of caution or questioned Bush's questionable war rationale and preparedness in any way, they were attacked.

The Republican propaganda machine would have made *Pravda* proud. But it was not a proud moment for America. Indeed, America's image in the world soon fell to an all-time low. The beacon of hope was becoming the bully of hype.

But perhaps no one was attacked harder, by more people, in more venues, and with more malice than the Democratic presidential nominee, John Kerry.

John Kerry. Three Purple Hearts. One Silver Star. One Bronze Star. John Kerry, who did two tours of Vietnam. John Kerry, who bled for his country. John Kerry, who killed for his country. John Kerry, war hero.

It didn't matter. When John Kerry had the audacity to question Bush's wartime policies, the Republican pretenders sprang into action.

George W., not one of the few or the proud, repeatedly questioned Kerry's commitment to the soldiers in the field. Vice President Dick Cheney called Kerry "unfit to serve" as commander in chief. Cheney even suggested that America would be hit with a terrorist attack again if Kerry were elected! The accidental Senate leader, Bill Frist, couldn't resist puffing out his patrician chest and accusing Kerry of playing politics with the war.

They were hell-bent on brainwashing America into thinking there was a new definition of patriotism. Their redefinitions and revisionist historical accounts were voluminous enough that, were George Orwell alive in 2004, his sequel to *1984* would have written itself.

Because by 2004 war was peace. "I just want you to know that, when we talk about war, we're really talking about peace." That's what George Bush actually said in a speech at the Department of Housing and Urban Development on June 18, 2002. God help us.

And by 2004 draft dodgers were being defined as patriotic warriors, and patriotic warriors were being defined as, well, some sort of antiwar, antitroops, antipatriotic wimps.

Even that political opportunist Zigzag Zell Miller, at the Republican National Convention, in a voice that suggested his shorts were far too tight, lambasted Kerry as nothing short of a traitor for challenging Bush on the war. (This was the same Zigzag Miller who, a couple of years earlier, had introduced Kerry as a true American hero. Zell, we did not know that heroes came with expiration dates.)

And when the leaders of the "redefine patriotism" movement were vomiting at full decibel levels, you could be sure their cheerleaders could not be far behind.

Sure enough, Rush Limbaugh put down his nanny-secured Oxy-Contin long enough to blubber into his microphone every day that these Democrats were traitors to America. Bill O'Reilly quit drooling body fluids over his Caribbean fetishes long enough to book guest after guest who could wax moronically about Democratic patriotism or lack thereof; and Ann Coulter exhaled her foot from her mouth long enough to spin her head in circles, emitting her putrid green vomit of lies faster than you could say "painted lady."

All of these attacks seemed to freeze America. Mainstream media appeared to fear the propaganda machine of the Republicans and either fell silent or, worse, capitulated and debated their lies on their warped terms. People in bars, restaurants, beauty shops, barbershops, grocery stores, schools, lunchrooms, you name it, seemed reluctant to raise voices of question or calls for reason because, as soon as they were out in public, some emboldened dipshit-head Rush Limbaugh fan was sure to be there to slap them down.

As a consequence, Democrats did not defend themselves nearly as vehemently as they should have or, worse, didn't defend their beliefs at all.

Saying you are unpatriotic, to us, is about the worst thing someone could do. Democrats have to get mad as hell and call these Republicans out on this issue.

They are wrong to distort the truth this way. And they threaten our country when they do it.

Let's look at how real leaders have defined patriotism over the years and how they viewed Americans speaking against injustice and for love of country.

That we are to stand by the president, right or wrong,
is not only unpatriotic and servile, but is morally
treasonable to the American public.
THEODORE ROOSEVELT

Patriotism means to stand by the country.
It does not mean to stand by the president
or any other public official.
THEODORE ROOSEVELT

May we never confuse honest dissent
with disloyal subversion.
DWIGHT D. EISENHOWER

Guard against the impostures of pretended patriotism.
GEORGE WASHINGTON

America will never be destroyed from the outside.
If we falter, and lose our freedoms, it will be because
we destroyed ourselves.
ABRAHAM LINCOLN

When the people fear their government, there is tyranny;
when the government fears the people, there is liberty.
THOMAS JEFFERSON

Criticism in a time of war is essential to the maintenance of any kind of democratic government.
U.S. SENATOR ROBERT TAFT (R–OHIO)

Before the war is ended, the war party assumes the divine right to denounce and silence all opposition to war as unpatriotic and cowardly.
U.S. SENATOR ROBERT LA FOLLETTE (R–WISCONSIN)

We must not confuse dissent with disloyalty. When the loyal opposition dies, I think the soul of America dies with it.
EDWARD R. MURROW

The cry has been that when war is declared, all opposition should be hushed. A sentiment more unworthy of a free country could hardly be propagated.
WILLIAM ELLERY CHANNING, UNITARIAN MINISTER AND ABOLITIONIST

It is no accident that four true giants of democratic thought—Thomas Jefferson, Theodore Roosevelt, George Washington, and Abraham Lincoln—had their faces carved in granite at Mount Rushmore in part because they all understood the absolute necessity of dissenting voices and indeed pleaded for them as the lifeblood of patriotism. By contrast, four pigmies of democratic thought—George W. Bush, Dick Cheney, Tom DeLay, and Denny Hastert—whose best hope for enshrinement would have been on the backs of milk cartons as missing from duty in Vietnam, all feared and rebuked dissent as *unpatriotic.*

Democrats have to remind America that this isn't acceptable. They have to scream loudly about this. They have to be unafraid to be patriots. They have to remind Americans that the great patriots throughout our history would have had these phonies for lunch with nary a hint of indigestion. Democrats must not let Republicans or anyone else attack their patriotism ever again.

Democrats must remind Americans that the American governmental system became the greatest in the world in no small part because true patriots loved it enough to speak out and make sure it did great things. Without dissent, we couldn't have been great. Let them know that this great government is their government. They own it. Democrats need to stand up and fight any attempts to usurp the voice of the people and do it in a loud voice.

George W. Bush as Commander in Chief: Throw Him a Life Jacket, He's in Over His Head

I go to bed every night feeling that I have failed *that day because I could not end the conflict in Vietnam.*
LYNDON B. JOHNSON
PRESS CONFERENCE, FEBRUARY 2, 1967

Press Conference, April 13, 2004

Reporter's Question: Two weeks ago, a former counterterrorism official at the NSC, Richard Clarke, offered an unequivocal apology to the American people for failing them prior to 9/11. Do you believe the American people deserve a similar apology from you, and would you be prepared to give them one?

George W. Bush: Look, I can understand why people in my administration are anguished over the fact that people lost their life. I feel the same way. I mean, I'm sick when I think about the death that took place on that day. And as I mentioned, I've met with a lot of family members, and I do the best to console them about the loss of their loved one . . . Here's what I feel about that: The person responsible for the attacks was Osama bin Laden. That's who's responsible for killing Americans. And that's why we will stay on the offense until we bring people to justice.

Reporter's Question: In the last campaign, you were asked a question about the biggest mistake you'd made in your life, and you used to like to joke that it was trading Sammy Sosa. You've looked back before 9/11 for what mistakes might have been made. After 9/11, what would your biggest mistake be, would you say, and what lessons have you learned from it?

George W. Bush: I wish you'd have given me this written question ahead of time so I could plan for it. John, I'm sure historians will look back and say, gosh, he could've done it better this way or that way. You know, I just—I'm sure something will pop into my head here in the midst of this press conference, with all the pressure of trying to come up with an answer, but it hadn't yet. . . . I hope—I don't want to sound like I have made no mistakes. I'm confident I have. I just haven't—You just put me under the spot here, and maybe I'm not as quick on my feet as I should be in coming up with one.

This April 13, 2004, press conference took place forty-one months after Clinton administration officials briefed the incoming national security adviser, Condoleezza Rice, telling her that the Bush administration would need to spend more time on al-Qaeda than on any other issue. (Yet Rice did not even get around to broaching the subject of al-Qaeda with Bush cabinet members until just days before September 11, 2001.) This press conference took place thirty-two months after President Bush received and ignored an August 6, 2001, daily briefing headlined "Bin Laden Determined to Strike in US." This press conference took place thirty-one months after the terrorist attacks of September 11, 2001, cost 3,000 Americans their lives. This press conference took place thirteen months after the beginning of the Iraq War, with over 700 American lives lost and over 4,200 Americans wounded. This press conference took place eleven months after President Bush landed on the USS *Abraham Lincoln* off the California coast and declared that major combat operations in Iraq had *ended*. This press conference took place three weeks after the U.S. counterterrorism official Richard Clarke looked into a camera at a 9/11 Commission hearing and apologized to the victims of 9/11 and their families for our government having failed them.

Need any more hints of mistakes made, Mr. President?

George W. Bush.

No apologies. No mistakes.

No guts.

The truth is, for thousands in our armed forces and millions of Americans, George Bush was a living, breathing mistake.

No mistakes, Mr. President?

What about your discredited rationale for going to war?

What about your faulty if not falsified claim that there were weapons of mass destruction in Iraq?

What about your blind zeal to enact revenge on Saddam's threats against your father?

What about your disdain toward military leaders who warned that American troop strength was far too low in Iraq, endangering our soldiers there?

What about your miscalculated belief that the Iraqis would throw away their arms and welcome Americans as liberators?

What about the scandalous lack of equipment and body armor supplied to our troops in Iraq and your almost insouciant response to those who confronted you about it?

What about your administration's indifference to pleas for reinforced Humvees in Iraq so our personnel there wouldn't have to ride in "cardboard coffins"?

Mr. President, what about 2,000 dead and scores of wounded Americans in Iraq and 3,000 dead Americans following an attack on American soil by a man you made it much, much harder to capture because of personnel, equipment, and funds diverted to attack Saddam Hussein, who did not pose an immediate threat to America?

How different this president has been from past American presidents. Presidents who understood that their actions had consequences. That lives were at stake. That wars are failures, not victories. Lyndon Johnson understood that. He said of the Vietnam War, "The guns and the bombs, the rockets and the warships, are all symbols of human failure." Dwight D. Eisenhower understood that. He told us that when a nation gets into a war, "you should win as quick as you can, because your losses become a function of the duration of the war. I believe when you get in a war, get everything you need and win it."

Facts are facts. Bush bungled the rationale for this war, bungled the planning for this war, and bungled the timetable and implementation of this war. He took his eye off of the greatest threat to America, Osama bin Laden, and as a consequence not only allowed him to escape prosecution but also emboldened his cause of hatred and destruction and expanded his base of disciples while marginalizing the world's opinion of our nation.

In his April 13, 2004, press conference, the president said about bin Laden, "The person responsible for the [9/11] attacks was Osama bin Laden. That's who's responsible for killing Americans. And that's why we will stay on the offensive until we bring people to justice." But at a press conference on March 13, 2002, he said, "I don't know where he [bin Laden] is. Nor, you know, I just don't spend that much time on him really. To be honest with you . . . I truly am not that concerned about him."

Bush sent mixed signals with regard to our policy in Iraq and indeed with regard to our entire foreign policy objectives. He sugarcoated the war, glamorized the mission, and misled America and the world. Other than our military and our National Guard personnel and their families, from whom he asked the ultimate sacrifice, he did not ask America to sacrifice for this effort. We do not believe that is an accident. He is not a man who has a personal history of sacrifice.

Following Bush's stunning April 13, 2004, press conference, the historian Doris Kearns Goodwin provided some cover for the president by suggesting he fumbled the "mistake" questions because "he was just out of practice," because he had held so few press conferences.

We don't believe that was his problem. We believe George W. Bush couldn't answer the "mistake" questions because he actually thought he hadn't made any.

Thomas Hobbes told us in *Leviathan* that "no man's error becomes his own Law; nor obliges him to persist in it." Unfortunately, this president appears to beg to differ. We fear that this president ran up a massive debt in the world community that we are now having to pay back. Unfortunately, the currency is blood.

Republicans' Record on Defense and Veterans' Issues——You'd Better Sit Down for This One

Not only are most GOP leaders and their bought-and-paid-for mouth-pieces draft-dodging, lip-quivering, turn-and-run cowards who have to attempt to redefine patriotism because their own existence does not fall under accepted definitions, but their own policies with regard to our military are scandalous charades.

The evidence is overwhelming. Starting with equipment. This is what George W. Bush said on October 8, 2003, about making sure our soldiers were the best equipped in the world: "Any time we put our troops into harm's way, you must have the best training, the best equipment, the best possible pay."

Let's see if the president practiced what he preached.

• Of the approximately 20,000 Humvees initially sent into Iraq, fewer than 6,000 were equipped with factory-installed armor. And of the 9,000 trucks sent in to transport our troops and supplies, over 8,000 lacked armor. They were literally cardboard coffins.

• According to Representative Gene Taylor, who sat on the House Armed Services Committee, fully one-half of American casualties in Iraq had been the results of homemade bombs, so-called improvised explosive devices. How do you counter these devices? Radio jammers. We had the jammers—we just hadn't deployed them to Iraq. According to Taylor, each radio jammer cost approximately $10,000—the same amount he projected it would cost to bury a dead American soldier. Of the 29,000 vehicles the United States sent to Iraq, how many had jammers? According to Taylor, virtually none. (Unless Defense Secretary Donald Rumsfeld or some other high-level U.S. official traveled to Iraq. The administration made sure their vehicles had them.)

When confronted with this glaring lack of preparedness, Rumsfeld shrugged it off. "If you think about it, you can have all the armor in the world on a tank and a tank can still be blown up." (Remember, around 50 percent of all U.S. dead and wounded came at the hands of roadside bombing attacks—most of these preventable with proper truck armor and jamming devices.) A week earlier, when confronted with questions about the chronic shortages of equipment and supplies for U.S. soldiers, Rummy showed an alarmingly similar indifference. "You go to war with the Army you have . . . not the Army you might want or wish to have at a later time." He then suggested that contractors simply were not keeping up with the demand for armored vehicles.

This really is offensive. Every bit of public documentation clearly shows that America had been planning for the invasion of Iraq for at least two years before Rumsfeld's comments. And public records show that, as of the fall of 2003, the military was having only fifteen armored Humvees produced a month, or less than 4 percent of production capacity. To put into perspective the lack of foresight of these lame excuses for military leaders, during roughly the same amount of time it took to produce 20,000 Humvees (without armor!) and 9,000 trucks (without armor!) for this war, America produced 296,429 aircraft, 102,351 tanks, 87,620 warships, and 2,455,694 trucks to fight World War II. So let's be clear. The lack of armored Humvees or enough radio jammers for our 30,000 total vehicles was not a matter of inability to produce them, it was a consequence of shortsighted leaders who had no real military experience and were running the war like some Three Stooges skit. So, Rummy, stop with the lies. This is America. We support our troops in battle. The president and Congress pretty much had a blank check for this one. If you needed to produce 100,000 armored Humvees a month and 1 million jammers for our vehicles, you could have done it.

But Rummy the Warrior wasn't merely indifferent. He continued to lie. "I think it's something like 400 [armored Humvees] a month are being done. And it's essentially a matter of physics. It isn't a matter of money. It isn't a matter on the part of the Army of desire. It's a matter of production and capability of doing it." Yet when the sole U.S. supplier of protective plates for the Humvee military vehicles, Armor Holdings, was contacted after Rumsfeld's comments on December 8, 2004, the president, Robert Mecredy, told reporters that his company was prepared to produce 50 to 100 *more* vehicles a month and was only waiting for the Army to give them the word to do so.

And what about the morale of the troops whose vehicles lacked the necessary protection when they saw Rummy pull up in a vehicle so well protected that it looked like something out of Bill Murray's movie *Stripes*? Colonel John Zimmerman was quoted saying that he and the other American soldiers "could not help fuming at the sight of the fully 'up-armored' Humvees and heavy trucks put on display here for Mr. Rumsfeld's visit. What you see out here [the equipment used to transport Rumsfeld] isn't what we've got going north [to Iraq] with us." Nice work, Larry.

But Rummy wasn't the only one of the Three Stooges who continued to lie about adequate body armor for our troops. The great military mind Dick Cheney, who reminds us of the Ignatius J. Reilly character in John Kennedy Toole's Pulitzer Prize–winning novel, *A Confederacy of Dunces,* assured the Fox News reporter Brit "Tennis Anyone" Hume in March 2004 that "all" American troops were fully protected with body armor. That claim was immediately countered by Major General Charles Swannack, who was on the ground in Iraq and said publicly that same month, "We are short a significant amount . . . of body armor to properly equip [soldiers]." Way to be on top of things, Moe.

Finally, how did Bush address this problem? Inexplicably, his 2004 defense budget proposed "zero" dollars for Humvee armor kits. Good work, Curly.

• At a town hall meeting with military personnel in Iraq, Rumsfeld was asked by a National Guard member from the 116th Calvary Brigade what he planned to do about antiquated equipment for National Guardsmen stationed in Iraq. Rummy at first stumbled over an answer, claiming it was early, he was an old man, and he was just gathering his thoughts. Then he gave the following response: "So any organization, any element of the Army is going to end up, at some point, with—you characterize it as 'antiquated.' I would say the older equipment, whatever it may be, in any category. Somebody is always going to be at that level." We're guessing that made the men and women of the guard feel very appreciated. Why didn't he just tell them the truth. "Yeah, you're right, we *are* sticking you guardsmen with really shitty equipment." Good work again, Larry.

• News reports out of Iraq indicated that there were chronic shortages of basic military equipment, including ammunition, night vision goggles, and radios. One guardsman told CBS's *60 Minutes* in October 2004 that men in his unit were using walkie-talkies their families had picked up at sporting goods stores in the United States. Of course, he noted, "anybody can pick up those signals," including enemy soldiers.

• For fear it would give support to the belief that his war efforts were failing, President Bush refused to support a permanent increase in the size of the Army, leading to extended stays and increased stress for deployed troops. Way to put politics first, Curly.

• Yet Secretary of State Colin Powell and other top military leaders had been warning the Stooges for years that the troop levels in Iraq were not adequate enough to fulfill our mission there. In 2002 Powell called Army General Tommy Franks, one of the architects of the Iraq War plan, and warned that troop levels in Iraq were insufficient. Paul Bremer, the administrator of the U.S.-led occupation force, flat out told the Stooges in October 2004, "We never had enough troops on the ground." And as a consequence we had created "an atmosphere of lawlessness" in Iraq. Then, in November 2004, Powell once again pleaded with both Curly and British prime minister Tony Blair to put more troops in Iraq or risk a military disaster. Curly stuck to his guns, and Powell announced his resignation. Blair stuck to *his* guns as well, causing his own foreign secretary, Robin Cook, to resign, saying, "There were no international terrorists in Iraq until we went in. It was we who gave the perfect conditions in which Al Qaeda could thrive."

• According to news accounts, Lieutenant General Ricardo Sanchez, the former top U.S. commander in Iraq, complained to Pentagon officials that supplies were so lacking that our soldiers' ability to fight was being compromised. Sanchez reported that parts for helicopters and tanks were so low he could "not continue to support sustained combat operations." He noted that units were having to wait an average of *forty days* for critical spare parts.

• Fifty thousand U.S. troops fighting in Iraq received no body armor at all. The administration's excuses were many. Orders for body armor were not filled, as many as 10,000 body armor plates were reported lost before they arrived in Iraq, and the Defense Department took almost six months before they even began shipping body armor. Knuckleheads.

• Perhaps part of the problem with equipment shortages was the Three Stooges' inability to oversee and run the Department of Defense. According to a General Accounting Office study in 2005, the DOD ranked as the federal government department with the most waste, fraud, and abuse. How did the Three Stooges respond? Yuk, yuk, yuk, yuk, yuk . . .

• How might there be excessive fraud? A Center for Public Integrity study found that a stunning 40 percent of the nearly $500 billion Pentagon budget for military contracting was awarded without competitive bids. The inmates had clearly taken over the asylum.

The truth is, this was no way to run a war. These Stooges had no clue what they were doing. They underestimated our opponent and sent American troops into harm's way woefully underequipped, and they clearly had no long-term plan for victory. And they claim they are pro-defense? In any other leading government in the world, these mistakes would have caused heads to roll. None rolled here. Not one.

Indeed, in a government in denial, you don't fire incompetent buffoons—at least not ones who do what you tell them, who don't ever question your motives or methodology, and who fear the dictator—you give them medals! That is exactly what Curly did. On December 14, 2004, George W. Bush actually presented the Presidential Medal of Freedom to Tommy Franks, the Army general who led the invasion in Iraq; CIA Director George Tenet, who had told Bush it was a "slam dunk" that Iraq had weapons of mass destruction; and L. Paul Bremer, who presided over the first months of the less than successful attempts to rebuild Iraq. It was a slap in the face to previous medal recipients, whose heroic deeds actually warranted the honor.

Many inside and out of the military cried foul. Paul Rieckhoff, an Army lieutenant who served in Iraq, told *The Washington Post* that giving the Medal of Freedom to these three buffoons was a "slap in the face to the troops" from "an administration that loves the big PR move. It validates how out of touch Washington is with the reality of what is on the ground in Iraq."

Maybe out of touch; or maybe Bush just thinks he is untouchable. Maybe Bush thinks he can say and do anything he likes. In the course of researching this book, we came across several quotations from W's gubernatorial days in Texas through his White House years in which he joked that things would be a lot easier if we had a dictatorial form of government and he was the dictator. We pretty much dismissed them as idle and rather pedestrian attempts at humor. Perhaps we shouldn't have.

The bottom line is that Democrats need to reveal all of this. Defense is an especially important issue to southern and rural Americans who voted for Bush. Shout about his massive failures to these voters. Stand up and demand that our troops in battle get the equipment, parts, personnel, and leadership they deserve. Point out the massive fraud, deception, and incompetence that is going on in our country's military. Cry out when they put medals around the necks of incompetent bunglers.

Here's some more hard data to make the point.

• Bush's 2005 budget called for cutting monthly imminent-danger pay from $225 to $150 and family separation allowances from $250 to $100 for troops in combat. He also proposed dropping 1 million children of military and veterans' families from the child tax credit passed in 2003.

• Refusing the pleadings of Veterans Administration hospitals, Republicans in Congress defeated a measure to provide $2 billion in health-care funding for veterans in April 2005.

• In 2004 the administration attempted to cut $1.5 billion for military housing and medical facilities. In the same budget, Bush proposed closing commissaries, cutting $174 million from schools near military bases, and totally eliminating aid to military base schools.

• The administration banned photographs of caskets of U.S. soldiers killed in Iraq and, according to news accounts, mandated that flights carrying wounded soldiers from Iraq be allowed to arrive in the United States only in the dead of night. Soldiers were then transported to hospitals in unmarked vans and unloaded at back entrances. Photographs of them were also forbidden.

• President Bush did not attend one funeral for a soldier killed in Iraq.

• Another published report indicated that letters of condolence from the secretary of defense to families of soldiers killed in Iraq were not being signed by Secretary Rumsfeld. Traditionally this is a sacred act. But Rummy didn't have time. So the letters were instead being signed . . . by a machine. According to *The Washington Post,* "One father bitterly commented that he thought it was a shame that the Secretary of Defense could keep his squash schedule but not find the time to sign his dead son's letter." After the public outcry, Rumsfeld agreed to sign all future letters personally.

• According to a Government Accountability Office report released in February 2005, over one-third of all wounded Army National Guard and Reserve soldiers were prematurely dropped from active duty status, thus losing medical care and thousands of dollars in pay because of a faulty personnel system.

• A Harvard University and Public Citizen study showed that between 2000 and 2003, 235,000 more veterans fell into the ranks of the uninsured—a total of 1.7 million American veterans were uninsured in 2003, a 14 percent increase from 2000. That same study showed that one-third of all veterans under the age of twenty-five had no health insurance, 15 percent of all veterans between twenty-five and forty-four had no health insurance, and 10 percent of veterans aged forty-five to sixty-five lacked health coverage.

Yet, when the Republican Representative Chris Smith declared publicly that the administration was underfunding and undermining the health care of America's veterans, the administration responded by pressuring leaders in Congress to strip Smith of his chairmanship of the Veterans' Affairs Committee.

• A report in February 2005 noted that soldiers at Walter Reed Army Medical Center in Washington, D.C., were asked to pay for their meals. This even applied to severely wounded outpatient soldiers who had been at Walter Reed for over ninety days.

• A scandalous 23 percent of America's homeless were veterans.

• President Bush proposed doubling copayments while he cut veterans' health benefits. Complaints and appeals to the U.S. Department of Veterans Affairs over unfavorable decisions on disability benefits nearly doubled from 2000 to 2004—from 60,000 to 109,000. Also, because of a slowed-down appeals process, veterans were told they would have to wait an average of three years to have their appeals heard, making some veterans lucky to have a hearing before they died.

• In 2002 President Bush ordered Veterans Administration centers around the country to quit informing veterans and their families about government health-care services and stop recruiting new veterans. This was a reversal of a program started under Bill Clinton, which instructed the VA to expand eligibility to include all veterans.

• President Bush opposed spending $275 million to reduce backlogs at VA medical centers. Veterans' organizations such as the American Legion had been calling for the funds to help move the more than 300,000 veterans new to the system off the waiting lists (some had been on them for more than a year) for the initial medical exams they needed to qualify for prescription drug benefits. In Florida alone, 42,000 veterans were on waiting lists to see a doctor.

• Under Bush budget requests, the Department of Veterans Affairs would lose 3 percent of its funding in 2006 and 16 percent by 2010.

• Not only did Bush's 2006 budget more than double the copayment charged to veterans for prescription drugs but it also required a new $250 a year fee to use government health care. Critics charged the move was designed to discourage people from enrolling in the health-care system.

• Remember the national shortages of flu vaccines in 2004? One would think that our soldiers heading into battle would be a priority. They weren't. At the height of the flu season, when 50,000 to 60,000 doses of flu vaccine were needed at the Navy hospital at Camp Lejeune in North Carolina, the hospital reported receiving zero.

• The suicide rate in the Marine Corps rose by 29 percent in 2004. All were enlisted men. Marine Corps Commandant Michael Hagee attributed the increase to "perceived overwhelming stresses associated with relationship, financial and disciplinary problems." Might we suggest that part of that stress came from being dropped into combat situations ill equipped, with lousy pay, poor housing, extended deployment periods, antiquated processing procedures that throw wounded soldiers off military payrolls and out of military hospitals, and dishonest scenarios for success from Washington policy makers.

This lack of support was scandalous. And we're clearly not the only ones to have noticed.

A poll of America's military personnel and their families conducted by the National Annenberg Election Survey and published in October 2004 found that 59 percent believed President Bush had far underestimated the number of troops needed to win peace in Iraq, while only 30 percent felt that veterans and their families were getting the medical care they needed. And this was from *military* families.

A study prepared by the Rand Corporation in early 2004 for the Department of Defense blasted the Pentagon for a lack of planning, unrealistic expectations, a dismal record of political-military coordination and cooperation, and the lack of a realistic reconstruction and exit strategy in

Iraq. The study concluded that this group of leaders clearly had not absorbed "historical lessons" with regard to fighting insurgencies.

Even the presidential commission appointed to look at intelligence failures leading up to the war in Iraq concluded in March 2005 that a major problem with our intelligence operation was an atmosphere that discouraged dissent from the president's positions as well as lack of competitive analysis and information sharing. It appeared Curly, Larry, and Moe were mandating that the intelligence community tell them only what they wanted to hear. Oh, that's right, their idea of leadership and their definition of patriotism is for all Americans—apparently even our intelligence agencies—to be yes-men and yes-women to the scandalously inept Three Stooges.

But at least the president was right when he said that our military actions were severely clamping down on terrorist activity—right?

Wrong.

According to the State Department, terrorist attacks have dramatically increased throughout the world. Indeed, government figures indicated that the number of serious acts of international terrorism had tripled in 2004, and there were more terrorist attacks in 2004 than in any year since 1985. The department was so embarrassed by its nineteenth annual report on terrorism that it announced it would no longer publish yearly statistics on international terrorist acts. Terrorist attacks in Iraq blew off the charts. In 2003 there had been 22. In 2004 there were 198—this after Curly, Larry, and Moe had repeatedly told the American people that the situation had stabilized significantly after the United States turned over political authority to an interim Iraqi government.

And look at what ArmyTimes.com said in an editorial on June 30, 2003, about President Bush's support of our armed forces:

In recent months, President Bush and the Republican-controlled Congress have missed no opportunities to heap richly deserved praise on the military. But talk is cheap—and getting cheaper by the day, judging from the nickel-and-dime treatment the troops are getting lately.

For example, the White House griped that various pay-and-benefits incentives added to the 2004 defense budget by Congress are wasteful and unnecessary—including a modest proposal to double the $6,000 gratuity paid to *families of troops who die on active duty. This comes at a time when Americans continue to die in Iraq at a rate of about one a day.*

Why was it only $6,000 to begin with? And Bush opposed raising this "modest" benefit to $12,000. He should have been impeached for that alone.

But the Army Times.com continued:

Similarly, the administration announced that on October 1 it wants to roll back recent modest increases in monthly imminent-danger pay (from $225 to $150) and family-separation allowance (from $250 to $100) for troops getting shot at in combat zones.

But the fun did not end here.

As Bush and Republican leaders in Congress preach the mantra of tax cuts, they can't seem to find time to make progress on minor tax provisions that would be a boon to military homeowners, reservists who travel long distances for training and parents deployed to combat zones, among others.

> *The chintz even extends to basic pay. While Bush's proposed 2004 defense budget would continue higher targeted raises for some ranks, he also proposed capping raises for E-1s, E-2s and O-1s at two percent, well below the average raise of 4.1 percent.*

Couple all of this with the proposed cuts in veterans' health-care programs, which among other things doubled the prescription drug cost and would have caused an estimated 200,000 veterans to drop out of the VA system and get their health care elsewhere. These callous cuts so incensed VA officials in spring 2004 that they threatened to challenge Bush's reelection efforts—a move unprecedented by a veterans' group when our country is at war.

As a consequence of the mismanaged Defense Department, Veterans Affairs Department, and the entire military effort, the Marine Corps missed its monthly recruiting goal for the first time in a decade in 2005. In January 2005 alone, the Army National Guard fell short 44 percent. The precipitous drop caused the General Accounting Office to warn that, if the trends persisted, the military would "run out" of reserve forces needed for war-zone rotations.

Enrollment in the Army's Reserve Officers' Training Corps, the program that trains and commissions 60 percent of our nation's Army officers each year, dropped 16 percent in 2004–5. This gives the corps its fewest members in a decade.

The Army began its fiscal year in October 2005 with only 18.4 percent of the year's target of 80,000 active-duty recruits, and the National Guard raised its maximum enlistment age from thirty-four to thirty-nine in an effort to bolster its alarmingly low numbers.

The Defense Department was even so nervous about wounded soldiers getting damning news about the war effort that they unveiled the Pentagon Channel in hospital rooms of wounded vets returned from Iraq. The twenty-four-hour channel offered "news" that had been created and vetted by the Defense Department. Big Brother must have been proud.

The Bush and GOP record in support of our troops was clearly suspect at best, and scandalous at worst. Yet delusional or perhaps merely cynical Bush campaign aides in 2004 had the audacity to compare W's reelection effort with Franklin Delano Roosevelt's during World War II. Say what? Let's be real clear: George W. Bush wouldn't make a pimple on Franklin Roosevelt's ass.

Democrats have to take on these Keystone Kops. This is inexcusable. Democrats, don't ever take a back seat to these fools. Stand up and support our troops and our veterans. It will cost money to do so, but do so proudly. Democrats have a rich tradition of supporting our military. Democrats include in their ranks some of the great military leaders of all time. Hold this current crop of Republican Stooges accountable.

But, Democrats, you have to do one other vitally important thing. You have to embrace the culture of the 18 percent of American voters who served or are serving in the military—60 percent of whom voted for the draft dodger Bush over the war hero Kerry. Something is wrong with that picture, and you have to make it right.

One way to start is to repeatedly lambaste the Republicans' dismal record on defense and veteran issues. Blast the hell out of these pretenders.

And, by the way, last we looked, bin Laden was still running around doing mischief. Can't we start some sort of clock that counts up how long Bush has let this son of a bitch go free? Three thousand American lives lost, and W has let this bastard off the hook. Let's remind the American public of this—daily. Democrats, you have to capture the attention of the American public and hammer this home.

And while you are beating the hell out of these half-wits, offer pro-military and pro-veteran legislation yourselves. It is time. Democrats began such a reaching out in April 2005, when they sponsored legislation that would, among other things, make sure federal employees in the National Guard were paid the equivalent of their full civilian salaries while on active duty, would let military families stay in military housing for a full year after the death of a spouse, and would allow $500,000 in death benefits to the family of a soldier who died on active duty. Democrats need to do more of this. We recommend a serious proposal to dramatically increase the pay of military personnel, particularly enlisted men and women as well as guard and reserve personnel. We would propose doubling it. Republicans have taken our military personnel for granted. Democrats must stand up for them. You can lead the charge. Democrats will earn respect from southern and rural America by simply addressing these issues and embracing military culture.

Another way to tap into the culture of the military is to begin a dialogue with military leaders, enlisted men and women, National Guardsmen, and so on. Democrats need to talk to them where they live, talk about their needs, their fears, their lives.

In order to reconnect with this important demographic, Democrats have to talk to these folks and listen to them. But then you must go further. Peter Beinart, editor of the *New Republic* magazine, suggests several ways for Democrats to break into the military culture. First, he advocates developing a group of military experts who can help the party shape national policy, can speak out on defense and veterans' issues, and can generally put a pro-defense and pro-veterans face back on the Democratic Party. People like Wesley Clark, Bob Kerrey, Pete Peterson, Sam Nunn, Max Cleland, former chairman of the Joint Chiefs of Staff William Crowe Jr. come immediately to mind.

Second, Beinart argues Democrats should admit that their anger over the Vietnam War has sometimes colored their support for and respect of the military. There is nothing wrong with that admission, and it is long overdue.

Finally, Beinart says Democrats should push America's colleges and universities to allow the military to recruit on campus. Broadening the perspective of future military leaders by broadening the ideological gene pool, if you will, is not a bad idea. In a *Washington Post* op-ed from March 6, 2005, Beinart makes this critical point: "Genuine multiculturalism is not just about race, ethnicity and gender. It's about embracing people whose culture differs from yours, in hopes of finding core principles that you share." Amen, brother.

Democrats have a long history of proven military leadership and respect for defense. Get back to it.

Republican Leadership—It Reads Like a Guest List at a Draft Dodgers of Foreign Wars Convention

It is only those who have neither fired a shot nor heard the shrieks and groans of the wounded who cry aloud for blood. . . . War is hell.
GENERAL WILLIAM TECUMSEH SHERMAN

You know what is perhaps most strange and unsettling about the hawkish nature of this current crop of Republican leaders and cheerleaders when it comes to their support of the war in Iraq? Virtually none of them served in the military.

Perhaps that's why they have no sense of how to run the war. Perhaps that's why they have no idea how to equip an army. Perhaps that's why they have no plan, no strategy, no international support to speak of—no clue. This group of phony military wannabes ought not to be questioning anybody who questions their actions.

Take a look at these guys.

- **President George W. Bush**—got into the National Guard thanks to Daddy pulling strings. W showed his appreciation to Daddy (and to the guard) by skipping town.
- **Vice President Dick Cheney**—received five deferments, the last because his wife had a baby almost nine months to the day the Selective Service announced that henceforth married men *without* children would be eligible for the draft. He was quoted as saying he "had other priorities in the sixties than military service."
- **Karl Rove**—did not serve.
- **Former Attorney General John Ashcroft**—did not serve. Had seven deferments. Nice touch, General.
- **Speaker of the House Dennis Hastert**—did not serve. Can you say "O Canada"?
- **Former House Majority Leader Dick Armey**—did not serve. No surprise here.
- **House Majority Leader Tom DeLay**—did not serve; actually claimed, "So many minority youths had volunteered . . . that there was literally no room for patriotic folks" like himself. Perhaps if a foreign lobbyist would have flown him over, he would have gone.
- **House Majority Whip Roy Blunt**—did not serve.
- **Senate Majority Leader Bill Frist**—did not serve. But offered to view a videotape of a battle and render judgment as to whether he thought it was real.
- **Senator Rick Santorum**—did not serve.
- **Senator George Allen**—did not serve. But had a wicked tan during most of the Vietnam War.
- **Rudy Giuliani**—did not serve. But would have been happy to come in after the war and claim it as his own.
- **Senator Saxby Chambliss**—did not serve. Had a "bad knee" and apparently no spine either. Had no problem attacking the war hero Max Cleland, who had both his knees blown off in Vietnam, as "unpatriotic."
- **Governor Jeb Bush**—did not serve.
- **Senate Majority Whip Mitch McConnell**—did not serve.
- **Former Speaker Newt Gingrich**—did not serve.
- **Former Senate Majority Leader Trent Lott**—did not serve. Perhaps, had Strom Thurmond been commander in chief, Trent would have felt the swell of patriotic duty.

- **Former Vice President Dan Quayle**—We're sorry, we know Mr. Potatoe Head is *soooo* eighties, but we couldn't resist. Mr. "Not to have a mind is very wasteful" had his wealthy newspaper publisher grandfather pull strings so he could get out of Vietnam and into the National Guard. Of course, Mr. "It's great to be in Latin America, I only wish I spoke Latin" may have gotten out of fighting in Southeast Asia anyway because he didn't speak Southeastern.
- **Bill O'Reilly**—did not serve. However, should America ever go to war with Barbados or Aruba, sign him up.
- **Sean Hannity**—did not serve.
- **Bill Kristol**—did not serve.
- **Ralph Reed**—did not serve.
- **Rush Limbaugh**—did not serve. He was classified 4-F with a pilonidal cyst—that's what the record shows. If you want to find out more about this condition, look it up—it isn't pretty.

Clearly, many of the Republican mouthpieces and the mouths who support them lack the backbone to stand up with when it comes to claiming oneness with those who serve in the military.

Now let's look at some Democrats who did serve:

- **Senator John Kerry**—Lieutenant, U.S. Navy, 1966–70; Silver Star, Bronze Star with Combat V, and three Purple Hearts, Vietnam.
- **General Wesley Clark**—Four-star general; former Supreme Allied Commander of NATO; led U.S. and allied troops in NATO's war in Kosovo in 1999 and retired from the military in 2000 after thirty-four years of service.
- **Representative Richard Gephardt**—Missouri Air National Guard, 1965–71.
- **Former Senator Bob Kerrey**—Lieutenant, U.S. Navy, 1966–69; Navy SEAL special forces; first Navy SEAL to be awarded a Medal of Honor, Bronze Star, Vietnam; inductee Army Ranger Hall of Fame; SEAL Team 1 training facility named in his honor.
- **Former Senator Tom Daschle**—First Lieutenant, U.S. Air Force Strategic Air Command, 1969–72.
- **Former Senator Max Cleland**—Captain, U.S. Army, 1965–68; Silver Star, Bronze Star, Vietnam.
- **Former Vice President Al Gore**—Enlisted, Army, 1969–71.

- **Former Representative David Bonior**—Staff Sergeant, U.S. Air Force, 1968–72.
- **Former Representative Pete Peterson**—Captain, U.S. Air Force, POW; Purple Heart, Silver Star; Legion of Merit; ambassador to Vietnam.

Democrats, you have no shortage of military leaders to praise, be proud of, run up the behinds of these Republican phonies and their sniveling apologists. We would take a John Kerry, a Wes Clark, a Bob Kerrey, or any one of a number of other Democrats over this entire batch of run-and-hide, afraid-of-their-shadows, antiveteran, weak-on-combat-strategy-and-needs military pretenders any time.

Oh, but before we close the chapter, we feel compelled to profile one other political "giant" who claims military credentials.

Zigzag Zell Miller

This is what America knows about Zell Miller.

He is a former "Democratic" senator from Georgia; he gave the keynote address at the 2004 Republican National Convention in support of George W. Bush while trashing John Kerry—particularly on defense issues; he claims he is a conservative; he suggests that he has a long military record (he often refers to himself as "this Marine" and even wrote a book titled *Corps Values: Everything You Need to Know I Learned in the Marines*); he threatened the MSNBC newsman Chris Matthews to a "duel" with pistols; and he says the Democratic Party left him, not the other way around. Miller flip-flopped on so many issues over the course of his political career that he picked up the nickname Zigzag Zell.

The truth about Zigzag Zell Miller is as follows:

Zigzag Zell is not a Democrat. Democrats support working Americans. Zigzag Zell voted with the Republicans for $2 trillion in tax cuts for the rich. Democrats protect our seniors and always lead the charge to protect Social Security. Zigzag Zell supported the Bush plan to gut Social Security and dramatically increase costs while obliterating any security for seniors. Democrats lead the charge for equal rights for all Americans. Zigzag Zell served as chief of staff to the segregationist governor Lester Maddox and, as a congressional candidate in 1964, attacked Lyndon Johnson for supporting the Civil Rights Act, saying that President Johnson "is a southerner who has sold his birthright for a mess of dark porridge."

And this is the same Zigzag Zell who wrote of his boot camp experience, "In the course of one season of the calendar, boot camp turns sometimes aimless youths into proud and self-disciplined Marines who have well-honed senses of self-esteem and dedication to themselves, their mission and their country. *The differences of economic classes and prejudices of race and religion, which they brought with them, have been transformed into respect for others* [emphasis ours] and the ability to follow orders to achieve mutual goals." Apparently Zigzag Zell's "respect for others" transferred back to "prejudices of race" ten years after he left the Marines and ran for Congress.

And this pretender says the Democratic Party left him? Let's get something straight here, Mr. Marine, the Democratic Party has not abandoned the principles of fairness, equity, equal rights, opportunity, and justice for which it has fought proudly since the days of George Washington and Thomas Jefferson. Our party did not leave anybody. It is pretty clear, however, that if you ever were a Democrat, you are not now. So please leave. You are an embarrassment to the party.

The truth is, Zigzag Zell is a fraud. Zigzag Zell is a shameless opportunist. The only reason Zell retains a Democratic Party registration is to attempt to sell his lame book attacking Democrats.

Zigzag Zell does not have a long, distinguished military career. He served three years in the Marine Corps, from 1953 to 1956. He joined the Marines in August 1953, one month *after* the Korean War ended. He saw no combat. He won no medals for valor. The only thing he ever shot at was paper targets.

Zigzag Zell Miller lied at the 2004 Republican National Convention. Zell Miller did speak at the Republican National Convention. He probably felt he had to. Democrats didn't want him to speak at theirs.

The Republicans knew Zell the Shell had his new book trashing Democrats to hawk, so the odds were pretty good that he would say anything they wanted. He did.

At the heart of Zell's speech was the claim that John Kerry had voted to kill the M-1 tank, the Apache helicopter, and the F-14 and F-18 jet fighters. If Zigzag Zell was to be believed, Kerry had apparently voted virtually to dismantle the entire Department of Defense. There is one problem. It did not happen. No vote ever occurred on the floor or in any of Kerry's committees to kill these weapons programs.

But somebody on a 2004 ticket *did* try to dismantle the M-1 tank program as well as the F-14 and F-18 jet fighter programs—it was Dick Cheney. The same Dick Cheney who spoke after Zigzag Zell at the Republican National Convention. As secretary of defense for George H. W. Bush, in 1992 Cheney told the Senate Armed Services Committee, "Congress has let me cancel a few programs. But you've squabbled and sometimes bickered and horse-traded and ended up forcing me to spend money on weapons that don't fill a vital need in these times of tight budgets and new requirements. . . . You've directed me to buy more M-1s, F-14s, and F-16s—all great systems . . . but we have enough of them."

In a speech in 2001, Zell the Shell called Kerry "one of this nation's authentic heroes, one of this party's best known and greatest leaders and a good friend. John Kerry has fought against government waste and worked hard to bring some accountability to Washington. . . . He fought for balanced budgets before it was considered politically correct for Democrats to do so. John has worked to strengthen our military, reform public education, boost the economy and protect the environment."

And you want to know the real evidence of Zigzag Zell's shameless attacks on Kerry's voting record? On several of the legislative measures upon which Zell the Shell attacked Kerry, Zell voted the same way Kerry did.

Former President Jimmy Carter, who indeed distinguished himself in and out of public life, chastised Zell the Shell for "unprecedented disloyalty," called Zigzag's speech "rabid and mean-spirited." Carter even sent Marine Miller a letter that said in part, "There are many of us loyal Democrats who feel uncomfortable in seeing that you have chosen the rich over the poor, unilateral preemptive war over a strong nation united with others for peace, lies and obfuscation over the truth and political technique of character assassination as a way to win elections or to garner a few moments of applause." Thank you, Mr. President.

If the Democrats ever again allow these shameful, despicable Republicans—with their disastrous personal, political, and policy credentials regarding military policy and caring for our military personnel—to label them as antidefense or unpatriotic, they deserve to lose.

The bottom line is this: On the three major issues of family values, fiscal conservatism, and military support, and on scores of other issues, Democrats have been giving Republicans a free pass and carte blanche. They have been letting the GOP define the issues. They have run away from their responsibility to hold the Republicans' feet to the fire for their dismal record.

Democrats must not let these guys get away with this stuff any longer. Make them pay—with their political careers, their most precious commodity—for their lousy service, for their lack of understanding of the responsibilities of elected officials in a representative democracy, for their blind eye to the consequences of their actions. When the Democrats do this, southern and rural America will take notice and will open up to the Democrats. Rural America will no longer feel that the Democratic Party is turning up its nose to them. If the Democrats speak to those issues and speak to them frankly, they will gain votes and win races.

Chapter 9

LIE 4: REPUBLICANS ARE THE PARTY FOR HUNTERS, ANGLERS, AND OUTDOOR ENTHUSIASTS

The intent of this chapter is to provide Democrats with a more realistic blueprint on how to deal with the issue of guns, and with hunting and other outdoor activities.

Just the Facts, Please

To begin, then, let's state a historical fact. From America's founding through the exploits of Lewis and Clark to the frontier days and the opening up of the West, hunting, fishing, and wildlife watching have been valued parts of America's culture and history.

They still are. Democrats can deny it all they want, but they do so at their peril.

It is also a fact that hunters, anglers, and wildlife watchers today face obstacles unlike any in our history. In the past fifty years they have seen their ability to practice and enjoy their culture face growing obstacles. They have witnessed unparalleled population growth and its inherent sprawl from urban to suburban and most recently to exurban population centers. They have endured unsustainable increases in our air, land, and water pollution. They have seen government and industry saddle them and our nation with poor conservation, preservation, and habitat management practices. In short, they have encountered reduced availability of unspoiled places to hunt and fish and watch wildlife. These obstacles have also reduced the numbers of hunting, fishing, and outdoor enthusiasts.

Democrats shouldn't be another obstacle to these good folks.

You don't believe us that this culture is alive and well in America in 2006?

Let's look at some more facts.

• Today it is estimated that as many as 256 million guns are owned by Americans.

• There are between 60 and 65 million Americans who own guns.

• Nearly half of all American households have at least one gun owner.

• Eighty-two million Americans, or nearly 40 percent of the entire U.S. population aged sixteen and older, fished, hunted, or watched wildlife in 2001; of those, 34.1 million fished, 13 million hunted, and 66.1 million participated in at least one type of wildlife-watching activity, including observing, feeding, or photographing wildlife.

• Over 10,000 organizations exist to promote interests ranging from hunting and fishing to conservation and preservation advocacy. These include groups such as Ducks Unlimited, the Izaak Walton League, Safari Club International, Pheasants Forever, National Wild Turkey Federation, Quail Unlimited, Trout Unlimited, Rocky Mountain Elk Foundation, and Bass Anglers Sportsman Society (BASS), to name just a few.

• According to a 2001 national survey conducted by the U.S. Fish and Wildlife Service (the service conducts an extensive national survey every five years; the next is due in 2006), sportsmen spent a total of over $70 billion in 2001—$36 billion on fishing, $21 billion on hunting, and $14 billion on items used for both hunting and fishing, while wildlife watchers spent an additional $38 billion on trips, equipment, and other items, for a total of over $108 billion.

• According to that same study, 16 percent of the U.S. population aged sixteen and older spent an average of sixteen days in 2001 fishing; 6 percent spent eighteen days hunting, and fully 31 percent fed, observed, or photographed wildlife in 2001. (The survey uses a strict definition of wildlife watching, by which participants must indicate they take a "special interest" in wildlife around their homes or take a trip for the "primary purpose" of wildlife watching.)

• In addition, there are 1.6 million hunters, 10.2 million anglers, and 12.6 million wildlife-watching children between the ages of six and fifteen.

• According to the National Shooting Sports Foundation, hunters and hunting directly support over 1 million jobs in the United States, and according to a May 2000 poll conducted for the foundation, 85 percent of Americans believe that hunting has a legitimate role in our society.

Democrats need to know that *40 percent* of our population hunt, fish, or watch wildlife, and *50 percent* of all homes have at least one gun. This is not some fringe element of our society. It is every other household. It is half the parents of kids who play on your son's baseball and your daughter's softball teams. It is half the people you work with; indeed, it is half the people you sit next to in church.

These are facts. We can deny them all we want. But guns and hunting as well as fishing and wildlife watching are significant parts of America's culture, and the passion of the people practicing these activities runs very deep. And, as we will illustrate shortly, while sport shooting, hunting, fishing, and related wildlife-watching activities are significant in the South and the Heartland, they involve hundreds of thousands of people in virtually every state in the union.

And don't kid yourselves. These sportsmen are as fervent in their love of the fishing, hunting, gun-owning, and wildlife-watching culture as any block of voters is about any other issue.

Part of the problem for Democratic candidates on these issues has been that they get pigeonholed on one or two secondary positions on guns and then are labeled not only antigun but antisportsman, even though their overall policy positions on guns, coupled with their conservation positions, are better than the overall gun and conservation positions of their Republican opponents. Why do Democrats so often get broadbrushed as antisportsmen?

They let it happen.

Too often Democrats allow the Republican Party to define the issue of sportsmen and guns. It is not unlike the family values argument. Just as the Republicans have done a better job of convincing the American public that people who favor abortion rights as well as gay rights do not possess family values, Republicans have convinced American sportsmen that the biggest threat to their right to hunt or enjoy the outdoors is someone who wants to register their pistols or ban assault weapons.

And just as the real threat to the American family is not abortion or gay rights but a lack of jobs, health insurance, and adequate income, the biggest threat to hunters and anglers, indeed to all outdoor enthusiasts, is not the ban of an AK-47 or the registration of a handgun but the astonishingly rapid rise of pollution and sprawl, and the loss of habitat and poor conservation and preservation practices that result from it.

Ask any true hunters or anglers, and they will tell you as much.

Democrats have also gained a reputation for being antigun and antisportsmen for a couple of other telling reasons. First, the face of Democrats on guns is too often that of leaders, particularly Democrats from urban centers, who have championed polarizing issues such as the Brady handgun control bill and the recently reversed assault weapons ban.

Second, and related to the first, phony pro-hunting groups like the National Rifle Association have jumped in bed with Republicans and offer significant financial and political support to Republican candidates. In fact, as the most prominent national organization promoting guns and hunting, the NRA is generally given carte blanche in setting the Republican campaign agenda when it comes to gun and sporting issues. Democrats don't seem to know how to get around this monopoly, and the media buy into the NRA's rhetoric that they are the barometer on anything that uses gunpowder.

The NRA's record speaks for itself. In the 2004 elections, the association endorsed 251 candidates for Congress; of those, 241, including 20 freshmen, won. Their Political Victory Fund also targeted six U.S. Senate seats in 2004, winning five of them, including John Thune's victory over Senate Democratic leader Tom Daschle in South Dakota. The NRA has to know they are supporting candidates whose conservation records ultimately damage gun owners' ability to hunt. In fact, the overall voting records of these NRA-backed members of Congress are for the most part devastating on the issues that matter most to hunters, anglers, and outdoor enthusiasts—habitat protection and conservation and preservation practices.

And if the NRA is such a pro-hunting group, why do they let this happen, indeed, facilitate it by supporting bad candidates? We believe it's because of two important trends in the past generation. First, the NRA increasingly aligned itself with partisan Republican candidates who were more than happy to carry NRA water on extreme gun issues in exchange for an endorsement. That endorsement then gave these candidates political cover on their generally dismal conservation and preservation records. Why did they have dismal voting records on conservation and preservation issues? Because a significant portion of their campaign funds came from corporate polluters and industries who were poor environmental stewards. And if these Republicans did not vote for the interests of the corporate polluters, the polluters quit writing them campaign checks. A vicious circle.

The second reason the NRA has no problem endorsing candidates and members of Congress who maintain scandalous conservation and preservation records is that the association's primary mission is to raise money through its direct-mail fund-raising machine. Leaders of the NRA know that scare tactics make millions more than a pitch for better conservation practices ever could.

An additional problem for Democrats on the gun issue is research indicates that people who are against guns do not feel as strongly about the issue as do people who are pro-gun. That is, people who are pro-gun are more likely to go to the polls and vote on that issue alone, whereas people who are against guns are more likely to have some other issue influencing their voting patterns. And because Democrats are much more likely to have been painted as against guns in recent election cycles, they are much more likely to lose with this pro-hunting, pro-gun block of voters.

The bottom line is that Republicans working hand in glove with the NRA are getting gun owners to vote for them whether they earned that vote or not.

In addition, much of the success the Republicans and the NRA have had in broad-brushing Democrats as antigun has to do with the candidates at the top of their tickets, who often are far less friendly to gun owners and hunters than are Democratic candidates down ballot. The negative publicity on guns gotten by, for example, Michael Dukakis, Al Gore, and John Kerry has tended to hurt down-ballot Democrats on the gun issue—regardless of the stance of the down-ballot Democrats. Exit polls from the 2000 presidential race, for instance, indicated that gun owners went for

Bush over Al Gore by a whopping 61 to 39 percent margin, and exit polls from 2004 showed that Bush *increased* that margin over John Kerry: 63 to 36 percent.

Moreover, Democrats too often do not even attempt to garner the support of the hunting, gun-owning, sportsmen groups of voters. This is another prime example of practicing the politics of subtraction instead of addition and conceding a voting block to the Republicans even though Democratic positions and votes address the real threats to this group far better than do those of Republicans.

Instead of fighting and too often *losing* on this issue, we suggest the Democrats be realistic and work to find areas of common ground to partner with and indeed fight for the tens of millions of Americans who embrace this culture. Instead of allowing Republicans to define the turf on guns and sporting issues, the Democrats need to define it first—exposing the glaring records and weaknesses of these Republicans on the real issues that affect hunters, anglers, and outdoor enthusiasts.

We offer the following seven guidelines for Democrats to consider. We believe that, were most Democrats to adopt these points, the upside would be significant while the downside would be minimal.

1. To tens of millions of Americans, hunting, fishing, and wildlife watching are still important parts of the culture of America, particularly in the South and the Heartland. Democrats and their candidates need to study this culture and understand and respect it.
2. Democrats should push to have gun laws and rules decided by states and not the federal government. Democrats should also adopt this as a party position.
3. Democrats should argue that enforcement of existing gun laws would solve virtually all our concerns about guns.
4. Democrats should make the case that the greatest threat to hunters today is not that someone (read Democrats) desires to take their guns but rather Republicans' policies that coddle corporate polluters, destroy habitat, and undermine responsible conservation and preservation practices.
5. Democrats and their candidates should offer a reasonable and proactive pro-sportsmen and pro-outdoor policy agenda. This should include

such positions as opening more federal land for hunting and increased funding to clean up polluted waterways.

6. Democrats should implement campaign practices and devices such as sportsmen committees, pro-sportsmen advertising campaigns, and relevant celebrity endorsements.

7. Democrats need to be honest with voters and tell them the truth—that the National Rifle Association has become a front group for the Republican Party and as such actually hurts the cause of hunters and outdoor enthusiasts in America by blindly endorsing Republican candidates whose policies are allowing unprecedented pollution and habitat destruction.

Hunting, Fishing, and Outdoor Activities—Right in Your Backyard

Many Democrats we know are surprised to learn how many people hunt, fish, and enjoy wildlife watching in the United States. And often they are downright shocked to learn how much of this activity is happening in their own states—in their own backyards.

From fishing at a favorite water hole through hunting in the woods to whale watching, bird watching, and wildlife photography, hunting, fishing, and outdoor wildlife activities are big business and favorite pastimes for tens of millions of Americans. How many Americans hunt, fish, and watch wildlife? How much time and money do they spend doing it? What are the numbers in your state?

To get the answers, look at the latest national survey by the U.S. Fish and Wildlife Service, in which over 80,000 households participated.

U.S. Fish and Wildlife Service, Results of 2001 Survey

Alabama

Total participants: 1.6 million★
Sportsmen:

Anglers:	851,000	Average days fished per angler: 13
Hunters:	423,000	Average days hunted per hunter: 18

Wildlife watchers: 1 million
Total spent on all activities: $2.3 billion**

Alaska
Total participants: 632,000
Sportsmen:
    Anglers: 421,000   Average days fished per angler: 8
    Hunters: 93,000   Average days hunted per hunter: 12
Wildlife watchers: 420,000
Total spent on all activities: $1.4 billion

Arizona
Total participants: 1.7 million
Sportsmen:
    Anglers: 419,000   Average days fished per angler: 10
    Hunters: 148,000   Average days hunted per hunter: 11
Wildlife watchers: 1.5 million
Total spent on all activities: $1.6 billion

Arkansas
Total participants: 1.4 million
Sportsmen:
    Anglers: 782,000   Average days fished per angler: 17
    Hunters: 431,000   Average days hunted per hunter: 20
Wildlife watchers: 841,000
Total spent on all activities: $1.3 billion

California
Total participants: 7.2 million
Sportsmen:
    Anglers: 2.4 million   Average days fished per angler: 11
    Hunters: 274,000   Average days hunted per hunter: 13

*The sum of anglers, hunters, and wildlife watchers in each state will exceed total participants because many individuals engaged in more than one wildlife activity while in the state.

**This figure includes trip-related expenditures, equipment purchases, and licensing.

Wildlife watchers: 5.7 million
Total spent on all activities: $5.7 billion

Colorado
Total participants: 2.1 million
Sportsmen:
    Anglers: 915,000   Average days fished per angler: 10
    Hunters: 281,000   Average days hunted per hunter: 9
Wildlife watchers: 1.6 million
Total spent on all activities: $2 billion

Connecticut
Total participants: 1.2 million
Sportsmen:
    Anglers: 346,000   Average days fished per angler: 14
    Hunters: 45,000   Average days hunted per hunter: 17
Wildlife watchers: 967,000
Total spent on all activities: $502 million

Delaware
Total participants: 407,000
Sportsmen:
    Anglers: 148,000   Average days fished per angler: 9
    Hunters: 16,000   Average days hunted per hunter: 14
Wildlife watchers: 232,000
Total spent on all activities: $130 million

Florida
Total participants: 4.9 million
Sportsmen:
    Anglers: 3.1 million   Average days fished per angler: 16
    Hunters: 226,000   Average days hunted per hunter: 21
Wildlife watchers: 3.2 million
Total spent on all activities: $6.2 billion

Georgia

Total participants: 2.2 million

Sportsmen:

Anglers:	1.1 million	Average days fished per angler: 13
Hunters:	417,000	Average days hunted per hunter: 19

Wildlife watchers: 1.5 million

Total spent on all activities: $1.7 billion

Hawaii

Total participants: 324,000

Sportsmen:

Anglers:	150,000	Average days fished per angler: 18
Hunters:	17,000	Average days hunted per hunter: 19

Wildlife watchers: 220,000

Total spent on all activities: $261 million

Idaho

Total participants: 868,000

Sportsmen:

Anglers:	416,000	Average days fished per angler: 10
Hunters:	197,000	Average days hunted per hunter: 11

Wildlife watchers: 643,000

Total spent on all activities: $982 million

Illinois

Total participants: 3.4 million

Sportsmen:

Anglers:	1.2 million	Average days fished per angler: 13
Hunters:	310,000	Average days hunted per hunter: 15

Wildlife watchers: 2.6 million

Total spent on all activities: $1.9 billion

Indiana

Total participants: 2.4 million

Sportsmen:

Anglers:	874,000	Average days fished per angler: 16
Hunters:	290,000	Average days hunted per hunter: 17

Wildlife watchers: 1.9 million
Total spent on all activities: $1.5 billion

Iowa
Total participants: 1.3 million
Sportsmen:
     Anglers: 542,000   Average days fished per angler: 14
     Hunters: 243,000   Average days hunted per hunter: 16
Wildlife watchers: 1 million
Total spent on all activities: $823 million

Kansas
Total participants: 1.1 million
Sportsmen:
     Anglers: 404,000   Average days fished per angler: 14
     Hunters: 291,000   Average days hunted per hunter: 13
Wildlife watchers: 807,000
Total spent on all activities: $591 million

Kentucky
Total participants: 1.8 million
Sportsmen:
     Anglers: 780,000   Average days fished per angler: 16
     Hunters: 323,000   Average days hunted per hunter: 14
Wildlife watchers: 1.4 million
Total spent on all activities: $1.8 billion

Louisiana
Total participants: 1.6 million
Sportsmen:
     Anglers: 970,000   Average days fished per angler: 13
     Hunters: 333,000   Average days hunted per hunter: 19
Wildlife watchers: 935,000
Total spent on all activities: $1.6 billion

Maine

Total participants: 975,000

Sportsmen:

    Anglers: 376,000   Average days fished per angler: 11

    Hunters: 164,000   Average days hunted per hunter: 15

Wildlife watchers: 778,000

Total spent on all activities: $916 million

Maryland

Total participants: 1.9 million

Sportsmen:

    Anglers: 701,000   Average days fished per angler: 11

    Hunters: 145,000   Average days hunted per hunter: 12

Wildlife watchers: 1.5 million

Total spent on all activities: $1.7 billion

Massachusetts

Total participants: 2 million

Sportsmen:

    Anglers: 615,000   Average days fished per angler: 12

    Hunters: 66,000   Average days hunted per hunter: 18

Wildlife watchers: 1.7 million

Total spent on all activities: $1.1 billion

Michigan

Total participants: 3.5 million

Sportsmen:

    Anglers: 1.4 million   Average days fished per angler: 14

    Hunters: 754,000   Average days hunted per hunter: 12

Wildlife watchers: 2.7 million

Total spent on all activities: $2.8 billion

Minnesota

Total participants: 2.9 million

Sportsmen:

    Anglers: 1.6 million   Average days fished per angler: 19

    Hunters: 597,000   Average days hunted per hunter: 14

Wildlife watchers: 2.2 million
Total spent on all activities: $2.7 billion

Mississippi

Total participants: 1 million
Sportsmen:
    Anglers: 586,000   Average days fished per angler: 16
    Hunters: 357,000   Average days hunted per hunter: 24
Wildlife watchers: 631,000
Total spent on all activities: $974 million

Missouri

Total participants: 2.5 million
Sportsmen:
    Anglers: 1.2 million   Average days fished per angler: 11
    Hunters: 489,000   Average days hunted per hunter: 14
Wildlife watchers: 1.8 million
Total spent on all activities: $1.8 billion

Montana

Total participants: 871,000
Sportsmen:
    Anglers: 349,000   Average days fished per angler: 12
    Hunters: 229,000   Average days hunted per hunter: 11
Wildlife watchers: 687,000
Total spent on all activities: $943 million

Nebraska

Total participants: 768,000
Sportsmen:
    Anglers: 296,000   Average days fished per angler: 11
    Hunters: 173,000   Average days hunted per hunter: 13
Wildlife watchers: 565,000
Total spent on all activities: $585 million

Nevada

Total participants: 657,000
Sportsmen:
    Anglers: 172,000   Average days fished per angler: 9
    Hunters: 47,000   Average days hunted per hunter: 10
Wildlife watchers: 543,000
Total spent on all activities: $681 million

New Hampshire

Total participants: 892,000
Sportsmen:
    Anglers: 267,000   Average days fished per angler: 12
    Hunters: 78,000   Average days hunted per hunter: 19
Wildlife watchers: 766,000
Total spent on all activities: $619 million

New Jersey

Total participants: 2.3 million
Sportsmen:
    Anglers: 806,000   Average days fished per angler: 13
    Hunters: 135,000   Average days hunted per hunter: 23
Wildlife watchers: 1.9 million
Total spent on all activities: $2.2 billion

New Mexico

Total participants: 884,000
Sportsmen:
    Anglers: 314,000   Average days fished per angler: 8
    Hunters: 130,000   Average days hunted per hunter: 13
Wildlife watchers: 671,000
Total spent on all activities: $1 billion

New York

Total participants: 4.6 million
Sportsmen:
    Anglers: 1.6 million   Average days fished per angler: 16
    Hunters: 714,000   Average days hunted per hunter: 18

Wildlife watchers: 3.9 million
Total spent on all activities: $3.5 billion

North Carolina
Total participants: 2.9 million
Sportsmen:

Anglers:	1.3 million	Average days fished per angler: 12
Hunters:	295,000	Average days hunted per hunter: 25

Wildlife watchers: 2.2 million
Total spent on all activities: $2.5 billion

North Dakota
Total participants: 322,000
Sportsmen:

Anglers:	179,000	Average days fished per angler: 12
Hunters:	139,000	Average days hunted per hunter: 12

Wildlife watchers: 190,000
Total spent on all activities: $351 million

Ohio
Total participants: 3.7 million
Sportsmen:

Anglers:	1.4 million	Average days fished per angler: 15
Hunters:	490,000	Average days hunted per hunter: 21

Wildlife watchers: 2.9 million
Total spent on all activities: $2.3 billion

Oklahoma
Total participants: 1.5 million
Sportsmen:

Anglers:	774,000	Average days fished per angler: 16
Hunters:	261,000	Average days hunted per hunter: 22

Wildlife watchers: 1.1 million
Total spent on all activities: $995 million

Oregon
Total participants: 2.1 million
Sportsmen:

Anglers:	687,000	Average days fished per angler: 13
Hunters:	248,000	Average days hunted per hunter: 12

Wildlife watchers: 1.7 million
Total spent on all activities: $2.1 billion

Pennsylvania
Total participants: 4.6 million
Sportsmen:

Anglers:	1.3 million	Average days fished per angler: 14
Hunters:	1.0 million	Average days hunted per hunter: 14

Wildlife watchers: 3.8 million
Total spent on all activities: $3 billion

Rhode Island
Total participants: 399,000
Sportsmen:

Anglers:	179,000	Average days fished per angler: 11
Hunters:	9,000	Average days hunted per hunter: 12

Wildlife watchers: 298,000
Total spent on all activities: $288 million

South Carolina
Total participants: 1.7 million
Sportsmen:

Anglers:	812,000	Average days fished per angler: 13
Hunters:	265,000	Average days hunted per hunter: 18

Wildlife watchers: 1.2 million
Total spent on all activities: $1.3 billion

South Dakota
Total participants: 518,000
Sportsmen:

Anglers:	214,000	Average days fished per angler: 14
Hunters:	209,000	Average days hunted per hunter: 12

Wildlife watchers: 358,000
Total spent on all activities: $562 million

Tennessee
Total participants: 2.7 million
Sportsmen:
    Anglers: 903,000   Average days fished per angler: 17
    Hunters: 359,000   Average days hunted per hunter: 19
Wildlife watchers: 2.1 million
Total spent on all activities: $1.7 billion

Texas
Total participants: 4.9 million
Sportsmen:
    Anglers: 2.4 million   Average days fished per angler: 14
    Hunters: 1.2 million   Average days hunted per hunter: 12
Wildlife watchers: 3.2 million
Total spend on all activities: $5.4 billion

Utah
Total participants: 1.1 million
Sportsmen:
    Anglers: 517,000   Average days fished per angler: 10
    Hunters: 198,000   Average days hunted per hunter: 12
Wildlife watchers: 806,000
Total spent on all activities: $1.4 billion

Vermont
Total participants: 569,000
Sportsmen:
    Anglers: 171,000   Average days fished per angler: 14
    Hunters: 100,000   Average days hunted per hunter: 15
Wildlife watchers: 496,000
Total spent on all activities: $386 million

Virginia

Total participants: 3 million
Sportsmen:

    Anglers: 1 million   Average days fished per angler: 14
    Hunters: 355,000   Average days hunted per hunter: 16

Wildlife watchers: 2.5 million
Total spent on all activities: $1.9 billion

Washington

Total participants: 3 million
Sportsmen:

    Anglers: 938,000   Average days fished per angler: 14
    Hunters: 227,000   Average days hunted per hunter: 13

Wildlife watchers: 2.5 million
Total spent on all activities: $2.4 billion

West Virginia

Total participants: 843,000
Sportsmen:

    Anglers: 318,000   Average days fished per angler: 13
    Hunters: 284,000   Average days hunted per hunter: 18

Wildlife watchers: 605,000
Total spent on all activities: $503 million

Wisconsin

Total participants: 3.2 million
Sportsmen:

    Anglers: 1.4 million   Average days fished per angler: 16
    Hunters: 660,000   Average days hunted per hunter: 15

Wildlife watchers: 2.4 million
Total spent on all activities: $3.6 billion

Wyoming

Total participants: 662,000
Sportsmen:

    Anglers: 293,000   Average days fished per angler: 9
    Hunters: 133,000   Average days hunted per hunter: 10

Wildlife watchers: 498,000
Total spent on all activities: $634 million

So, not only are there hundreds of thousands, if not millions, of people in virtually every state in the union who hunt, fish, and watch wildlife, and spend a lot of money to do it, but look at the time these people put into their passion—sixteen, eighteen, twenty, twenty-four days a year! We love major league baseball, but we don't get to sixteen games a year—if we get to two or three games a year we feel lucky. People love opera, soccer, the theater, collegiate athletics, rock-and-roll or country music concerts, but they don't normally spend sixteen or more days a year acting on those passions. We hate to say it, but there are adults who do not spend sixteen days a year with their children. But outdoor enthusiasts spend an amazing amount of time practicing the culture of fishing, hunting, and wildlife watching. No wonder a politician's position (perceived or otherwise) on issues that affect this culture carries a lot of weight with these individuals.

How important politically, then, are hunting, fishing, and wildlife-watching activities in regions where Democrats are currently getting trounced by Republicans?

Look at the numbers for the Old Confederacy, eleven states that George Bush swept in 2004.

- **Alabama**—If you asked John Kerry to find an issue on which he could connect with Alabama voters, he likely would have drawn a blank. Yet as a fellow hunter and outdoor enthusiast, he had a wonderful cultural connection with the 1.6 million participants there who enjoy the same activities.
- **Arkansas**—Kerry lost Arkansas by 100,000 votes out of 1.1 million cast. Had he reached out to hunters, anglers, and outdoors enthusiasts, might he have found the 50,001 votes he needed in the 1.4 million who participate in hunting, fishing, and wildlife watching to win the election?
- **Florida**—Kerry lost Florida by 375,000 votes out of 7.3 million cast. Had he reached out to the 4.9 million people there who hunt, fish, and watch wildlife, might he have found the 187,501 votes he needed to win the election?
- **Georgia**—In Georgia 2.2 million people enjoy an average of sixteen

days a year engaging in outdoor activities. John Kerry spends that much time enjoying the outdoors as well. The problem was that no one in Georgia knew it.

- **Louisiana**—Kerry lost Louisiana by 280,000 votes out of nearly 2 million cast. Had he reached out to the 1.6 million people who hunt, fish, or watch wildlife in Louisiana, might he have identified the 140,001 votes he needed to win the election?
- **Mississippi**—Perhaps had Kerry gone to Mississippi and spoken to the 1 million people who spent an average of twenty days enjoying the outdoor activities, he would have had a reason to go South to campaign.
- **North Carolina**—Kerry lost North Carolina by 430,000 votes out of 3.5 million cast. Had he reached out to the 2.9 million people who hunt, fish, and watch wildlife in North Carolina, might he have found the 215,000 votes he needed to win the election?
- **South Carolina**—Instead of windsurfing alone off Nantucket, perhaps Kerry could have joined some of the hundreds of thousands of South Carolinians who fish the same Atlantic waters—1.7 million people can't be wrong.
- **Tennessee**—Perhaps Kerry could have joined the 2.7 million Tennessee residents on some of their outdoor adventures. In doing so, he wouldn't have looked so elitist and they might have been more receptive to his strong record of preservation and conservation.
- **Texas**—In Bush's own backyard, Kerry could have reminded the 4.9 million outdoor enthusiasts of their former governor's disastrous record on conservation and habitat protection.
- **Virginia**—Kerry lost Virginia by 260,000 votes out of 3 million cast. We know for a fact that in a statewide poll in early summer 2004, he trailed Bush by only 2 percentage points. Had Kerry reached out to the 3 million hunters, anglers, and wildlife enthusiasts in Virginia, might he have found the 130,001 votes he needed to win the election?

Now remember that, twenty-five years from now, there will be 40 million *more* people living in the South than there are today.

As we indicated, Bush swept these eleven states in 2004. The question is, did he have to? Ten of these were states that either Kerry initially conceded to Bush or his campaign publicly wrote off following the Democratic Convention in July. The lone exception was Florida, which Kerry lost but in which he did spend money and might have won with a different strategy toward sportsmen.

What if Kerry had come to the voters of this region with a toned-down antigun message and a toned-up pro-conservation, preservation message, coupled with a scathing indictment of Bush's programs and policies that were literally destroying the great outdoors before the eyes of its greatest enthusiasts? What would that kind of message have meant to down-ballot Southern Democratic candidates who were being skewered on the sword of an antigun national Democratic image? As the numbers indicate, Kerry would not have had to turn too many votes in any of these states to have been competitive and even to have won. At a minimum, he would have given political cover to down-ballot Democrats and forced Bush to spend tens of millions of dollars in these states instead of concentrating it in a few targeted swing states.

Now look at some of the additional seventeen states Kerry conceded to Bush.

- **Alaska**—Kerry lost Alaska by 65,000 votes out of approximately 240,000 votes cast—seemingly an insurmountable margin of 62 to 35 percent. Yet had Kerry turned only 32,501 votes, he would have won Alaska. Might those 32,501 votes been found in the 632,000 who hunted, fished, and watched wildlife there?

- **Arizona**—Kerry lost Arizona by 180,000 votes out of over 1.6 million cast. Had he found just 90,001 votes in the 1.7 million who hunt, fish, and watch wildlife in Arizona, he would have won here.

- **Colorado**—Even though Kerry wrote off Colorado early on, he lost the state by only 120,000 votes out of nearly 2 million cast. Had he found 60,001 votes among the 2.1 million people who hunt, fish, and watch wildlife, he would have won this state.

- **Missouri**—Kerry lost the Show Me State by 200,000 votes out of 2.8 million total cast. Had he found just 100,001 votes among the 2.5 million people who hunt, fish, and watch wildlife in Missouri, he would have won the state.

- **Nevada**—Kerry lost Nevada by 20,000 votes out of 800,000 votes cast. Had he found just 10,001 more votes, he would have won the state.

- **West Virginia**—Kerry pulled out of West Virginia early, yet he lost the state by only 96,000 votes out of 750,000 cast. By turning 48,001 votes, he would have won the state. Might he have found those votes among the 843,000 people who hunt, fish, and watch wildlife in West Virginia?

Finally, look at six so-called swing states, where Kerry and Bush were very close or relatively close.

- **Iowa**—Kerry lost Iowa by approximately 12,000 votes. A change of just 6,001 votes, and he would have won Iowa. There had to have been 6,001 votes in the 1.3 million people who hunt, fish, and watch wildlife in Iowa Kerry could have switched had he courted these voters.
- **Michigan**—Kerry won Michigan by 165,000 votes out of 2.8 million cast, or a 51 to 48 percent margin.
- **Minnesota**—Kerry won Minnesota by 98,000 votes out of 2.7 million cast, or a 51 to 48 margin.
- **New Hampshire**—Kerry won New Hampshire by 10,000 votes out of nearly 700,000 cast, or a 50 to 49 percent margin.

  Wouldn't it have made more sense to hedge his bets in these slightly blue states by reaching out to the millions who engage in hunting, fishing, and wildlife-watching activities?
- **New Mexico**—Kerry lost New Mexico by 12,000 votes out of over 700,000 cast, or a 50 to 49 percent margin. Just as with Iowa, there had to have been 6,001 votes among the 884,000 who hunt, fish, and watch wildlife in New Mexico that he could have gotten had he reached out to them.
- **Ohio**—Kerry lost Ohio by 135,000 votes out of almost 5.5 million votes cast. Had he courted the 3.7 million people who hunt, fish, and watch wildlife in Ohio, he might well have found the 67,501 votes he needed to win this state and become the next president of the United States.

This is not some fringe, whacked-out group. These are mainstream Americans. And the biggest threat to this huge number of people is not that some politicians will take their guns but that too many politicians support misguided conservation, preservation, and habitat management practices. Yet, right now, Republicans have convinced this group that Democrats, not they, are the enemy.

It's time to change that.

By the way, we both hunt and fish, and have done so all our lives. Indeed, one of the major reasons we are Democrats is that Democrats have such a superior track record on the conservation, preservation, and habitat management issues that we know are vital to the hunting culture and, conversely, that Republicans and their corporate-polluting-influenced votes have been the single most devastating detriment to the hunting and fishing culture in American history.

For Democrats to win these voters back, they will have to continue to educate themselves on their culture; they have to redefine the turf on which the debate is framed, including advancing much friendlier positions on guns and hunters in particular; they will have to expose groups like the National Rifle Association and the candidates and elected officials they endorse for the forgeries that they are. Doing so will not be as hard as Democrats may think. As they do with family values, fiscal conservatism, and national defense arguments, Democrats have a lot with which to work.

A Democratic Agenda on Guns, Hunting, Fishing, and Other Outdoor Issues

Let's begin by tackling a myth that exists in Democratic Party circles: If Democrats moderate themselves on gun and hunting issues, they will lose votes among the staunchly antigun constituencies.

That is false for a couple of reasons.

First, we are not advocating that all Democrats moderate their positions on guns. We understand that most of the staunchly antigun advocates and constituencies live in urban centers, and their representatives tend to be securely antigun. We are not suggesting that those representatives change a thing.

By contrast, few staunch antigun advocates live in rural or less urban areas. Instead, most voters in these areas tend not only to tolerate a more pro-gun stance but often mandate it.

Second, our experience in states that have both large urban and significant rural areas (Pennsylvania, Ohio, Virginia, for instance) is that candidates have been and can continue to be successful in reaching out to hunters and gun owners without losing the support of antihunting, antigun activists. The best example we know is Virginia Governor Mark Warner. When Warner was running in 2001, he took a fairly strong position in favor of gun owners and hunting rights. When asked what he would do about guns were he elected, a question that came up with some frequency in a state with a couple of million gun owners, 350,000 of whom hunted, he typically replied, "Nothing. We have enough gun laws." That response, as you might imagine, did not enthrall antigun enthusiasts, particularly in the Washington, D.C., suburbs in Northern Virginia, but these voters did not abandon Warner. Indeed, the antigun voters stayed with Warner while his strong push to reach out to gun owners and sportsmen garnered significant increases in these communities. In fact, Warner won rural Virginia, receiving 51.4 percent of the vote there—significantly ahead of past Democratic performance in these regions.

The point is, whether Washington, D.C., should ban handguns is up to the people who live in Washington, D.C. Conversely, if people in Mitchell, South Dakota, or Roanoke, Virginia, want to allow shotguns or rifles in gun racks in pickup trucks, that is their prerogative as well, and the national Democratic Party and its leaders ought not stand in their way.

We are also suggesting that, on the national level, Democrats too often seem to push a gun agenda that severely hamstrings hundreds of Democratic candidates every election cycle. That has got to stop.

We propose that Democrats need to give their elected representatives and their candidates in more rural and pro-gun districts and states the blessing to support their constituencies and their cultures. Don't make them explain why they are different from the party on this issue. Don't make them apologize for the party on this issue. Don't let their opponents stigmatize them with stereotypes on this issue. Be the big tent that the Democratic Party has always professed to be, and let these differing opinions all reside in it together. What a powerful signal such a stance would send to individuals who want to support Democrats but have not been able to get over the gun debate issue for the past couple of generations.

Second, we propose that Democrats, particularly in the more rural areas of the country, should take the position that we have enough gun laws and we should be enforcing the ones we have now. It is vital that

Democrats not begin their campaigns debating the narrow, trumped-up issues and policy stances put forth by the Republican Party and their mouthpiece, the NRA.

Third, Democrats should propose a pro-hunting and pro-gun agenda that includes ideas such as opening up more federal and state land to hunting and fishing; offering tax incentives to land owners who allow public hunting; reining in development that lacks mandated set-asides for wildlife habitat and sound conservation and preservation practices; committing to cleaning up pollution that threatens our streams, our forests, and our air and land; and allowing Sunday hunting in places where that is still prohibited. Whatever the issues, Democrats should establish a pro-sportsman platform and proudly run on it.

Finally, Democrats need to take the lead in identifying the true threats to hunters and sportsmen—that is, Republicans and their policies that coddle corporate polluters, destroy habitat, and undermine responsible conservation and preservation practices.

Democrats must hammer the pro-gun and pro-hunting constituents with these points:

You will not take their guns. You respect their culture. You come to the table with a solid agenda. And, indeed, the greatest threat to their pro-gun, pro-hunting culture is Republican-supported anti-conservation and -preservation policies.

This education will not be easy. Pro-gun and pro-hunter groups have been bombarded for generations with the notion that their right to possess guns is under attack (wrong), that Democrats are leading the charge to take their guns (wrong), that Republicans are fighting for them (wrong), and that, if they elect more Republicans, their problems will evaporate (really wrong!). It will take time, but the facts are on your side. The current Republican leaders have generally been the greatest enemies of hunters, anglers, and outdoors enthusiasts in American history.

We encourage all Democratic candidates for congressional, statewide, even local office to establish sportsmen committees on their behalf. Find hunters, gun owners, outdoors enthusiasts who are willing to commit their names to a list that will be made public. Establish such a committee in each county, district, whatever. Find some high-profile, well-respected person to head up each committee.

Commit a portion of the campaign budget to materials indicating support of hunting, fishing, and gun ownership. Then find other creative ways to connect with this group of voters. South Dakota senator Tim Johnson hosts pheasant hunts each fall and has had the South Dakota media personality and hunter Tony Dean cut television ads for him. Mark Warner brought three live Boone and Crockett white-tail bucks to a hunting store in Roanoke, Virginia, and drew 7,000 people to a two-day viewing. Finally, make absolutely sure you have credibility on the issues, or your visibility will turn into a joke—à la John Kerry goose hunting in Ohio in the fall of 2004.

All of this is not to say that there are not and will not be polarizing gun issues on which Democrats will be asked to take a stand. But if the Democratic Party and its candidates very early in the campaign make a concerted effort to respect the culture of gun owners and hunters, if they put forth a legitimate, friendly pro-gun and pro-sporting agenda, if they broaden the turf on which gun and hunting issues are being played to include key issues such as conservation and habitat protection, then Democrats will be much more credible on these difficult issues—even if they are not always perceived to be 100 percent pro-gun.

Bush and the Republicans: An Unprecedented Assault on Our Air, Land, and Water, and the Fish and Wildlife They Are Killing There

Question: Name the greatest toxic waste site in America—the site that has polluted more land, air, and water than any other; the site that has destroyed more habitat and more fish and wildlife than any other, indeed has destroyed more habitat and more fish and wildlife than all other toxic waste sites combined.

Give up?

Answer: The Bush White House and the Republican-controlled Congress.

You think we're kidding?

We're not.

The evidence is mind-numbing. Failing to enforce environmental laws and regulations, clear-cutting, gutting toxic waste cleanup, undermining the Clean Air Act, selling out to big oil and to the power plants, rewriting Environmental Protection Agency rules and guidelines, destroying wetlands, dumping raw sewage, drilling for oil in our nation's most pristine and sensitive areas, appointing corporate polluting shills to our environmental policing agencies—the list is massive and nauseating, literally.

We won't attempt to mention all the assaults on our air, land, and water, as well as the fish and wildlife that live there, which have occurred as consequences of the policies of George W. Bush and his bobble-headed Republican members of Congress—there are volumes and volumes of data. As you will see, the destruction of air, land, and water resources by the Bush administration and Republicans in Congress is nothing short of criminal.

So the next time people tell you they hunt or are big outdoors enthusiasts and therefore are voting for a Republican, tell them this:

• According to the U.S. Fish and Wildlife Service, between 1971 and 2001, the number of hunters in America declined by almost 1 million, dropping to under 14 million. The percentage of Americans hunting dropped from 10 percent in 1980 to 6 percent in 2001. In the past fifteen years alone, hunting in America has declined by 22 percent.

• Hunting demographics experts, in a study conducted at the University of Wisconsin, predict that because of pollution and habitat destruction, which will lead to rapidly declining numbers of game and birds to hunt, sport hunting will cease to exist in the United States by the year 2050.

• According to the Fish and Wildlife Service, by 2001 there had been a 22 percent decline in hunting of small game and a 31 percent decline in hunting of large game in the past fifteen years.

• The service notes that the number of Americans who fish has dropped 10 percent in the past twenty years.

Why are the millions of people who love this culture finding it harder and harder to practice it?

Let's let everyone in on a little secret: *It's not because someone wants to take their guns!*

It's because of pollution.

• As a result of increased and uncontrolled pollution, species of fish, snails, amphibians, mussels, and other animals that live in our rivers and streams are dying out five times faster than animals that live on land, and three times faster than marine mammals. In fact, freshwater species are disappearing in the United States as fast as tropical rainforest species, which are considered to be the most imperiled species on earth.

• In America today, seventeen species of freshwater fish have disappeared, as have one in ten freshwater mussels—forever. Today 65 percent of crayfish, 35 percent of amphibians, and 67 percent of mussels are imperiled. Forty percent of all freshwater fish in this country are imperiled.

• Almost 30 percent of bird populations in the United States are facing "significant decline," according to an extensive National Audubon Society study released in 2004. That study also indicated that 70 percent of grassland species of birds were doing "poorly," as were 36 percent of shrubland species, 25 percent of birds in forests, 23 percent in urban areas, and 13 percent in wetlands.

• In 2004, a numbing 79 percent of *male* smallmouth bass tested from the South Branch of the Potomac River near Moorefield, West Virginia, were found to have developed *female* organs and were producing eggs. The apparent cause? Unchecked dumping of chicken droppings coupled with human hormones dumped into the river with processed sewage.

• And for the deepsea fishing aficionados, 90 percent of the world's large predator fish have disappeared in the past fifty years; at least 33 percent of fish stocks monitored by the federal government are overfished; there is a dead zone, caused in large part by nitrogen from agricultural runoff, in the Gulf of Mexico the size of Connecticut. Speaking of the Gulf of Mexico, the white-tipped sharks there have declined by 99 percent.

• Today fully 40 percent of America's rivers, 45 percent of our lakes, and 51 percent of our estuaries are too polluted to fish or swim in.

• Of our 840,000 miles of assessed rivers and streams, 300,000 do not meet minimum water quality standards.

• Over one-half of all America's lakes, reservoirs, and ponds are now polluted, according to the Environmental Protection Agency, and only 16 percent—about *one-sixth*—of all America's watersheds have "good" water quality.

• According to the EPA, 96 percent of the shoreline of the Great Lakes has a toxicity level that now exceeds water quality standards to protect human health.

• A National Coastal Condition Report projects that, by 2020, 70 percent of all U.S. estuaries will see dramatic and dangerous increases in pollution under current practices.

The list goes on and on. But it is not just our waterways that are dying, it's happening to our land as well.

• From 1982 to 1997, the U.S. population grew by 17 percent, while urbanized land grew by 47 percent. Over the past twenty years, the acreage per person for new housing has almost doubled, and since 1994, ten-plus-acre housing lots have accounted for 55 percent of the land developed.
• In the 1990s, America lost farmland and ranch land 51 percent faster than in the 1980s. The rate of loss for the period 1992–97 alone was 1.2 million acres—an area the size of the state of Maryland—per year.
• Every single minute, America loses two acres of farmland.
• Between 1982 and 1997, 39,000 square miles, or 25 million acres, of rural land was converted into subdivisions, malls, workplaces, roads, and parking lots. That is equal to the landmass of Maine and New Hampshire *combined*.
• The rate of rural land lost to development in the 1990s was about 2.2 million acres per year. If this rate continues to the year 2050, the United States will have lost an additional *110 million acres* of rural countryside—equal to the combined land areas of Connecticut, Massachusetts, Rhode Island, Vermont, Delaware, Pennsylvania, New York, New Jersey, and Virginia.

And who and what are causing all of this pollution and sprawl?
George W. Bush and his lapdog Republican check cashers in the U.S. Congress.

• In his first act as president, on January 20, 2001, George W. Bush froze all Clinton term rules, including tougher rules for dumping raw sewage into our nation's waterways. On the same day, Bush proposed opening the Arctic National Wildlife Refuge to oil drilling.
• Barely three weeks into office, the Bush administration told the Energy Department to put off enforcing new efficiency standards for air conditioners.
• That same week, the administration told the EPA to delay new rules protecting wetlands from mining and development; 20 million acres became imperiled.

• Barely one month into office, the administration mandated that the Fish and Wildlife Service withdraw a report that called for protecting a variety of endangered fish.

• That same week, Bush appointed an oil and mining lobbyist as deputy secretary of the Department of Interior.

• Also that week, the administration refused to defend in court a rule protecting 58 million acres of wild forest.

• Two months into his administration, George Bush refused to sign the Kyoto Protocol on climate change. That international effort to curtail global warming had been years in the making. It went into effect on February 16, 2005. One hundred and forty countries signed the agreement. The United States and Australia were the only two industrialized nations that did not. This even though world leaders including British Prime Minister Tony Blair pleaded with Bush to take the lead on this rapidly growing world problem.

The prime minister's sense of urgency was ratified by the findings of a 2005 task force cochaired by Senator Olympia Snowe and Stephen Byers, a British MP and an adviser to Blair, which warned that global warming was becoming such a severe problem that, unless actions were taken immediately, the resulting harm would be *irreversible.* The report said "widespread agricultural failure, water shortages, and major droughts, increased disease, sea-level rise and the death of forests" would result. Blair even warned world leaders at a G-8 industrialized nations' conference that climate change was the single greatest issue the world faced. Study after study confirmed that the generation of so-called greenhouse gases, particularly from automobiles and power plants, which keep heat from escaping into space, was literally overheating the world. And the United States, which alone produces one-quarter of all greenhouse gases in the world, refused to participate in the Kyoto Protocol.

What have been the consequences so far? According to the Millennium Ecosystem Assessment, a study by 1,300 scientific experts from ninety-five countries published in March 2005, most of the world's ecosystems are in danger and likely will not sustain future generations unless drastic measures are taken. A U.S. Geological Survey study in 2005 showed that 212 of the 244 glaciers surrounding the Antarctic Peninsula have shrunk as temperatures have risen more than 4.5 degrees Fahrenheit since the 1950s. At the other end of the world, a study by more than 300 scientists found that sea ice in the Arctic is projected to shrink by one-half by the end of this century, with some computer models indicating it could disappear altogether. Melting with it would be all the life that it sustains—including, for instance, polar bears. A December 2004 study by the Global Coral Reef Monitoring Network found that only about 30 percent of the world's coral reefs are healthy, down from 41 percent just two years earlier. The primary cause? Higher water temperatures from global warming. An Arctic Council study of November 2004 warned that global warming would have a devastating impact on agriculture, ranges for terrestrial and marine plants and animals, and global shoreline flooding because of increases in sea level caused by melting ice.

In October 2004 the journal *Science* published a study involving over 500 scientists from more than sixty countries which showed that as many as 122 species of frogs, toads, and salamanders have disappeared *since 1980,* and 1,900 more species were in danger of becoming extinct. The study also found that 32 percent of all amphibian species faced extinction as well as 12 percent of bird species and 23 percent of mammal species. The scientists noted that this was tens of thousands of years' worth of extinctions in just one century. The causes? Deforestation, pollution, habitat loss, and climate change. Scientists were particularly concerned because amphibians such as frogs and toads are not unlike the "canary in the coal mine"—the first species to die because they are the most sensitive to environmental changes.

Yet the Bush administration routinely altered reported scientific results in an attempt to change pollution and conservation practices and justify their indifference to global warming threats. A General Accounting Office study confirmed that the EPA was issuing "dubious" reports to justify its rewriting of rules governing mercury emissions from coal-fired power plants. In fact, Bush rolled back a 2000 plan that would have reduced toxic emissions from power plants by 90 percent in three years using existing technology. His replacement program, misnamed the Clear Skies Act, did nothing of the sort. According to a National Academy of Sciences study, the act resulted in *more* air pollution, not less. No wonder. In 2005 it was revealed that a group of eight power plant companies actually wrote the sections of the act dealing with power plant pollution controls.

Oh, yeah, those same eight companies gave nearly $100,000 to Bush's presidential campaigns; power plants in general gave him $6.6 million for his reelection campaign. Meanwhile, the toxic mercury from these coal-fired power plants was literally killing streams and forests at record levels up and down the East Coast—not exactly good for deer hunters and trout fishermen.

This is how it works. Power plants burn enormous amounts of coal. When the coal burns, it releases toxic mercury into the air. The mercury-laced air rises into the atmosphere and returns to earth on raindrops. That mercury then settles in our streams, rivers, and lakes, and on our treetops. It proceeds to kill the tops of the trees as well as killing and deforming land animals and fish. In fact, mercury poisoning was so prevalent in our fish that by 2004, forty-five states had warnings against eating certain types of fish. Ohio advised its citizens not to eat more than one serving of fish caught in *any* of its rivers or lakes because of mercury contamination. Toxic levels of mercury had even been found in birds living high in the Green Mountains of Vermont.

It is not just birds and animals that are being poisoned. Mercury poisoning from these power plants has been showing up in our nation's infants. Six hundred thousand babies are now born every year with dangerously high levels of mercury in their systems—often leading to physical deformities and learning disabilities. A 2004 University of North Carolina at Asheville study found that an alarming 21 percent of women of childbearing age have mercury levels in their bodies that exceed federal health standards. That was up from 12 percent in a study conducted by the Centers for Disease Control and Prevention just *four* years earlier.

Bush's message to the power plant industry: Smoke 'em if you got 'em.

And the president was relentless.

In 2001 alone, he proposed dramatic cuts in the EPA budget; opposed stricter limits for arsenic in drinking water; took scientific participation out of the decision-making process of the Forest Service; proposed that oil drilling off the Florida coast be allowed; proposed cutting 270 EPA inspector jobs; ordered the Army Corps of Engineers to loosen permit requirements for wetland protection; ordered massive new road building and logging in the national forests while he ordered the EPA to delay tougher rules for power plant emissions and the Interior Department to weaken rules for mining operations and reopen national parks to snow-mobiling.

In 2002, Bush ordered the EPA to propose a two-year exemption for the oil and gas industry from storm-water pollution rules while they weakened Clean Air Act rules for power plants; he gutted the federal panel on lead poisoning and replaced members with officials from the lead industry; he ordered the Bureau of Land Management to approve the largest oil and gas drilling exploration ever in the state of Utah while a report showed that Superfund cleanups had dropped to forty-two per year, nearly one-half the number during the Clinton administration; another study showed that EPA air quality inspections had dropped under Bush by a staggering 34 percent; Bush also directed the Interior Department to sign oil drilling leases on 500,000 acres in Alaska while he ordered them to reject a proposal to limit offshore oil drilling in California; he also ordered the EPA to weaken clean air rules for 17,000 power plants and he cut funding by one-half for toxic-waste site cleanup; Bush also missed the deadline to set new fuel-economy standards; he also shocked the world scientific community when he granted U.S. power plants ten more years to cut mercury and sulfur dioxide emissions.

In 2003 the assault continued. Bush began the year by proposing to cut federal protection from 20 percent of U.S. wetlands; he ordered the EPA to relax standards on toxic air pollutants and to exempt the oil and gas industry from tougher water pollution rules; in March 2003, he ordered the EPA to continue to allow sludge dumping on the Potomac River for seven additional years and to propose a postponement of smog-control rules; Bush then tripled the logging limits in California's Sierra Nevada and ordered the Department of Agriculture to reverse a Clinton administration ban on logging and road building on nearly 60 million acres of protected forest land, and he ordered the EPA to implement new rules ignoring mercury pollution from chlorine plants; Bush then ordered the EPA to exempt 17,000 factory facilities from upgrading pollution controls and mandated that they not regulate dioxins in sewage sludge dumped on land; he also ordered the Interior Department to discontinue limiting where gold mines could dump their waste.

By 2004, Bush had this attack down to a science. He opened the year by overturning a long-standing ban on mining near streams; he ordered the Interior Department to triple the number of gas drilling permits in Wyoming and to open 9 million acres to oil drilling on Alaska's North Slope; he mandated that the Forest Service increase its logging on 3 million acres of Appalachian forests and he cut $10 million in funding for endangered species; Bush also mandated that the EPA approve a plan to inject toxic waste into underground wells in Michigan and he mandated that the Fish and Wildlife Service oppose protections for Yellowstone trumpeter swans; he also ordered the Department of Agriculture to weaken rules on organic food, allowing hormones and feed raised with pesticides, while he commanded the Interior Department to reduce designations of critical habitat for endangered species; Bush also directed the EPA to allow additional fine-particle pollution from 1,000 industrial plants and he zeroed out funding for research on climate change while he pushed through one of the largest timber sales in U.S. history.

Who needed an apocalypse? The earth had George W. Bush.

It seems that no state, no ecosystem, no bird, no animal, no fish would be spared Bush's fanatical crusade to undermine sound conservation, preservation, habitat protection, clean air, land, or water policy. This was a veritable scorched-earth plan, and George Bush and the Republican Congress would stop at nothing to fill the pockets of their greedy campaign contributors and polluters with ill-gotten profits so that these irresponsible corporate citizens would in turn give campaign contributions in record-breaking amounts to ensure that all these Republicans would be reelected in November 2004.

It worked.

Bush was reelected. So (you might want to send the kids to bed now) he plowed forward.

• In 2005, George Bush and the Republicans cut more than $500 million from conservation programs.

• George Bush and his band of merry men proposed changing rules to allow wastewater treatment facilities to dump partially treated sewage into our nation's waterways routinely—instead of only when there is no alternative.

• The administration refused to mandate that the EPA set guidelines for the dumping of pharmaceuticals in discharged water. The result? A study at Baylor

University in Texas showed that antidepressants, birth control drugs, and other medications were showing up in fish tissue in alarmingly high amounts, causing neurological, biochemical, and physiological changes.

•   Under Bush and the Republicans, forests could now be "harvested" of trees without environmental impact studies. And just to show wildlife lovers how powerless they were, the administration implemented a new rule eliminating the requirement to ensure that viable populations of native species are maintained in our national forests.

•   Under Bush and the Republican "pro-sportsmen" in Congress, hunters would now have to set up tree stands not on trees but on oil rigs in Alaska's pristine Arctic National Wildlife Refuge. That's right, in 2005 the oil companies were given yet another gift by Bush, Cheney, Hastert, and Frist, the Four Horsemen of the Environmental Apocalypse—the right to drill for oil in the Arctic National Wildlife Refuge. Of course, we are not sure that any caribou will still congregate there to be hunted with all the people and noise and equipment. What we do know is that the projected oil reserves there are minuscule compared with our energy demands, and virtually every study of the impact of drilling in ANWR indicates that our dependence on foreign oil will not be reduced, our national security will not be enhanced, and consumers will not save a nickel at the pumps.

We'll say it again: The biggest threat to hunters and sportsmen in America is *not* that someone wants to take their guns. The Bush record on coddling industry polluters, the logging industry, developers, oil and gas interests, mining interests, power companies, and on and on is the worst by far of *any* American president. And these misguided, profit-driven, corporate-coddling Republican policies have done more harm to hunting, fishing, and outdoor enjoyment than anything a Democrat ever did to a sportsman.

The truth is, the issue of out-of-control pollution is much bigger than politics. It is about a way of life. It is about a future not just for birds and animals and fish and ecosystems and habitat but for all of humanity. When America's and indeed the world's scientific community issues warning after warning about the perils of the litany of practices we have just outlined, it behooves us to listen. When twenty Nobel Prize winners stand and warn that the Bush administration policies are undermining our very ability to exist on this planet, what part of that shouldn't cause us to rise up and throw the bastards out?

Where is the outrage? The Democrats need to get mad and get in some people's faces. This one is too important. If some brainwashed moron attempts to claim that Republicans are better for him as a sportsman, Democrats need to stand up and tell the truth.

Most hunters, anglers, and wildlife observers already know the damage being done. They are the best stewards of the land. Democrats just need to show them they are fighting for these folks' culture and their cause. Outdoors enthusiasts need an alternative to the biased, jaded, manipulated rhetoric coming from the other side, or they may begin to believe the rhetoric. They need a party with a plan, with compassion for the culture of preserving our air, land, and water.

One way to start getting these people back in the fold is to change the focus of the sportsmen debate. The turf has to shift from the hollow and unsubstantiated claims that the greatest threat to sports people is that someone wants to take their guns to the real pollution and conservation problems we have outlined.

The second way Democrats need to challenge those who are spewing the lies and establishing the turf is to challenge the way the gun and wildlife issue has been typically debated. We propose starting with exposing the phony, corporate-pollution-coddling, fund-raising-first fools at the National Rifle Association.

The NRA—Now Republican Altogether

That the NRA has had a rather turbulent transformation over the past fifteen years or so from a gun-safety, pro-hunter organization to a much more strident and narrow guns-only lobbying and fund-raising group is fairly well documented. With this transformation came high-profile defections from the organization, extreme positioning on several high-visibility issues, money problems, and ultimately stark evidence that the NRA cares little about the real issues confronting hunters and outdoor enthusiasts.

One of the first public indications that the NRA was becoming an extreme fanatical organization was a controversial fund-raising letter the group sent to members in 1995. In that letter, signed by the longtime executive vice president, Wayne LaPierre, the NRA referred to agents of the Bureau of Alcohol, Tobacco, and Firearms as "jack-booted thugs" who wear "Nazi bucket helmets and black storm trooper uniforms." There was a collective fear that attacks on law enforcement officials in the letter might suggest it was acceptable for radical elements to strike out against the government—not unlike the attack on the Alfred P. Murrah Federal Building in Oklahoma City, which killed 168 people shortly after the letter was mailed. The comparison of American law enforcement officials to Nazi storm troopers drew harsh rebukes from newspaper editorial writers, political pundits, and government officials. But perhaps the greatest rebuke came in the form of a symbolic gesture by former President George H. W. Bush, who announced that he was canceling his lifetime membership in the NRA in protest of the letter.

How did the NRA respond? LaPierre issued a weak apology but then was quick to note that Bush's resignation would be a cash windfall for the group. In a story in the *St. Louis Post-Dispatch* that month, he was quoted as saying, "This [fund-raising letter] is going to do very, very well and will raise well over a million dollars."

Further, the NRA announced that the letter had drawn more than 900,000 responses from its claimed 3.5 million members. That would be a response rate of over 35 percent, with an average contribution of only a little over one dollar per respondent. (Normal returns on direct mail are lucky to hit 5 percent, and average contributions are much more likely to be in the twenty-to-forty-dollar range.)

The money might have been good, but the publicity for the NRA was not. So the association placed a full-page advertisement in several major daily newspapers asking Bush to reconsider his resignation. And in a public relations ploy that defies rational judgment, they also paraded the washed-up and weirded-out rock music guitarist Ted Nugent, who was a member of the NRA board of directors. Nugent said Bush "can kiss my ass."

President Bill Clinton weighed in, praising Bush the Elder for standing up to the NRA and calling on the association, if they were truly sorry for the wording of the letter, to donate the money it raised to the families of police officers slain in the line of duty.

LaPierre declined.

House Speaker Tom Foley would soon follow with his resignation from the NRA, and Phoenix mayor Skip Rimsza announced that he had also let his membership lapse. Rimsza was quoted in the *Houston Chronicle* saying, "I can support a reasonable NRA, but not this one." It was also announced that the staunch pro-gun supporter Representative John Dingell had resigned from a seat on the NRA board of directors the previous year because he felt the group was becoming too extreme.

Yet apparently there was no end to NRA insensitivity. The next major public relations debacle came in 1999, when the group refused pleas from elected officials and parents to cancel its annual meeting in Denver as a show of respect for the twelve students and a teacher killed by two heavily armed fellow students who also took their own lives at Columbine High School only days before the NRA's national convention was to come to nearby Denver.

Although the association scaled back the meeting, they refused to cancel it. The NRA president and aging tough-guy actor Charlton Heston informed the media, "We will not be silent or be told, 'Do not come here, you are not welcome in your own land.'"

We think you missed the point, Chuckles.

Heston also proposed this simple solution to the Columbine shootings: "If there had been even one armed guard in the school, he could have saved a lot of lives and perhaps ended the whole thing instantly." The actor had to be told that an armed sheriff's deputy *was* at Columbine and had actually exchanged gunfire with one of the student gunmen.

As the NRA was solidifying its image as an extremist organization, it also began to take heat from pro-gun organizations and supporters. A lawyer representing gun companies was even quoted in an April 1999 *Washington Post* story saying, "The NRA, with its millions of members, has always served the firearms industry as a vast human shield, but people in this business now have to ask themselves whether the NRA is becoming ground zero, whether it is becoming more a target than a shield."

By 2002, in a story in the *Chicago Tribune,* the NRA admitted publicly that it was shifting its focus away from hunters and toward advocating Second Amendment gun-carrying rights.

The group's strident public relations missteps also began to take their toll in the pocketbook. By the end of 2000, the NRA was $20 million in debt. In 2001 the organization doubled its line of credit to $12 million, and according to news reports, it quickly drew that down to next to nothing. By the end of 2002, the NRA pension plan had a $10 million deficit, and it was reported that the group had sold investments at a loss that year—suggesting an urgent need for cash. Indeed, LaPierre's ability to manage NRA assets had been under attack since 1997, when the association's first vice president, Neal Knox, led an internal battle to fire LaPierre and other officers. While Knox was ultimately unsuccessful, he shined a spotlight on NRA mismanagement. The group saw its assets drop from $80 million in 1991 to $42 million in 1995.

And it isn't just financial problems that have dogged the NRA. From a reported high membership of 4.2 million following the 2000 presidential election, the group had witnessed a 20 percent drop by 2004 to a reported 3.4 million members.

But perhaps the crown jewel of evidence that the NRA had sold out to extreme interests, politicians, and causes came in June 2004, when the conservation group the Sierra Club proposed a program called Natural Allies that would have had the two join forces with other hunting and environmental organizations to stop the destruction being done to nature.

The NRA's response? No way.

During a speech to the Outdoor Writers Association of America (OWAA), a group that historically had been extremely friendly to the NRA, in Spokane, Washington, NRA president Kayne Robinson vilified the Sierra Club proposal and said his group would have no part of it. Robinson claimed the reason the NRA was refusing to join with other hunting groups like the National Wild Turkey Federation and the U.S. Sportsmen's Alliance—a pro-hunting group—was that the effort had a hidden agenda against hunters.

Robinson, apparently in an attempt to give the NRA cover for his outlandish remarks, then opened his mouth only to change feet. He said the NRA did not want to join with environmental groups because part of their hidden agenda was to support the Clinton administration's closure of "26 million acres" of land to hunting. When the reporters in the audience pressed him to offer an example of land closed to hunters, Robinson could not cite a single case. When reporters asked the former Forest Service chief Michael Dombeck about the charges, he said that Robinson was "dead wrong."

The outdoor writers subsequently panned the speech, and many OWAA members accused the NRA of becoming wildly out of touch with the real problems facing hunters and outdoor sports enthusiasts. A *San Francisco Chronicle* story about Robinson's speech said that it "fell flat." The story then quoted several OWAA board members, including Pat Wray of Oregon, an avid hunter and gun owner, who said, "I was embarrassed and appalled [by the NRA]." To *The Washington Post,* Wray summed up the NRA's problems this way. "Its primary purpose in life is protecting Americans' right to keep and bear arms, but they are trying to play that game in a hunter's realm. The NRA will make a push on behalf of politicians who are strong supporters of gun rights, but very often these are the same people who are the least supportive of efforts to protect hunting habitat from roads, logging and mining. . . . [There are] a great many hunters out there like me. I am a registered Republican. I am a longtime member of the NRA. But George Bush's administration scares me to death when it comes to the environment."

Steve Griffin of Michigan, also on the board of the OWAA, said, "The NRA made a complete ass of themselves." Calling Robinson's comments "inappropriate," the OWAA board of directors voted 11 to 4 to send him a letter "expressing our disappointment in your harsh criticism of fellow OWAA supporting member the Sierra Club."

The Washington Post quoted Tom Stienstra of the *San Francisco Chronicle* as saying, "The National Rifle Association locked, loaded and fired its best shot at the Sierra Club . . . only to have the blast explode in its face." The story also quoted Rich Landers, the outdoors editor of *The Spokesman-Review* in Spokane, saying, "The NRA continues to blindly advocate 'Vote your gun.' So narrow. So sad." Landers then said that Robinson's comments were "bull-headed polarizing rhetoric," which had caused a "good deal of eye-rolling" at his group's convention.

And remember, these writers historically had been very strong backers of the NRA and its mission.

All of this recent history would seem to suggest that the curtain has been pulled back from the NRA's Wizard of Oz, and what the public now sees is a dramatically morphed organization. Instead of a pit bull defending the rights of hunters, it is a neutered lapdog gorging itself on direct-mail-funded excesses while licking the hand of the Republican Party and treating hunters like fire hydrants. This is clearly not your daddy's NRA.

The NRA doesn't represent the needs of hunters anymore. Perhaps the most damning evidence of this fact is that the group is contributing millions of dollars to people like George W. Bush and a couple of hundred members of Congress whose voting records have hastened, not delayed, the advent of a hunterless society.

In 2002, the NRA gave an A+, A, or A- grade to 227 candidates or members of the House of Representatives who were elected in the fall of 2002. Two years later, according to the League of Conservation Voters (LCV), their voting records on key conservation and preservation issues averaged a paltry 17.2 percent. That means on all conservation and preservation issues, these members voted against the interests of hunters and outdoor enthusiasts 82.8 percent of the time. Even more alarming, 137 of these 227 members had voting records of *6 percent or less* on key conservation and preservation issues, and nineteen of them actually got a 0 rating from the league.

Shame on the NRA, and shame on those phony members of Congress who claim to be friends of hunters. Shame on those who run television ads and send direct mail telling hunters to vote for them because they got an A grade from the NRA when their records show that on average they vote *against* the wishes of hunters on conservation and preservation issues 82.8 percent of the time; in fact, 137 of them vote against hunters and outdoor enthusiasts over 94 percent of the time.

Throw the bastards out.

Here are the 227 members who received A grades from the NRA, along with their corresponding LCV scores. You be the judge as to whether these members indeed have strong enough conservation records to be returned to Congress. Some of them do. Most of them clearly don't. (The names of the nineteen **Asses** who received A grades from the NRA while receiving 0 ratings from the LCV are in bold type.)

NAME	STATE	NRA GRADE	LCV RATING
Aderholt, Robert	AL	A	3
Akin, Todd	MO	A	6
Alexander, Rodney	LA	A	23
Baca, Joe	CA	A	61
Bachus, Spencer	AL	A	10
Baker, Richard	LA	A	6
Ballenger, Cass	NC	A	3
Barrett, Gresham	SC	A	3
Bartlett, Roscoe	MD	A	19
Barton, Joe	**TX**	**Ass**	**0**
Bass, Charles	NH	A	39
Beauprez, Bob	CO	A	6
Biggert, Judy	IL	A	23
Bilirakis, Michael	FL	A	19
Bishop, Sanford	GA	A-	35
Blackburn, Marsha	**TN**	**Ass**	**0**
Blunt, Roy	**MO**	**Ass**	**0**
Boehner, John	OH	A	3
Bonilla, Henry	TX	A+	3
Bonner, Jo	AL	A	6
Boozman, John	AR	A	3
Boswell, Leonard	IA	A	65
Boucher, Rick	VA	A+	81
Boyd, Allen	FL	A	55
Brady, Kevin	TX	A	3
Brown, Corrine	FL	A	94
Brown, Henry	SC	A	6
Brown-Waite, Ginny	FL	A	3
Burgess, Michael	TX	A	3
Burns, Max	GA	A	6
Burr, Richard	NC	A	6
Burton, Dan	IN	A	6
Buyer, Steve	IN	A	6
Camp, Dave	MI	A	3
Cannon, Chris	UT	A+	3
Cantor, Eric	**VA**	**Ass**	**0**
Capito, Shelley	WV	A	23
Carson, Brad	OK	A	42

Carter, John	TX	A	3
Chabot, Steve	OH	A	16
Chandler, Ben	KY	A	100
Chocola, Chris	IN	A	6
Coble, Howard	NC	A	3
Cole, Tom	OK	A	3
Collins, Mac	GA	A	3
Costello, Jerry	IL	A	68
Cox, Chris	CA	A	3
Cramer, Robert	AL	A+	35
Crane, Philip	IL	A	6
Crenshaw, Ander	FL	A	6
Cubin, Barbara	WY	A+	3
Culberson, John	TX	A	6
Cunningham, Randy	CA	A+	13
Davis, Jo Ann	VA	A	6
Davis, Lincoln	TN	A	58
Deal, Nathan	GA	A	3
DeLay, Tom	TX	Ass+	0
DeMint, Jim	SC	A	3
Diaz-Balart, Mario	FL	A	6
Dingell, John	MI	A+	97
Doolittle, John	CA	A+	3
Dreier, David	CA	Ass	0
Duncan, John	TN	A	10
Ehlers, Vernon	MI	A-	52
Emerson, Jo Ann	MO	A	3
English, Phil	PA	A	19
Everett, Terry	AL	A	6
Feeney, Tom	FL	A	6
Flake, Jeff	AZ	A	6
Foley, Mark	FL	A-	16
Forbes, Randy	VA	A	6
Franks, Trent	AZ	A	3
Gallegly, Elton	CA	A	6
Garrett, Scott	NJ	A	13
Gerlach, Jim	PA	A	52
Gibbons, Jim	NV	A	3
Gillmor, Paul	OH	A	13

(continued)

NAME	STATE	NRA GRADE	LCV RATING
Gingrey, Phil	GA	A	3
Goode, Virgil	VA	A+	16
Goodlatte, Bob	VA	A	3
Goss, Porter	FL	A-	16
Granger, Kay	TX	A	6
Graves, Sam	MO	A	6
Green, Gene	TX	A	61
Green, Mark	WI	A	29
Gutknecht, Gil	MN	A	3
Hall, Ralph	TX	A	13
Harris, Katherine	FL	A	10
Hart, Melissa	PA	A	3
Hastert, Dennis	IL	A	(No grade)
Hastings, Doc	WA	Ass	0
Hayes, Robin	NC	A	6
Hayworth, J. D.	AZ	A	3
Hefley, Joel	CO	A	13
Hensarling, Jeb	TX	A	3
Herger, Wally	CA	A+	3
Herseth, Stephanie	SD	A	56
Hill, Baron	IN	A	94
Hobson, David	OH	A	3
Hoekstra, Peter	MI	A	6
Holden, Tim	PA	A	71
Hostettler, John	IN	A-	13
Hulshof, Kenny	MO	A	3
Hunter, Duncan	CA	A+	10
Isakson, Johnny	GA	A	3
Issa, Darrell	CA	A	6
Istook, Ernest	OK	A	3
Jenkins, William	TN	A	3
John, Christopher	LA	A+	13
Johnson, Sam	TX	Ass	0
Johnson, Timothy	IL	A	65
Jones, Walter	NC	A	10
Kanjorski, Paul	PA	A	68
Keller, Ric	FL	A	10
Kennedy, Mark	MN	A	16

King, Steve	IA	A	6
Kingston, Jack	GA	A	3
Kline, John	MN	A	3
Knollenberg, Joe	MI	A	6
Kolbe, Jim	AZ	A-	6
LaHood, Ray	IL	A	19
Lampson, Nick	TX	A	71
Latham, Tom	IA	A	6
LaTourette, Steven	OH	A	10
Lewis, Jerry	CA	A	6
Lewis, Ron	KY	A	10
Linder, John	GA	A	3
LoBiondo, Frank	NJ	A-	81
Lucas, Frank	OK	A	3
McCotter, Thaddeus	MI	A	3
McCrery, Jim	LA	A	6
McHugh, John	NY	A	13
McInnis, Scott	CO	A	10
McIntyre, Mike	NC	A	68
McKeon, Howard	CA	A	3
Manzullo, Donald	IL	Ass	0
Marshall, Jim	GA	A	58
Mica, John	FL	A+	6
Michaud, Michael	ME	A	87
Miller, Candice	MI	A	6
Miller, Gary	CA	A	3
Miller, Jeff	FL	A	6
Mollohan, Alan	WV	A+	42
Moran, Jerry	KS	A	10
Murphy, Tim	PA	A	3
Murtha, John	PA	A+	55
Musgrave, Marilyn	CO	A	3
Myrick, Sue	NC	A	3
Nethercutt, George	WA	A+	6
Neugebauer, Randy	TX	A	5
Ney, Robert	OH	A+	3
Norwood, Charlie	GA	A	6
Nunes, Devin	CA	A	3
Nussle, Jim	IA	Ass	0

(continued)

NAME	STATE	NRA GRADE	LCV RATING
Obey, David	WI	A	97
Ortiz, Solomon	TX	A	42
Osborne, Tom	NE	A	6
Otter, C. L.	ID	A	3
Oxley, Michael	OH	A	3
Paul, Ron	TX	A	13
Pearce, Stevan	NM	A	3
Pence, Mike	IN	A	6
Peterson, Collin	MN	A	19
Peterson, John	PA	A+	6
Petri, Thomas	WI	A-	39
Pickering, Charles	MS	Ass+	0
Pitts, Joseph	PA	A	6
Platts, Todd	PA	A	19
Pombo, Richard	CA	A+	3
Porter, Jon	NV	A	10
Portman, Rob	OH	A	13
Putnam, Adam	FL	A	3
Radanovich, George	CA	A	3
Rahall, Nick	WV	A	90
Regula, Ralph	OH	A-	3
Rehberg, Dennis	MT	Ass	0
Renzi, Rick	AZ	A	10
Reynolds, Thomas	NY	A	6
Rogers, Harold	KY	A	3
Rogers, Mike	MI	A	6
Rogers, Mike	AL	A	3
Rohrabacher, Dana	CA	A	10
Ross, Mike	AR	A	42
Royce, Edward	CA	A	13
Ryan, Paul	WI	A	13
Ryan, Tim	OH	A	100
Ryun, Jim	KS	Ass	0
Sandlin, Max	TX	A	39
Schrock, Edward	VA	A	3
Sensenbrenner, James	WI	A	26
Sessions, Pete	TX	Ass+	0
Shadegg, John	AZ	A	3

Sherwood, Don	PA	A	6
Shimkus, John	IL	A	6
Shuster, Bill	PA	A	3
Simmons, Rob	CT	A	68
Simpson, Michael	ID	A+	6
Skelton, Ike	MO	A	61
Smith, Lamar	TX	A+	3
Smith, Nick	MI	A	6
Souder, Mark	IN	A	10
Stenholm, Charles	TX	A	19
Stearns, Cliff	FL	A+	10
Strickland, Ted	OH	A	90
Sullivan, John	OK	A	3
Sweeney, John	NY	A	16
Tanner, John	TN	A	48
Tauzin, Billy	**LA**	**Ass**	**0**
Taylor, Charles	NC	A	3
Taylor, Gene	MS	A	52
Terry, Lee	NE	A	6
Thomas, William	CA	A	10
Thornberry, Mac	TX	A	3
Tiahrt, Todd	KS	A	3
Tiberi, Patrick	OH	A	3
Toomey, Patrick	**PA**	**Ass**	**0**
Turner, Jim	TX	A	32
Vitter, David	**LA**	**Ass**	**0**
Walden, Greg	OR	A	10
Wamp, Zach	TN	A	6
Weldon, Dave	FL	A	6
Weller, Jerry	IL	A-	10
Whitfield, Ed	KY	A	13
Wicker, Roger	MS	A+	6
Wilson, Heather	NM	A	16
Wilson, Joe	**SC**	**Ass**	**0**
Young, Don	**AK**	**Ass**	**0**

In the Senate, it is even worse. There the NRA gave A+, A, or A–grades to forty-seven senators. Wanna know what their average League of Conservation Voters score was? It was 7.3 percent. The NRA gave A grades to forty-seven members whose LCV scores averaged 7.3 percent.

That means that these phonies in the Senate voted against hunters and outdoors enthusiasts 92.7 percent of the time. Of these forty-seven senators, thirty-six had LCV scores of 9 or less. The average score of these fools was 3. That means that the NRA gave A's to thirty-six U.S. senators who voted against hunters and outdoors enthusiasts on average 97 percent of the time. *Ninety-seven percent of the time.* And of the forty-seven senators who received an A from the NRA, twenty-one voted against hunters and outdoors enthusiasts 100 percent of the time—that's right, twenty U.S. senators to whom the NRA gave A's received 0 ratings on conservation and preservation issues.

Here are the forty-seven members of the U.S. Senate who received A grades from the NRA along with their League of Conservation Voter scores. You be the judge as to whether these members indeed have strong enough conservation records to be returned to Congress. Some of them might. Absolutely most of them don't. (The names of the twenty-one **Asses** who received A grades from the NRA while receiving 0 scores from the LCV are in bold type.)

NAME	STATE	NRA GRADE	LCV RATING
Alexander, Lamar	TN	A	4
Allard, Wayne	CO	Ass	0
Allen, George	VA	Ass	0
Bennett, Robert	UT	Ass	0
Bond, Christopher	MO	Ass	0
Brownback, Sam	KS	A	4
Bunning, Jim	KY	Ass	0
Burns, Conrad	MT	Ass	0
Burr, Richard	NC	Ass	0
Chambliss, Saxby	GA	Ass+	0
Coburn, Tom	OK	A	13
Cochran, Thad	MS	Ass	0
Coleman, Norm	MN	A	16
Cornyn, John	TX	A	4
Craig, Larry	ID	Ass+	0
Crapo, Mike	ID	Ass	0

FOXES in the HENHOUSE

DeMint, Jim	SC	A	9
Dole, Elizabeth	NC	A	8
Domenici, Pete	NM	Ass	0
Ensign, John	NV	A	16
Enzi, Mike	WY	Ass+	0
Frist, William	TN	A	8
Graham, Lindsey	SC	A	8
Grassley, Chuck	IA	Ass	0
Hagel, "Up" Chuck	NE	Ass	0
Hatch, Orrin	UT	A	4
Hutchison, Kay	TX	A	8
Inhofe, James	OK	A+	4
Isakson, Johnny	GA	A	14
Kyl, Jon	AZ	A	12
Lott, Trent	MS	A+	8
Martinez, Mel	FL	A	No grade yet
McConnell, Mitch	KY	Ass	0
Murkowski, Lisa	AK	A	8
Nelson, Benjamin	NE	A	32
Roberts, Pat	KS	Ass	0
Santorum, Rick	PA	Ass+	0
Sessions, Jeff	AL	A+	0
Shelby, Richard	AL	A	4
Snowe, Olympia	ME	A-	68
Specter, Arlen	PA	A	28
Stevens, Ted	AK	A+	4
Sununu, John	NH	A	36
Talent, Jim	MO	A	4
Thomas, Craig	WY	Ass	0
Thune, John	SD	A	9
Vitter, David	LA	Ass	0

These numbers in both houses of Congress are offensive. How the National Rifle Association can give A's to most of the people who are on these lists is a sham. Anybody on this list who scored a 0, 3, 6, 10, 13, 16, 19—name the number—is not a friend of hunters. To vote against conservation issues 100, 90, 80 percent of the time is indefensible. Most of these numbers should outrage every hunter and outdoors enthusiast in Amer-

★ 271 ★

ica. The numbers should indeed create a backlash against these individuals when they run for reelection in 2006 as friends of hunters. Moreover, these numbers are so stark in exposing the NRA for the pretenders they are that it is almost laughable—except that there is nothing funny about these selfish jerks. Let's be real clear: For the NRA to give A's to the vast majority of the people just listed is an indictment of their entire organization and mission. Hunters, if you vote for the vast majority of the individuals named here, you get what you deserve—a nation without hunting in your lifetime or in the lifetimes of your children.

And if Democrats ever again let Republicans, or the NRA, say that Republicans are better on issues that affect hunters, they deserve to lose. Democrats must expose the charade that the NRA has been playing with hunters and organize to beat them on the real issues that affect hunters most.

The bottom line for Democrats is this: All the empirical evidence suggests that hunting and gun owning are indeed important parts of America's culture and heritage. They are not merely the domain of some fringe elements of our society but rather are quite mainstream. Yet, Democrats too often ignore this massive group of people or, worse, join a chorus of mostly urban political leaders who categorically condemn this group and their culture. In doing so, Democrats allow fanatical groups like the National Rifle Association to dictate the terms of the debate while rewarding Republican elected officials for supporting a very narrow policy agenda. These Republican politicians then gain great political benefit even though their policy positions ultimately are devastating to the outdoors and those who enjoy it.

Democrats have the power to turn this situation around. As this chapter has demonstrated, there is overwhelming empirical evidence that the Republicans and their policies are devastating the hunting, fishing, and outdoor culture. There is damning data to illustrate that the chief Republican mouthpiece on hunting and outdoor issues, the NRA, has transformed itself into a group whose political agenda now is devastating to hunters and outdoors enthusiasts. Take this evidence and mount a counterattack. Set the terms of the debate. Rally the millions who love hunting, fishing, and the outdoors. Adopt a more reasonable national position on the hunting and gun culture. Create a reasonable pro-hunting, pro-conservation agenda. Crush the sacrosanct NRA, with its destructive, narrow agenda. And throw out the phonies in Congress who have been having it both ways on hunting and outdoors issues for a generation.

Epilogue

The preceding pages document a crisis of leadership in American politics. It tells the story of two political parties who have lost their way. One, the Republicans, drunk on power and gorged with special interest money, seem to have forgotten the meaning and importance of public service, and have made a calloused and indifferent mockery of it. The other, the once proud Democrats who for half a century boldly lit the torch of hope and opportunity for all Americans and indeed for much of the world, have become inexplicably cautious and largely silent, condemning themselves to irrelevance. The result is a ship of state run adrift, irresponsibly captained by a mob of Rasputin-like Republican leaders who have left the American people shell-shocked and confused as they drown in a sea of dispassion, inattention, and silence.

This misguided Republican leadership, hell-bent to erase generations of obscurity, sold out to record amounts of special interest money in exchange for granting those interests unprecedented and virtually unfettered access to federal monies, federal programs, and federal policy initiatives. These narrow-interested Republican leaders viewed government as an acquisition. Once captured, it became their political playground, complete with an ATM machine stocked with taxpayer dollars to be looted as they wished. And loot they did. In just a few short years, the Bush administration and the Republican-controlled Congress turned record surpluses into record deficits and orchestrated the largest redistribution of wealth from the working classes to the richest Americans in our history. The irresponsibility of the Republicans' giveaway programs were so massive in scale, and their eagerness to pay back special interest benefactors so grand, that the number of special interest lobbyists mushroomed from 16,000 to over 34,000 in Bush's first four years in office. During this same time, poverty rates exploded, wages were suppressed, benefits were slashed, unemployment ballooned, and the number of Americans unable to afford health insurance skyrocketed. Without question, the Republican assault on the American family was unlike anything ever witnessed in modern American history.

Meanwhile, without the political will or courage to pay for their federal orgy, deficits blew through the roof and government debt piled higher than at any time in American history. At the same time, Republicans rendered the American worker a disposable commodity; turned America's air, land, and water into sewage lagoons; undermined the security of our senior citizens; and ignored the fact that record numbers of children went to bed hungry. The cycle of Republicans gorging themselves at the table of record contributions from corporations, who piled up record profits while record numbers of Americans feared for their very capacity to survive, repeated itself over and over. And to help ensure that this cycle would be unbroken, the Republicans adopted a platform largely designed to divide Americans, cast a veil of fear over them, divert their attention, and co-opt them with a series of polarizing issues.

On top of this, George W. Bush's Don Quixote–like march into war continued with an untempered rubber stamp from his bobble-headed Republicans in Congress and a largely muted and supportive Democratic cast. These were the same Democrats who were impervious to any notion of caveat emptor in the first place, when they were convinced to purchase the rationale for war based on a false marketing campaign. It was a campaign complete with a guarantee that if it were purchased, the enemy would be found to possess weapons of mass destruction. Inexplicably, once no weapons of mass destruction were found, when Bush's own military leaders chastised the administration for embarking on a war without enough troop strength, and when reports surfaced that American soldiers were often purchasing their own protective gear back home because the military was not providing it, Democrats largely still cowered. They seemed muted by fears that free speech in a free society would be deemed unpatriotic and by a bizarre argument that they could not condemn a war they had largely voted for—even though they had voted for the war under false pretenses.

EPILOGUE

In the meantime the fury of the war raged on. In the fall of 2005, the death toll, fed by the lies, lack of courage, and lack of a countervailing voice, mounted eerily and almost silently past the 2,000 mark. Yet, as so often happens when power is too concentrated in too few people who possess too little courage and too little conviction—it corrupts.

At the same time, the wheels began to come off the Republican juggernaut. First it was disclosed that Senate majority leader and presidential wannabe Bill Frist was being investigated to determine whether he might have received inside information, causing him to sell considerable stock he held in his family's health-care company. This he did just prior to a sharp drop in the value of the shares. Frist feigned innocence and ignorance, claiming his stock was held in a blind trust, but the subsequent disclosure of numerous letters which kept Frist up to date on his holdings seemed to suggest that Frist was not ignorant and his trust was not blind.

And then Tom "the Hammer" DeLay, the blowtorch Republican leader in the House, got blindsided by his own arrogance and was indicted for money laundering. The charges were that DeLay violated Texas campaign finance laws by intentionally laundering corporate money through the Republican National State Elections Committee back into Texas state legislative elections in violation of a Texas law banning corporate contributions. It was a long time coming, and against his protests and worst efforts DeLay was forced to resign from his leadership position.

But the fun did not stop there. Both Vice President Dick Cheney's chief of staff, Lewis "Scooter" Libby, and Bush political mastermind Karl Rove, then the White House deputy chief of staff, were long thought to have been the individuals responsible for illegally disclosing the identity of covert CIA operative Valerie Plame to the news media in retaliation for criticism her husband, Ambassador Joe Wilson, publicly leveled at Bush's rationale for invading Iraq.

After a two-year investigation in October 2005, Libby was indicted on five felony counts of obstructing justice, perjury, and making false statements in illegally disclosing Plame's identity. Special Counsel Patrick Fitzgerald reserved the possibility that Rove too could still be indicted in the case. Finally, as 2006 opened, the Jack Abramowitz lobbying scandal threatened to snare untold members of Congress in one of the largest political scandals ever.

EPILOGUE

Clearly, ugly patterns of corruption and deceit had been exposed and a stench was settling around the Republican leadership. The public began to recoil. Polls showed Bush's approval rating as president had reached an all-time low. The public's belief that Bush and the Republicans could be trusted to run their government was unraveling at an alarming pace.

This growing pattern of Republican arrogance, callousness, and indifference, coupled with muted minority-status Democrats, seemed to be hurtling out of control, until an act of God—the winds and water of Hurricane Katrina—gave shocking perspective and put a disturbing face on the consequences of the abuses and excesses of the Republican-controlled government. In August 2005, this storm left a path of death and destruction unseen in our nation's history. Wind and water leveled a city and a region, and left 800,000 people homeless, exposing the great underbelly of poverty in America and a government that was broken and seemingly unable or unwilling to take care of its own.

Those winds and waters also opened America's eyes. In the searing third-world-like images on television and in news photos of the unprecedented death and destruction, Americans saw their government fail its citizenry. Instead of a president showing leadership and heeding the dire pre-hurricane warnings, they found out the president was attending a birthday party. And then only after the worst had happened did they see this "I'd rather be fishing" president reluctantly take charge when he ambled into New Orleans to praise "Brownie" while bodies floated in the streets and thousands clung to rooftops. Americans would later find out that the political appointee "Brownie," who possessed no real training in emergency management, spent his hours during the height of the devastation e-mailing coworkers and asking for fashion assessments of his television appearances and where to find dog-sitters. But the callousness did not stop here. Americans had to be stunned when they heard the House Speaker, Dennis Hastert, demonstrate his compassion by suggesting that America simply bulldoze New Orleans. Americans also saw the Republican Senate leader Bill Frist wail for tax cuts for the wealthy as the nation's first post-Katrina order of business. And Americans must have been embarrassed when the Republican-controlled Congress added their final insulting mark on the devastation when—oblivious to their own failings as legislators, as leaders, and indeed as human beings—they proposed paying for the devastation by cutting programs for the poor.

And in the midst of all of this, Americans also witnessed a governmental coup of sorts by the far right and a vice president who had apparently lost his mind. George Bush nominated a conservative, Harriet Miers, for the position of associate justice on the U.S. Supreme Court to replace the retiring Sandra Day O'Connor, only to see her forced to withdraw her name—not because liberals or Democrats complained but because the far right crazies in the president's own party determined that she might not be conservative enough. This made it clear that Bush was not in control of his own party or his own government. Then, while Bush was being shackled by the far right, his vice president proposed that Congress violate the Geneva Convention and authorize the use of torture by the CIA. Not to be outdone, Bush, who had exactly zero vetoes in his first five years as president, vowed to veto the annual defense spending bill if it did not allow for Cheney's torture provisions. Finally, it was disclosed that W had authorized our government's spying on American citizens. In these stunning moments, Americans were beginning to suspect, if not finally see, that the inmates had officially taken over the asylum.

America's government was reaching new lows. But something else was happening too. Out of this corruption, polarization, devastation, and indifference we believe seeds of new hope were sown. We think Americans are tired of the corruption and polarization brought to them by the Republican leadership. We think Americans once again want a government that unites its people, not divides them in cynical attempts to retain and enhance political power. We believe that Katrina was a stark reminder that a government *of* the people must work *for* the people. We believe Katrina showed millions of Americans that they can no longer allow politicians to convince them that government has to be bad. We believe that millions of Americans will now demand that government once again treat its citizenry with dignity and respect, and once again adopt policies that build wealth and opportunity for the American people. We believe that millions of Americans will now see the importance of public service as a vehicle to improve lives and fulfill dreams. We believe that hundreds and thousands of Americans will now rise up and tell uncaring and sanctimonious politicians it is time for them to go. We believe in the midst of this chaos, fear, corruption, and despair, there have been hints that the Democrats are again finding their voice. We were proud of Senate Democratic leader Harry Reid for invoking little-used Rule 21 in the fall of 2005, forcing the Senate to shut down so that Democrats could demand the long overdue investigation into the Bush administration's handling of intelligence about Iraq's weapons in the run-up to the war. (And we were embarrassed frankly for the continually out-of-touch Senate Republican leader Bill Frist, who stormed out of the closed session to tell waiting cameras that he had never been "slapped in the face with such an affront to the leadership of this grand institution." Please, Senator, this "institution" has been far less "grand" since you Republican "leaders" turned it into your own private country club. And incidentally, when you broke long-standing tradition and actually traveled to South Dakota to campaign against fellow leader Tom Daschle in 2004, what kind of an "affront" was that to the leadership of your "grand institution"? The truth is, Senator, you deserved to be slapped.)

We believe the moment is at hand for an American revival. The abuses and excesses of Republican control of all branches of government have embarrassed our country and diminished our people. They have given Americans pause and, for the first time in half a century, caused the world community to question whether America remains the model for governments everywhere.

We believe Americans once again want to trust in their government. They want to believe that their government will again look to the spirit and imagination of the American people as its greatest resource.

We also believe that the time is at hand for a revival of the spirit that made the Democratic Party the greatest hope for its citizenry of any political party in world history. It is time for the Democratic Party, the oldest political party in the world, to take its rightful place as the beacon of hope, the voice of opportunity, and the warrior for the common good. We believe the Democratic Party is ready to lead America and the world in pursuit of the ideals of justice, equality, liberty, and freedom.

We believe that the voice is coming back. It is a voice that says all people in our nation matter, wherever they might live, whatever their culture, whatever their needs. It is a voice that says we will be impassioned, we will shed any notion of elitism, we will be strong, we will look to all people in all regions as our greatest resources, we will stand up and define the playing field that best represents the needs of our people, and we will take on and expose our opponents for their deception and cynicism on some of the most important issues of the day. We believe the Democratic leaders of tomorrow are among us today. It is a belief that says we will always fight for the least among us as we strive to reach the absolute heights of our God-given abilities. We believe the time is now.

Foxes in the Henhouse

2006 ABSOLUTE ARROGANT ASSES AWARDS

Before we closed this book that has detailed just how damning the Republican takeover of the White House, the Congress, and ultimately the American agenda has been, we wanted to highlight several of the more extreme instances of the consequences of Republican arrogance. Because since these foxes entered the henhouse, they have tended to gorge until there was nothing left to gorge upon.

So, from the literally hundreds of macabre, distorted, jaw-dropping asinine instances of Republican and Republican-leaning abusers of power in 2005, we decided that *Foxes in the Henhouse* would offer an award to the top ten instances of Republican and Republican-leaning scoundrels from the previous year in politics. So with no further ado, here are the

Foxes in the Henhouse
2006 Absolute Arrogant Asses
Medal of Dishonor Awards

Medals of Freedumb

From all we have documented, George W. Bush is clearly the village idiot of world military history and not a very good friend of the men and women in uniform. So, in 2005, what did the village idiot, who has bungled all things military, do to cover up his inadequacies?

He gave medals.

That's what Bush did on February 14, 2005, when he conferred America's highest civilian medal, the Medal of Freedom, upon Tommy Franks, George Tenet, and L. Paul Bremer.

In a bizarre scene reminiscent of a medal-granting ceremony in the old USSR, where Soviet leaders routinely received chests full of medals seemingly in direct correlation to their military and political blunders, there was George W. Bush, the draft-dodging bungler of the war in Iraq, conferring the Medal of Freedom on three individuals who arguably had screwed up the war in Iraq more than any other three individuals not named Bush, Cheney, or Rumsfeld.

The Medal of Freedom, whose past recipients included such luminaries as Mother Teresa and Pope John Paul II, now added to its list of recipients these three men:

George Tenet: The former CIA director who advised Bush in the weeks before the war that his vaunted CIA had "slam dunk" evidence that Iraq possessed weapons of mass destruction—even though the CIA had been warned by relatives of Iraqi scientists that there were no weapons of mass destruction. George Tenet, whose inept oversight of America's intelligence operations prior to the attacks on America on September 11, 2001, factored largely in the 9/11 Commission's recommendation of a complete overhaul of America's intelligence activities.

L. Paul Bremer: The man who oversaw and presided over America's rebuilding of Iraq—which included creating a powder-keg atmosphere when he disbanded the Iraqi army and ran the Baathists from government, igniting unprecedented unrest, unprecedented bombing of Iraqi civilians, and unprecedented death and destruction. The same L. Paul Bremer who, after his return from Iraq, lambasted America's military policy in Iraq, contending the United States did not have enough troops in Iraq to accomplish its mission there.

Tommy Franks: The Army general who put together the flawed Iraqi war plan—the one that had too few troops to accomplish our mission there. As a consequence of this undermanned force, unprecedented looting and destruction took place, and insurgents were emboldened and gained a foothold in their terror operations, allowing them to become a daily deadly threat to the American troops who were on the ground there.

These Three Blind Mice, this Confederacy of Dunces, these Paragons of the Peter Principle, were rewarded for their failures.

Mr. President, you did not fool anybody. In honoring these architects of anarchy, you were really attempting to honor yourself by obfuscating your military failures. So, to George Tenet, L. Paul Bremer, Tommy Franks, and especially to George W. Bush: Congratulations! You each are the recipient of a 2006 Foxes in the Henhouse Absolute Arrogant Asses—Medal of Dishonor. Wear it with shame.

Armstrong Williams, Maggie Gallagher, Michael McManus, and Prepackaged Government-Produced News: Putting the "da" Back in *Pravda*

Early on in the Bush administration, Bush and his sleazy group of politics-first advisers decided that America's "free" press was being too honest with the American public when it wrote and commented on flawed programs within the Bush administration. So these primordial backroom moles decided they would violate federal law and even subvert the First Amendment protections of a "free" press by creating their own "free" press organization to churn out press releases and DVD videos as though they were independently produced by legitimate news organizations. Then they decided they would even pay off syndicated columnists, reporters, and radio and television talking heads who would then report and comment exactly what the administration told them to report and comment.

In Bush's first term, the Bush team ordered our federal departments and agencies to pay an unprecedented $254 *million* TAXPAYER dollars to public relations firms to create and send out hundreds of press releases, newspaper columns, and audio- and videotapes to thousands of news organizations, spinning and attempting to justify the administration's position on dozens of issues. The one constant? The press releases, DVDs, syndicated columns, etc., that were being sent did not disclose that they were being provided by a federal-government-purchased public relations firm posing as a legitimate news organization.

There were only two problems with this little scheme.

First, Bush got caught.

In early January 2005, it was revealed that the Department of Education was paying a public relations firm called Ketchum Incorporated more than $1 million to promote and defend Bush's flawed "No Child Left Behind" program.

On top of that, in March 2005 *The New York Times* ran an eye-opening story that detailed the unbelievable length to which the Bush White House had gone to manipulate and propagandize the American public. *The Times* reported that in Bush's first term alone, at least twenty different federal agencies and departments had produced literally hundreds of fake TV news stories and sent them to television stations nationwide, where they were broadcast in significant numbers on stations across the nation.

It was also revealed that the State Department had produced sixty prepackaged stories justifying Bush's war in Iraq. These efforts clearly violate federal law, but when the Government Accountability Office, the internal government watchdog organization, called the fake news stories "covert propaganda" and called on all federal agencies and departments to stop the practice, Bush had the Justice Department send a memo to all agencies instructing them to ignore the GAO mandate.

It then came to light that part of Ketchum's deal was to pay conservative commentator and radio show host Armstrong Williams, who was also a frequent guest on CNN, $241,000 to discuss, promote, and defend Bush's controversial "No Child Left Behind" law. That would be $241,000 of taxpayer money.

Then there was the case of syndicated columnist Maggie Gallagher. It seems that all the way back in 2002, the Department of Health and Human Services paid her a reported $41,500 to promote, defend, and discuss—in any and all venues—Bush's $300 million "healthy marriage" initiative. That initiative, in and of itself a propaganda effort, would entail an advertising campaign as well as such things as teaching materials in high schools on the value of marriage. (Gallagher didn't deny being paid by the government. Instead, she contended she was "hired" by the government for her ideas, which just happened to mirror Bush administration ideas.)

When the mainstream media (the real guys) asked her why she did not disclose that she was being paid to write propaganda, she contended she had "forgotten" about the contract when she wrote the propaganda! Forgot $41,500?

Finally, Salon.com, an Internet news source, revealed that there was yet another syndicated columnist, Michael McManus, who was paid to regurgitate government propaganda. McManus, like Gallagher before him, had been paid $10,000 (he clearly should have held out for more) to promote and defend the same marriage initiative on which Gallagher had sold out.

Which brings us to the second little problem with Bush's *Pravda*-type propaganda scheme . . .

It's illegal.

U.S. Code states, "Appropriated funds may not be used to pay a publicity expert unless specifically appropriated for that purpose." On top of that, there are numerous laws on the books that prohibit the expenditure of funds for "covert propaganda." When the Government Accountability Office investigated the legality of these fake news stories, it concluded they amounted to illegal propaganda and they noted that the Bush administration must report these misspent funds to Congress. The Bush administration promptly ignored the GAO ruling.

A pox on all their houses.

So to Armstrong Williams, Maggie Gallagher, Michael McManus, and to George W. Bush and all of the dolts in the Bush White House and in the various departments and agencies who concocted and carried out these miscarriages of legal and constitutional practices, congratulations, you are each a recipient of a 2006 Foxes in the Henhouse Absolute Arrogant Asses—Medal of Dishonor. Wear it with shame.

Michael Powell's Vasectomy

In March 2005, Federal Communications Commission (FCC) Chairman Michael Powell stepped down. That was good news. But it is the neutered agency Powell left behind that warrants his receiving an Arrogant Asses medal. Instead of monitoring America's media groups, Powell jumped in bed with them. During his tenure the FCC changed its rule to allow corporations to own two stations in most television markets and three in the largest markets (the rule had previously been only one television station in most markets and two in the largest markets), severely curtailing independence and stifling competition. Moreover, the FCC tore up rules that prevented cross-ownership of print and broadcast media in any single market. The commission also changed the rules stating that a single media company could not own a group of individual stations reaching over 35 percent of the national audience or they would be forced to sell stations until they got under that percentage. Powell's FCC increased that percentage to 45 (Congress reduced it to 39 percent—still high enough for the media monsters to get what they wanted), which was seen as a windfall for the media conglomerates and a blow to consumers.

On top of Powell's selling out to the corporate elites, it was revealed that Powell, who was known for cozying up to industry groups and trade associations during his entire four-year tenure, had met with top corporate media personnel dozens of times in closed-door meetings prior to the sweeping new rule changes.

The bottom line on the FCC's consolidation of the media on Powell's watch is this: In America, the public is supposed to own the broadcast airwaves—that means they will remain free, that means we will have competition and a diversity of views, that means one major conglomerate should not control all of the means of dispersing the news in any one market. The FCC is supposed to be the watchdog that makes sure these principles are upheld. Under Michael Powell, these principles were eviscerated.

So, to Michael Powell for ramming through George Bush's Politburo FCC policies—congratulations! You are the recipient of a 2006 Foxes in the Henhouse Absolute Arrogant Asses—Medal of Dishonor. Wear it with shame.

Bill Frist—Hoping Malpractice Makes Perfect

In 2005 Senate Majority Leader Bill Frist of Tennessee was desperately trying to be the perfect 2008 presidential candidate.

He just wasn't doing a very good job of it.

First, in 2005 there was the case of poor Terri Schiavo, the Florida woman who was taken off life support on March 18, 2005, and who died

FOXES IN THE HENHOUSE

two weeks later. Schiavo had been in a vegetative state since suffering a heart attack in 1990. Schiavo's husband had argued that his wife would not want to live in her condition, but there was no living will. Schiavo's parents fought to keep their daughter on life support and claimed her state was not completely vegetative and could improve with therapy. Numerous neurologists, who had personally examined Schiavo over the many years, strongly disagreed and contended she was effectively brain-dead. The whole drawn-out battle was a terrible and painful tragedy.

But then Republican politicians caught wind of the case and smelled political opportunity. They started speaking out. They traveled to Florida. They took to the floors of the House and the Senate. The legal counsel to Senator Mel Martinez (R-Fla) even wrote a memo for Republican senators outlining the great *political* advantages Republicans could get out of exploiting Schiavo's plight. These advantages included firing up the Christian right by contending that Schiavo was being "murdered" by activist "liberal" judges who needed to be reined in, and attempting to paint Democrats as opponents of the sanctity of life if they did not join in the chorus of those calling for reinstituting life support for Schiavo.

The cable news network *CNN* even obtained an audiotape of House Majority Leader Tom DeLay telling a conservative group that God had sent Terri Schiavo to help the conservative movement.

Make no mistake: Republicans believed that the Schiavo case was political gold and conservative Republicans were falling all over themselves to mine some political capital for themselves.

Enter cardiologist-turned-senator Bill Frist from Tennessee—the man who wanted to be president. He had to figure out a way to jump on this political gravy train. He did. But he had to stomp on his Hypocritical Oath to do it.

On Thursday, March 17, 2005, Bill Frist took to the floor of the United States Senate and said the following: "I question it [the diagnosis that Schiavo was in a persistent vegetative state] based on a review of the *video footage* [emphasis ours] which I spent an hour or so looking at last night in my office."

Excuse us.

Cardiologist Bill Frist looked at a family *videotape* of Terri Schiavo, and based on that *evidence,* announced that numerous neurologists who had examined Schiavo in person over many years were all mistaken in their diagnosis of Schiavo's neurological condition!

Cardiologists don't make medical diagnoses on heart patients using family video footage, much less make medical diagnoses on brain-damaged patients using family video footage.

Bill Frist, we trust you are a much better doctor than that. Bill Frist, you were not making a medical diagnosis, you were making a political diagnosis. And the diagnosis was this—pander to the far-right religious elements of the party and you would have a better shot at becoming the Republican nominee in the 2008 presidential race.

Shame on you for attempting to use Terri Schiavo's sad story for your own political gain.

We should note that when results of an autopsy on Schiavo's brain were released in June 2005, it showed that Schiavo's brain had shrunk to half its normal size. It showed conclusively that Schiavo had indeed been in a persistent vegetative state and had indeed suffered severe, irreversible brain damage.

So, to Dr. Bill Frist, the Dr. Kevorkian of the U.S. Constitution—congratulations! You are a recipient of a 2006 Foxes in the Henhouse Absolute Arrogant Asses—Medal of Dishonor. Wear it with shame.

Momma, Don't Let Your Babies Grow Up to Be Environmental Neglection Agency Guinea Pigs in Pesticide Experiments

There are so many reasons the people running the Environmental Neglection Agency deserve an Absolute Arrogant Asses—Medal of Dishonor award for 2006. The damage these Neanderthals are doing to our air, land, and water and to our fish and wildlife of all kinds is colossal in scope and may be irreversible.

But we gave the Environmental Neglection Agency a 2006 Medal of Dishonor because of one shocking, calloused, insensitive, stupid program they devised in conjunction with the American Chemical Council to pay impoverished Florida families $1,000, as well as giving them a camcorder, in exchange for the *right* to expose their babies and children for a two-year period to increased levels of pesticides in their homes to determine pesticide links to birth defects, lung damage, neurological damage, and other physical and neurological problems.

We kid you not.

Isn't that illegal, you ask? Not anymore. Upon entering office, George W. Bush—the protector of all that is oil, chemical, or corporate—reversed the government's ban on the gruesome practice of using human guinea pigs for government experiments.

And if this isn't enough, *The Washington Post* obtained an e-mail from an EPA regional toxicologist that said that EPA researchers in the Florida program would "not tell participants that using pesticides always entails some risk, and not using pesticides will reduce that risk to zero." Well, that's special. Woo the impoverished, struggling parents with money and electronics, then expose the kids and babies, but God, don't let the parents know that the pesticides could physically and mentally harm their children. Nice work, EPA.

On top of that, when the public became aware of the macabre plan, an EPA official from the Human Exposure and Atmospheric Sciences Division (they really have this division) of the EPA's Office of Research and Development actually tried to defend the "gas our impoverished children and babies plan." The official told *The Post,* "We are developing the scientific building blocks that will allow us to protect children." Yeah, that's right, Mother Teresa, and what about the children you are exposing to pesticides for two years—how again are you protecting them? Then, in response to the criticism that the whole program was morbid and sick in light of the fact that it preyed on children and babies and on children and babies of poor families on top of that, the official gave the following imbecilic response, "Nobody can go into this study just for that amount [$970 per family] of money."

Yeah, right. These are people who just want to expose their kids and babies for the sheer delight of potentially watching their skin fester, their lungs begin to wheeze, and their language skills taper off because their brains are atrophying. What an unjustifiably stupid comment. Let's get something real clear, Hannibal Lecter, parents do not as a rule put their children and babies at risk unless they are really hurting financially and are really desperate. So don't try to justify your macabre human experiments as some sort of good-citizen exercise for middle- and upper-income yuppie families who just want to help the good ole EPA and American Chemical Council. Can we assume, then, that you enrolled your family in this program so you could have your kids exposed to pesticides? Finally, Dr. Mengele inexplicably tried again to soften the perverse practice by telling *The Post* that the families would be informed if their children's urine showed risky levels of pesticides.

That's just sick.

The call must go something like this:

"Yes, Ms. Weaver, hi, I'm calling from your kid-friendly EPA. No big deal, but I just wanted to let you know that your kid's got more dioxin in his piss than the Orkin Man's truck, and his kidneys should fail within the week, but on a brighter note, how's that camcorder working out?"

So, to George W. Bush for overturning a ban on using humans as guinea pigs and to the EPA along with the American Chemical Council for trying to justify and carry out such sick experiments—congratulations! You are each recipients of a 2006 Foxes in the Henhouse Absolute Arrogant Asses—Medal of Dishonor. Wear it with shame.

Wanted: An Exterminator to Exterminate the Exterminator— The Case to Rid Congress of Tom DeLay

It seems that every generation of Congress has its face of evil, its poster child for an unethical, self-serving, arrogant, defiant, delusional, power-hungry, nepotistic, nihilistic, sinister, despotic, self-indulgent, self-important, egomaniacal, venal, gluttonous, cynical, acerbic, churlish, misanthropic, malicious, spiteful, caustic, virulent, invidious, insidious, cold-hearted, inhumane, truculent, pernicious, malodorous jerk.

America, meet former Houston exterminator–turned–Republican leader—Tom DeLay.

Look at the lowlights of House Republican Leader Tom DeLay's tenure, as compiled by the congressional watchdog group *Common Cause:*

- Indicted for using one of his political action committees to illegally launder corporate money.

- Admonished by the House Ethics Committee for threatening the Electronic Industries Alliance for not hiring a Republican as president.

- Admonished by the Ethics Committee for creating "at least the appearance" that Westar Energy company executives were given special treatment at a golf retreat because they gave $25,000 to one of DeLay's political action committees. At the time of the retreat, the House was soon to consider a bill that Westar hoped to influence.

- Admonished by the House Ethics Committee for unlawfully using government resources in attempting to locate Democratic members of the Texas House of Representatives who had left Austin so as to deny the Texas House a quorum.

- Admonished by the House Ethics Committee for offering to endorse the son of a Republican congressman who would be running to replace his father, but only if his father voted in favor of a drug bill DeLay supported.

- Was forced to return contributions to his legal defense fund from registered lobbyists because the contributions violated House ethics rules.

- Attempted, at the 2004 Republican Convention, to use the IRS tax-exempt status of a charity with which he was associated to circumvent the ban on soft money. DeLay withdrew his illegal scheme when the House Ethics Committee threatened an investigation.

- Took a trip to Moscow costing almost $60,000, paid for when money was transferred from a mysterious company registered in the Bahamas to a non-profit group that "officially" paid for the trip.

- Had his political action and campaign committees pay his wife and daughter over $500,000 since 2001.

- Illegally took a golf trip to England costing $70,000, paid for by lobbyist Jack Abramoff, who was involved in a federal investigation of bank fraud. Abramoff got two of his clients, the Mississippi Band of Choctaw Indians and eLottery Inc., to pay for the trip. Two months later, DeLay helped both companies by killing legislation on gaming that they opposed.

- Took a trip to South Korea funded by a foreign lobbyist in violation of House rules.

- Believe it or not, the list goes on and on.

So, to Tom "The Hammer" DeLay—congratulations! You are an easy recipient of a 2006 Foxes in the Henhouse Absolute Arrogant Asses—Medal of Dishonor. Wear it with shame.

The Inmates Have Taken Over the Asylum: The Alarming Attempt to Intimidate and Take Over the Judiciary

In 2005, after the inmates had effectively taken over the White House and the Congress, they set their sights on the federal judiciary.

And perhaps the most outrageous and sickest dishonor of 2005 came from the mouths of far-right wackos who moved to intimidate and even threaten federal judges, and who began a process to attempt to destroy the American judicial system by totally undermining its capacity to function and exist as the Founders envisioned it.

This stuff is real and it is scary. Here's what happened.

On the heels of the Terri Schiavo case, conservative leaders met in Washington, D.C., for a couple of days in April 2005 for a conference they called "Confronting the Judicial War on Faith."

What they said and did there should outrage every American.

First, they actually paraded out guys like Edwin Vieira, a lawyer who told the crowd of a hundred or so nut jobs that, when dealing with federal judges, they should do what Joseph Stalin (now there's a guy after whom you want to model the behavior of your organization) did when someone did not act the way he wanted them to—"He had a slogan, and it worked very well for him, whenever he ran into difficulty: 'no man, no problem.' "

Isn't that special. While we don't believe Eddie really meant that judges should be killed, he actually suggested to these lobotomized Neanderthals language they could interpret to mean that they should kill judges who did not hand down rulings acceptable to their definitions of good and bad. (Stalin's actual quote was "Death solves all problems; no man, no problem." Which makes Eddie's statement even more disgusting.) Yet, according to media accounts, nobody walked out at this point. Nobody booed Eddie's sick suggestion. Nobody did anything—but applaud.

On top of that, according to Max Blumenthal of *The Nation,* psycho Republican senator Tom Coburn's chief of staff, Michael Schwartz, even announced to anyone within earshot that "I'm a radical! I'm a real extremist. I don't want to impeach judges. I want to impale them!"

Oh, but Eddie and Michael were in good company. Phyllis Schlafly, the black widow spider of the far right, was also there in her full bouffant regalia. And to the cheering throng she called for the impeachment of Supreme Court Justice Anthony Kennedy (a Reagan appointee), because he had written an opinion saying the death penalty should not be an option in cases involving juveniles. Schlafly's rationale for impeachment was that Kennedy's opinion had not fulfilled a "good behavior" requirement for judges.

Then this Princess of Dorkness crossed into even scarier territory for those who believe in a constitutional system of government. According to *The Washington Post,* she called on Congress to pass laws removing the court's ability to rule on such things as religious displays, the Pledge of Allegiance, same-sex marriage, and the Boy Scouts.

Let's be real clear: The only people other than Michael Jackson who should *not* be looking after our children is this group of freaks.

Then, just to remind everyone how absolutely insane and delusional she was, the *Post* quoted Schlafly as saying, "The Constitution is not what the Supreme Court says it is."

And don't think that this was just a few cockroaches scurrying out of their holes under the cover of darkness only to scurry back when the light of day breaks through the window. These people were playing their threatening cards boldly and menacingly in broad daylight. And these wack jobs, frankly, were emboldened by the comments from elected Republican leaders in Congress.

Remember, House Majority Leader Tom DeLay, in a threatening statement following Terri Schiavo's death, warned that "the time will come for the men [judges] responsible for this to answer for their behavior." And that was not the first time DeLay threatened judges. In 1997, DeLay told reporters, "Judges need to be intimidated." (DeLay also was one of two House members who addressed this conference—his appearance was by videotape.) Then, shortly after DeLay's salvo, Texas U.S. Senator John Cornyn took to the floor of the U.S. Senate and declared the following: "I don't know if there is a cause-and-effect connection, but we have seen some recent episodes of courthouse violence in this country . . .

and I wonder whether there may be some connection between the perception in some quarters, on some occasions, where judges are making political decisions yet are unaccountable to the public, that it builds up and builds up and builds up to the point where some people engage in, engage in violence." Who is this fool? He clearly should know better. Yet, here was a past Supreme Court justice from Texas, making statements that would seem to give a justifiable excuse for some sick idiot to physically harm or even kill a federal judge.

Finally, the wackos were moving forward. They got members of Congress to introduce a bill called the Constitution Restoration Act, which allows Congress to impeach judges whom they deemed to have violated the "standard of good behavior." (Read: "Their standard of good behavior.") This bill also said judges could be impeached if they did not agree that God is the "sovereign source of law, liberty, or government."

So, to Eddie Vieira, Michael Schwartz, Phyllis Schlafly, Tom DeLay, John Cornyn, and to all of the freaks who attended this conference—congratulations! You are each the recipient of a 2006 Foxes in the Henhouse Absolute Arrogant Asses—Medal of Dishonor. Wear it with shame.

The Wicked Witch of the Patuxent Research Refuge

It is no secret that George W. Bush does not like to work. It is also no secret, as evidenced from his days at Yale University, where he spent more time as a pom-pom waving cheerleader than he did pushing pencils in a classroom, that Boy George likes simple leisure exercise more than he can tolerate exercising any mental muscle.

This propensity to screw off during working hours, on taxpayer time, in and of itself is somewhat galling, yet it alone would not warrant a medal of dishonor for W.

But when the White House was evacuated on May 11, 2005, because a small Cessna 150 aircraft had unknowingly and illegally entered White House air space, and the media realized that George W. Bush was not one of the evacuees because he was playing hooky that morning riding his mountain bike—at a place his own budget cuts were destroying, the Patuxent Wildlife Research Reserve near Waldorf, Maryland—we felt that George W. deserved a Medal of Dishonor.

The Patuxent Wildlife Research Reserve is 12,790 acres of beautiful woods, ponds, and outdoor splendor. It lies in the fly route of hundreds of thousands of migratory birds and provides habitat for numerous other bird and animal species. It is the perfect spot for hikers, anglers, hunters, bird watchers, outdoor enthusiasts, and other *friends of nature* to connect with the environment. This is what George W. Bush, who hypocritically uses Patuxent for his own private pleasure, is doing to Patuxent and all of the nation's 545 wildlife reserves:

Bush's severe budget cuts to America's parks and reserves means that for the rest of America, who don't travel with a Secret Service detail and who cannot demand to use a wildlife reserve at their will, reserve access has been limited and office hours have been cut while service has been severely curtailed. According to Marc Fisher of *The Washington Post,* at Patuxent alone, staff cuts meant that the Reserve had to shut down and boot people out at 4:00 P.M. So much for allowing hard-working Americans in the Washington, D.C., area who could not play hooky, to enjoy the Reserve after work. And according to *The Post,* 200 national refuges now had no staff at all and there was a $2 billion maintenance backlog at our nation's reserves.

According to *The Post*'s Fisher, the trail Bush liked to ride on at Patuxent was not even open to other riders—ever. Fisher noted that there were twenty miles of trails on Patuxent's North Tract that, again due to Bush budget cuts, had to close four hours earlier. He pointed out this was a particular problem for fishermen, whose only access to a prime fishing pond was from these trails.

Also, due to Bush budget cuts at Patuxent, two major science buildings had to be closed—one of them was the facility where studies on the dangers of the pesticide DDT had been conducted in the 1960s, which had inspired Rachel Carson's eye-opening book *Silent Spring.* That groundbreaking work was credited with spearheading the environmental movement in America—a pivotal moment in the Earth's history, a pivotal moment through which Bush sleepwalked.

Again, due to staff cuts, Patuxent also had to end its Boy and Girl Scout camping programs—there goes that family values thing again.

Finally, on top of all of this, when Bush rode at Patuxent, which he had apparently been doing for several years, the Secret Service required scientists to vacate their laboratories.

Unbelievable.

So, to George "W stands for Wicked Witch of the West" Bush—congratulations! You are the recipient of a 2006 Foxes in the Henhouse Absolute Arrogant Asses—Medal of Dishonor. Wear it with shame.

Wal-Mart—A Transformation from "Buy American" to "Bye, America"

Some of you might remember an advertising campaign initiated by old Sam Walton, the founder of the Wal-Mart department stores. It was a campaign to "Buy American." Whether old Sam actually intended to fulfill that pledge or not, we will never know—he never lived long enough. But his kids apparently had different ideas than those expressed by his advertising compaign.

Kids these days, they just don't listen. With Sam dead, Wal-Mart not only seemed to shift its emphasis from "Buy American" to one that said, "Bye, America," because Wal-Mart would soon become the world's largest retail importer of foreign products.

Today, Wal-Mart imports over $15 billion worth of goods from China, making it China's eighth-largest trading partner. Wal-Mart's imports from the Chinese alone make up 10 percent of the entire trade deficit the United States has with China. Wal-Mart is a larger trading partner with China than the entire nations of Canada, Australia, Russia, and Great Britain. While Wal-Mart today is the largest seller of apparel in the nation, the majority of its private-label clothing is manufactured in at least forty-eight countries around the world—but not in the United States. Today, Wal-Mart has more than 1,100 international operations. According to a 2001 story in *USA Today,* workers in Bangladesh earned as little as nine cents an hour making shirts for Wal-Mart. There are similar reports coming out of "sweatshops" making clothing for Wal-Mart in China and El

Salvador, where the pay is pennies per hour and the workdays can be twenty hours long.

Not apparently what old Sam had envisioned. But the results of selling foreign products made with slave or near-slave labor have been staggering.

Wal-Mart today is the richest and largest corporation in the world. It is the largest corporation and private employer in the United States. It has nearly 4,000 stores in the United States employing 1.2 million people. It is the largest employer in twenty-five states. It is also the world's largest retailer. In the United States, Wal-Mart opens an average of two stores a day. By 2010, Wal-Mart plans to have 3,000 supercenters, up from 1,600 in 2005, and they expect sales to top $500 billion. By the end of 2005, Wal-Mart was the number one seller of food, apparel, home furnishings, and jewelry. In 2004, Wal-Mart did $259 billion in sales. It has topped the Fortune 500 list of America's largest corporations for four years running.

Pretty impressive.

But there are huge downsides.

Wal-Mart has become so dominant a corporate giant that some sectors of the retail industry are literally considering shutting down because they cannot compete with Wal-Mart's purchasing power. In late 2004, Toys "R" Us announced it was considering getting out of the toy business because it could not compete with . . . Wal-Mart.

And because of its dominance in the labor force, Wal-Mart is setting the wage and benefit practices for much of the nation.

It's doing a pretty poor job of it.

Wal-Mart pays its employees notoriously poorly. It is certainly one of the major reasons Wal-Mart has an astonishing annual turnover rate for its employees—some estimate as high as nearly 60 percent, although Wal-Mart denies this figure. According to a study by the United Food and Commercial Workers Union, Wal-Mart pays an average hourly wage of $8.23 an hour—a full-time salary that puts its workers below the U.S. poverty line. (Wal-Mart claims it pays an average hourly wage of $9.68, but at $17,114.24 yearly, that still falls below the poverty level for American workers, which according to the U.S. Department of Labor is $23,705 per year.) Most of its workers make less. A sales associate, the most common job, pays $8.23 an hour or $13,861 annually; a cashier, the second most common job, pays $7.92 an hour or $11,948 annually. Remember, Wal-Mart is the largest private employer in America and the largest employer in twenty-five states. They literally are setting a horrible wage standard in much of the country.

On top of this, Wal-Mart has no real retirement or 401k accounts for its employees. It claims to contribute 4 percent of its earnings into these accounts. But to give an example of how little this is per worker, in 2003, this would amount to a $302 contribution for the entire year per employee. That's a joke. The only way you can retire on that paltry amount of money is to retire to the poorhouse and force the government to support you. Which is exactly what Wal-Mart apparently intends—keep profit margins sky-high, salary and benefits rock-bottom—and let the government pay for the health care and other benefits of people who work for Wal-Mart.

It's working.

Almost two-thirds of all Wal-Mart employees are *not* covered by its health insurance plan. (This compared to almost two-thirds of the employees at other large American companies who *are* covered by a health insurance program; Wal-Mart disputes these figures as well and claims that close to half of its employees are covered by its health insurance plan, about the same rate as other retailers, Wal-Mart says.) Wal-Mart offers a health insurance plan to its employees, but its employees on average are paid so poorly that most of them cannot afford to buy into it. The average Wal-Mart worker would have to pay up to 20 percent of his or her paycheck to afford health-care coverage on Wal-Mart's health plan. Employees would have to pay an estimated $218 per month for family health coverage with deductibles ranging from $350 to as high as $3,000. Since 1993, Wal-Mart has increased its premium costs per worker by over 200 percent even though health-care costs during this period rose by 50 percent.

On top of that, in 2002 Wal-Mart made it even more difficult for its employees to get health insurance. Under tougher coverage policies, now full-time Wal-Mart employees are not even eligible for health-care coverage until they have been on the job for six months and part-time employees are not eligible for health-care coverage until they have been on the job a numbing *two years!* Oh, and if the part-time employee can afford to stay at Wal-Mart for two years, only that employee, *not* his or her spouse or children, can get coverage.

So where do these workers go to get health insurance? Because they cannot afford it themselves, if they get any at all, many are likely to go to the state. In Alabama, Wal-Mart employees with children on Medicaid cost the state more than $8 million to cover nearly 4,000 children annually. In California, the state pays an estimated $32 million to provide health insurance for Wal-Mart workers and their children. (Wal-Mart, which disputes the California figures, and says it cannot verify the Georgia figures below, claims it did a survey showing only 5 percent of its hourly workers receive coverage through Medicaid.) According to the *Washington Post*'s Harold Meyerson, a study of health care in Las Vegas showed that a plurality of the city's employed Medicaid recipients worked at Wal-Mart. In Georgia, 10,000 children of Wal-Mart employees have to get health insurance from the state. (The next largest company has 734 of its children getting government assistance.) This means that one in five Wal-Mart employees in Georgia has a child on the State Children's Health Insurance Program (CHIP). According to government watchdog organization, The Progress Report, Washington State taxpayers have to pay several million dollars a year to subsidize health care for Wal-Mart employees who do not earn enough to be able to afford to purchase it on their own.

In addition, because Wal-Mart doesn't offer legitimate health coverage for its workers, that forces other companies to cut health-care benefits to its employees in order to compete with the megagiant—so when Wal-Mart screws its employees, it is very likely screwing employees throughout a community as well as screwing all taxpayers, whose tax dollars are going from state coffers to subsidize the health care of Wal-Mart workers and their children.

Wal-Mart employees have also filed a class-action lawsuit against the company, contending the corporate giant regularly "engaged in a systematic scheme of wage abuse." The suit contends that Wal-Mart "pressured hourly employees not to report all their time worked, failed to keep true time records . . . failed to give employees full rest or meal breaks, threatened to fire or demote employees who would not work off the clock [and] required workers to attend unpaid meetings and computer training." (Wal-Mart, of course, denies the employees' claims.) In Maryland, when the state legislature in 2005 proposed legislation to make companies like Wal-Mart spend at least 8 percent of its payroll on health benefits, which would have affected 15,000 employees in Wal-Mart's fifty-two stores there, Wal-Mart threatened to scrap plans to build a one-million-square-foot distribution center in the state and potentially to pull other stores and jobs out of the state as well. For Wal-Mart, these are not empty threats.

When a Wal-Mart store in Quebec, Canada, voted to form a union so that their employees could compete with the nearly 40 percent of the workforce in Quebec that is unionized, Wal-Mart shut down the store. Employees be damned. Wal-Mart's anti-employee practices are particularly alarming in Canada because today Wal-Mart there takes a jaw-dropping 52 percent of all retail market share.

In America, it's not any better.

None of Wal-Mart's 4,000 American stores are unionized. Wal-Mart won't allow it. But they do allow their 40 Chinese stores and 20,000 Chinese employees to join a union—a trade union run by the Chinese Communist Party, that is—which as we know doesn't have the best reputation in standing up for workers' rights. But if the communist China's government wants a union, by God, Wal-Mart is happy to capitulate.

On top of not paying its employees worth a damn and offering no real benefits to speak of, Wal-Mart also has problems with its hiring practices. In February 2005, Wal-Mart worked out a deal to settle child-labor violations with the Department of Labor. In March 2005, Wal-Mart was fined $11 million (pretty light slap on the wrist, if you ask us, for a company with $250-plus billion in sales) for repeated instances of hiring illegal immigrants to do janitorial work in its stores. A federal sting operation found that Wal-Mart was violating federal law using illegal immigrants in stores nationwide.

In addition, Wal-Mart is being sued for gender discrimination in the largest class-action lawsuit ever filed in U.S. history. Although about 72 percent of its total workforce are women, only about 38 percent of Wal-Mart's salaried managers are women and only around 15 percent of store managers are women. By contrast, women make up nearly 60 percent of the management positions at Wal-Mart's competitors. Wal-Mart female workers earn 5 to 15 percent less than their male counterparts for the same work.

Wal-Mart has had just as poor a record with hiring the disabled. In one sick instance, the company pulled a man with cerebral palsy from working in their pharmacy department after one day and moved him to the parking lot to pick up trash. Wal-Mart did this even though the man had had prior experience as a pharmacy assistant. The man sued, Wal-Mart lost. We wonder if their stupid little smiley face logo was still smiling when that decision came down.

It would seem that old Sam Walton's apparent affection for the American worker has been exported about as fast as foreign goods have been imported and have filled Wal-Mart's store shelves.

But the lousy pay, benefit, and employee practices coupled with the purchasing of slave labor products have one other profound consequence.

They have made the Walton kids very rich.

The Walton family today is the wealthiest family in America— worth an estimated $102 billion. For all that worth, the family has yet to display a willingness to give back to the people and the country that made them rich. According to the numbers compiled by the UFCW, the Walton family's lifetime charitable giving is a paltry 1 percent of their net worth. By contrast, the next richest family, Bill and Melinda Gates, have donated nearly $28 billion or 58 percent of their entire net worth. Bill and Melinda Gates graced the cover of *Time* magazine as two of its three (rock star Bono was the third) "people of the year" in 2005 for their generous giving to world causes. The Walton kids didn't make honorable mention.

One other thing. Wal-Mart is the single largest donor to the Republican Party in America.

Shame on you. We thought Sam raised you better than that.

So, to the Walton family and your un–Sam Walton–like "Buy It Wherever We Can Get It Cheapest Regardless of Child Labor and Sweatshop Issues" program, and your un-American poverty wages program as you turn phenomenal profits—congratulations! You are the first family to become a recipient of a 2006 Foxes in the Henhouse Absolute Arrogant Asses—Medal of Dishonor. Wear it with shame.

Charles Grassley, Jim Sensenbrenner, and the Republican Party: Bankrupt of Compassion

One of the worst pieces of legislation in American history, the misnamed Bankruptcy Abuse Prevention and Consumer Protection Act, passed the Congress and was signed into law in 2005 by President Bush.

It was a sham.

It was nothing more than a gift to major credit-card companies. And Charles Grassley, who sponsored the bill in the Senate, and Jim Senseless-brenner, who did so in the House, and all the members of Congress who voted for it should be ashamed for their lack of courage to stand up to the excessive money-grabbing scumbags in the credit-card industry. These members need to be held accountable at the ballot box in the fall of 2006 and beyond.

These are the facts:

One million six hundred thousand Americans filed for personal bankruptcy in 2004. Yet, according to the American Bankruptcy Institute, only 3.6 percent of those who filed Chapter 7 bankruptcy in 2004 could actually afford to pay the money back. That is, only 3.6 percent were frauds. Instead, the vast majority of people who filed Chapter 7 bankruptcy did so because of financial ruin due to family illness (over 50 percent of those who declare bankruptcy do so because of family illness), loss of a job, or divorce—and had no money to pay anyone back.

When one of the three tragedies occurs, families often are late with a credit-card payment, go over their credit limits to buy essentials upon which to live, or miss a payment while they are trying to regroup financially from the personal disaster. And when this happens, it is a bonanza for the credit-card companies. It's when they make their real money. Because late or missed payments or the exceeding of a credit-card limit typically allows credit-card companies to charge exorbitant monthly fees and to raise interest rates from as little as zero percent to 20 percent *for a single late or missed payment*. So, credit-card companies cared much less about people who defrauded them (they were too few) than they did about a bankruptcy law that allowed people devastated, through no fault of their own, to start over. Credit-card companies, in fact, then wanted to change the law so that they could force people who were financially ruined by family illness, divorce, or job loss to keep paying these huge interest and penalty fee charges for as long as possible—even if it meant taking funds out of these people's pockets that were needed for basic necessities. So be it. There were profits to be made.

So the credit-card companies bought off Congress and the White House to get what they wanted.

Led by MBNA, the credit-card companies showered Congress and President Bush with $25 million in campaign contributions in the past four years. Indeed, MBNA was the largest single contributor to President Bush's reelection campaign in 2004, giving him over $240,000.

The move paid off handsomely. They got their bill—MBNA alone will make an estimated $75 million a year off the financially devastated. Nice work, Congress.

When some members of Congress tried to separate out the real credit-card cheaters from those in financial crisis as a result of family medical illness, their effort was defeated.

When some members of Congress tried to exempt service men and women from this bill, the exemption was defeated.

When some members of Congress tried to exempt individuals who were the victims of identity theft, the exemption was defeated.

When some members of Congress tried to protect seniors by shielding their homes from being seized were they to declare bankruptcy, the protection was defeated.

But when Democrats tried to close a loophole in the law that allowed the very wealthy to shield millions of dollars in assets by setting up bogus trust funds, the amendment was defeated—the greedy were protected.

It was unconscionable. Republicans in Congress (and to be fair, some fool Democrats) and Bush claimed they were rooting out freeloaders. But if that was the case, why did they not just go after the small percentage of freeloaders? No, they instead went after the vast majority of people who filed for bankruptcy because their lives had been devastated by family illness, loss of a job, or a financially crippling divorce, because MBNA and the other credit-card companies wanted it that way, that's why.

Why didn't Congress say to the credit-card companies that they would protect and demand payment for what was owed them by their cardholders, but that they found it just plain wrong that these credit-card companies could charge these poor souls 30 percent interest rates and late fees of upwards of $25 to $50 a month! A late payment by some poor schmuck who was going through a family illness became a license for credit-card companies to steal people blind—and Congress institutionalized this thievery by making it the law of the land.

Listen to this story as told by reporters Kathleen Day and Caroline E. Mayer from *The Washington Post:* "For more than two years, special education teacher Fatemah Hosseini worked a second job to keep up with the $2,000 in monthly payments she collectively sent to five banks to try to pay $25,000 in credit-card debt. Even though she had not used the cards to buy anything more, her debt had nearly doubled to $49,574 by the time the Sunnyvale, California, resident filed for bankruptcy last June. This is because Hosseini's payments sometimes were tardy, triggering late fees ranging from $25 to $50 and doubling interest rates to nearly 30 percent. When the additional costs pushed her balance over her credit limit, the credit card companies added more penalties."

"I was really trying hard to make minimum payments," said Hosseini, whose financial problems began in the late 1990s when her husband left her and their three children. "All of my salary was going to the credit-card companies, but there was no change in the balances because of the interest and those penalties."

Or look at another example from Day and Mayer's report. It is the story of Ruth M. Owens from Cleveland. "Owens tried for six years to pay off a $1,900 balance on her Discover card, sending the credit company a total of $3,492 in monthly payments from 1997 to 2003. Yet her balance grew to $5,564.28, even though, like Hosseini, she never used the card to buy anything more."

Congress, you gutless wonders. You sold out these two women and literally hundreds of thousands more all so that credit-card companies could continue to soak them with highway robbery fees and interest rates that you did not have the guts to rein in—you probably were too busy cashing their massive campaign checks.

Shame on George W. Bush and all the spineless members of Congress who lacked the testosterone or estrogen to stand up to the callous vultures in the credit-card industry. Millions of Americans who already are hurting due to the devastation brought on by family illness, divorce, or job loss will now have another heartache to deal with—Congress and George W. Bush just told them they cannot start over. Congress not only did not outlaw, they institutionalized those stratospheric, unfair interest rates and penalties that have been eating people up financially. Nice work.

This bill was Congress at its worst. Hold them accountable.

So to Charles Grassley, Jim Senselessbrenner, and all who voted for this soldout piece of legislation—congratulations! You are all recipients of a 2006 Foxes in the Henhouse Absolute Arrogant Asses—Medal of Dishonor. Wear it with shame.